Sustainable Gardening for the Southeast

UNIVERSITY PRESS OF FLORIDA

Florida A&M University, Tallahassee
Florida Atlantic University, Boca Raton
Florida Gulf Coast University, Ft. Myers
Florida International University, Miami
Florida State University, Tallahassee
New College of Florida, Sarasota
University of Central Florida, Orlando
University of Florida, Gainesville
University of North Florida, Jacksonville
University of South Florida, Tampa
University of West Florida, Pensacola

Sustainable Gardening *for the* Southeast

Susan M. Varlamoff

Foreword by Allan Armitage

University Press of Florida

Gainesville / Tallahassee / Tampa / Boca Raton

Pensacola / Orlando / Miami / Jacksonville / Ft. Myers / Sarasota

Library of Congress Control Number: 2015938080
ISBN 978-0-8130-6180-1

The University Press of Florida is the scholarly publishing agency for the State
University System of Florida, comprising Florida A&M University, Florida
Atlantic University, Florida Gulf Coast University, Florida International
University, Florida State University, New College of Florida, University of
Central Florida, University of Florida, University of North Florida, University
of South Florida, and University of West Florida.

University Press of Florida
15 Northwest 15th Street
Gainesville, FL 32611-2079
http://www.upf.com

To my sister Karen, who left the earth too soon,

and

to my children, Pierre, Neil, and Paul,

my daughter-in-law, Susie, and my grandchildren, Sidney and Alec,

who inspire me to garden to protect the earth

Contents

Tables

Foreword

There is no lack of people telling us about a host of environmental problems and how we should respond. I have heard them, I have read them, and I admire some of them. But I now have my resource of choice—a book promoting sustainable gardening that is practical and concise.

Sustainable Gardening for the Southeast is a pragmatic and practical manual that provides step-by-step instructions leading us on a path to protect and enhance the surrounding environment. The practical steps in this book are backed up with scientific research data. I, like most gardeners, enjoy a well-marked path, but I also have a healthy dose of skepticism when told what to do and how to do it. As I read Susan's book, my skepticism dissolves with each chapter.

People often use the term *incredible* with little thought, but I am most deliberate when I call Susan Varlamoff's book about sustainable gardening an incredible resource. I am struck by the insight necessary to provide a simple game plan that allows us to do a better job of sustaining our planet through thoughtful, sensible gardening practices. It is easy to talk about doing a better job, but her book is so clearly written and so thorough that it empowers us to make positive choices in our gardens and landscapes. Susan's book is not only a marvelous teaching tool for my own kids and grandkids but also for a host of other gardeners who want to be planet-friendly.

Allan Armitage
Former professor of horticulture at the University of Georgia

Sustainable Gardening

for the

Southeast

Introduction

Creation is a gift, it is a wonderful gift that God has given us, so that we care for it and we use it for the benefit of all, always with great respect and gratitude.

Pope Francis

We are the ones we've been waiting for.

The Elders, Oraibi, Arizona Hopi Nation

The Southeast has always been a mecca for gardeners. The long growing season and generally copious rainfall (except during droughts) provide gardeners with many opportunities to indulge their hobby. From the antebellum plantation gardens to the modern weekend warriors who mow, plant, and weed so they can indulge their friends with an outdoor barbecue, gardening is a way of life in the Southeast.

Americans, in general, love to garden. In fact, it's their favorite hobby, according to a 2013 survey by the National Gardening Association. Homeowners, particularly, like to connect with the earth by mowing their grass, tending their flower beds, and cultivating vegetable gardens. According to the survey, approximately 74 percent of U.S. households participate in one or more gardening activities. When gardeners were asked in a 2011 survey how knowledgeable they were about maintaining their home landscapes in an environmentally friendly way, most homeowners said that they weren't very knowledgeable. However, 79 percent of all U.S. households in the survey said that it was important to them that residential, commercial, and municipal lawns and landscapes be maintained in an environmentally friendly way.

A 1999 University of Georgia survey mirrored these results, confirming that interest in earth-friendly gardening is not a new trend. The survey revealed that Georgia homeowners were very concerned about protecting the earth's resources, but they wanted more information about doing the right environmental thing. At the time, water-quality tests showed that pesticide levels in Georgia urban areas exceeded those in rural or farm areas. And since Georgia farmers and professional pesticide applicators are trained to apply garden chemicals properly by Georgia Cooperative Extension agents, the finger pointed to home gardeners who receive no training and who often believe that *if a little is good, more must be better.*

As a result of these findings, in 2000 I began working with a group of scientists to develop best-management practices for Georgia homeowners to reduce pollution in lakes, streams, and rivers. The information was disseminated through the media, in workshops, and on the Internet. The demand for and interest in green gardening practices was more than we could have imagined. Fact sheets were reproduced by the thousands, and homeowner workshops were standing-room-only events—even on snowy Georgia nights.

Over time, more environmental issues have cropped up to change the way Georgians and southeasterners think about maintaining their landscapes. For example, as a result of two serious droughts, we learned to collect rainwater from rooftops to irrigate our plants and keep our gardens alive. Many of us asked plant nurseries and retailers to stock more drought- and heat-tolerant native species. Armed with thirty years of research by a University of Delaware professor on the benefits of native plants, we began using more native flora in our landscaping. Such plants are adapted to the climate and also help to restore biodiversity—the backbone of a healthy ecosystem. Some native plant enthusiasts even race ahead of bulldozers on construction sites to rescue native plants and transplant them in their gardens. And we're getting smarter about selecting cultivated plants for our southern landscapes while targeting invasive plants such as kudzu and Chinese privet, which are capable of overtaking southern native forests and gardens, for removal.

In the midst of transforming our landscape plants and practices, we are embracing the local food movement that has swept the nation. Instead of buying West Coast lettuce to serve on our East Coast tables, more homeowners are growing their own veggies and fruits—the ultimate fast-food fad that reduces greenhouse gas emissions from long transports.

Just as Americans recycle, buy more efficient cars, and adjust thermostats to reduce energy use, we also want more sustainable ways to garden. We must act in concert to farm and garden in ways that not only feed us but also protect and restore our natural resource base. Gardeners and scientists alike are well aware that the burgeoning population of our planet is taxing our natural resource base. Climate change, water scarcity, biodiversity loss, and polluted streams and rivers are of tremendous concern. That's why much of the information in this book is gleaned from the best research conducted at our country's land-grant universities.

Many gardening books address only one environmental issue, such as designing a water-wise landscape, using natural pest control, or even growing organic vegetables. But what is missing is an integrated, concise gardening handbook that provides sustainable practices for all environmental issues—water quality and quantity, biodiversity, energy, and soil improvement, to name a few—and is organized in topics familiar to gardeners, from landscape design to natural pest management.

This book grew out of my lifelong passion for both gardening and environmental protection, interests I inherited from my father, John. Back in the 1960s, Dad created "paradise" in our yard by planting an artful array of shade trees, shrubs, flowers, and even a vegetable garden that delighted the neighbors as well as his children and eventually his grandchildren. He also took his five children for weekly walks in the woods to discover nature by learning about plants and their habitats, identifying trees by their leaves and bark, and observing tracks made by various animals.

I gardened in my early married years just as I saw my father do. As a young bride living abroad, I tended roses in our Tehran townhouse garden. After moving back to the United States, I cultivated home gardens in the deep, rich topsoils of Minnesota and Pennsylvania, then the sands of South Carolina. For the past twenty-one years, I have been trying to coax flowers, trees, and shrubs from Georgia red clay. In 1982, however, my gardening was abruptly put on hold as concerns for the health and safety of my three young sons led me to join my neighbors to shut the polluting landfill just two blocks from my home. Ironically, the city of Eden Prairie, Minnesota, where we lived, was named by early settlers who perceived it as a paradise on the prairie. This precedent-setting environmental case, chronicled in my book *The Polluters: A Community Fights Back*, showed me the fragility of the earth's resources and spurred me to take action to protect our land, air, and water. The landfill teemed with unauthorized toxic waste that polluted the groundwater and emitted methane into the neighborhood. Pollutants tumbled into the nearby wildlife refuge and also fouled the air. Today, that landfill is closed and capped; it no longer presents a hazard to either the nearby residents or the environment.

My foray into environmental activism led me to understand how a group of committed people can become change agents. After securing a master's degree in environmental pollution control to give me the educational credentials I needed, I eventually landed a position at the University of Georgia Research and Education Garden. In the Garden, scientists researched ways to minimize the impact of gardening on the environment. It was here that I worked with colleagues to write best-management practices for Georgia gardeners to safeguard water quality and quantity.

Eventually, I was promoted to the position of director for the Office of Environmental Sciences at the University of Georgia College of Agricultural and Environmental Sciences in Athens. I am based in the Department of Horticulture, which boasts world-class gardening experts such as Dr. Allan Armitage, an authority on annuals and perennials, and Dr. Michael Dirr, a specialist in woody ornamentals. It didn't take long for me to realize that other departments had their share of global experts in water conservation, lawn management, and natural pest management. These scientists often collaborate and share information about their latest research with other southeastern universities so it seemed natural to me that I would tap their talent to write a book about how southern gardeners could restore functioning ecosystems in their landscapes.

My ideas about southeastern planet-friendly gardening are also rooted in field experiments in my Lilburn, Georgia, yard. It became apparent that soil would be an issue after my three adolescent sons broke two shovels digging a hole for a koi pond one July. It dawned on me that the red clay used for the bricks in stately southern homes became nearly impenetrable during the hot, dry summers. The soil in my yard would require serious amending before I could plant anything and expect it to grow.

I noticed, too, that the hot, humid summers bred bugs in abundance.

Japanese beetles devoured my roses and crape myrtle. A Japanese beetle trap I purchased managed to attract what seemed like the entire Lilburn beetle population to my yard. Obviously, I needed to find a better solution.

The original shrubs in my yard included rhododendron, a plant found in Georgia forests and at higher latitudes such as New Jersey, where I grew up. I planted more and then noticed that the increasingly hot, dry summers gave them heat stroke.

As in most urban landscapes, turf occupied most of the yard. My husband and I voluntarily reduced the front lawn size when a serious drought left barely enough drinking water in area reservoirs, and outdoor watering was banned. When trees eventually covered the backyard, we eliminated the grass there entirely. In its place we put in native plants, bird feeders, and pebble paths to enjoy the wildlife-filled wooded area.

After twenty-some years of making mistakes and finding better ways to minimize my environmental impact, I believe I am moving in the right direction. Here's why:

- My garden is a certified wildlife habitat. At least twenty species of birds frequent the yard. Pest infestations are no longer a problem. Birds and bugs do the job of keeping those pests in check.
- Mother Nature irrigates my garden. During drought, rain collected in barrels supplies water needed for my thirsty annuals and perennials.
- My home, which is shaded by hardwood trees, is often ten degrees cooler in summer than Atlanta, which is twenty miles away. My energy bill is the envy of the neighborhood.
- I switched from a chemical lawn service to one that uses organic products, thus eliminating brown patch and other diseases associated with synthetic fertilizers.
- When I am gardening, my neighbors often stop by and ask for tips to improve their landscapes. As a Master Gardener, I have a ready stash of soil sample bags and begin the lesson from the ground up.

The more I learn about gardening and the environment, the more convinced I become that gardeners could and should be part of the solution to restore our native habitats, pull greenhouse gases out of the atmosphere, store carbon in the soils, return pollinators to plants, purify the air, and cool our cities. Collectively, we can become change agents to transform the landscape for tomorrow's children. My hope is that this book will serve as a guide and an inspiration.

1

Design with Nature

Whether it's the air we breathe, the water we drink, or the soil in which we plant, a steady stream of dire scientific findings continues to pinpoint many human activities as having a negative impact on the health of the planet. A constant barrage of bad news about the natural world can make us feel powerless to protect and safeguard the environment despite our best efforts to live a "green" life and reduce our environmental footprint. But in these times of decreasing biodiversity, declining green space, habitat loss, and increasing levels of water and atmospheric pollutants, landscapers and gardeners can take steps to promote the health of the earth.

This book is for people who want to extend their environmentally friendly practices to their landscapes, be it a pocket garden, a typical backyard, or a vegetable and fruit garden. It presents many ideas and practices that can help gardeners and landscapers create and maintain sustainable landscapes that work in harmony with nature. Whether created by nature or helped along by human hands, a sustainable landscape—one that nourishes and sustains all life within its boundaries—is achievable. A planet-friendly garden or landscape can be defined as a functioning ecological unit. And even if it includes the built environment, such as a house, a deck, or a driveway, these man-made elements can work in harmony with the natural processes that maintain the earth's natural balance.

Among the many benefits of a sustainable garden or landscape are:

- Maintaining fertile soil
- Enhancing the local biodiversity

- Recycling water and nutrients
- Purifying the air and water
- Absorbing and storing excess carbon dioxide produced by people and machinery
- Augmenting the food supply for wildlife and humans
- Offering a safe and attractive place to live and play
- Reducing the use of artificial pesticides and fertilizers

Through thoughtful design, gardeners can begin the process of enhancing their landscapes to become attractive, inviting, planet-friendly places to relax, play, and enjoy. And all who take pleasure in them also get the additional satisfaction of knowing that these landscapes are working in harmony with nature.

But before we plunge right into these planet-friendly practices, a refresher on how ecosystems operate is in order, especially since these principles form the basis of environmentally friendly gardening practices. Understanding how ecosystems function will help gardeners recognize not only why specific practices are recommended but also why and how they help reduce global warming and city smog, increase biodiversity, provide a greater variety of habitats, and protect water quality and quantity. If you are already familiar with the basic principles of ecology, you might want to skim over the next section of this chapter and jump ahead to the section about cultivating a sustainable landscape.

Anyone who has ever studied ecology knows that ecosystems are immensely complex. Many of their physical components—such as water, air, nutrients, and carbon—are recycled through a maze of complex biogeochemical processes that interact with one another, as illustrated in figure 1.1.

Through a process called photosynthesis, plants use carbon dioxide, sun, water, and nutrients from the soil to make carbon-rich starches and sugars. Thus, carbon becomes part of the plant tissue, and the oxygen, a by-product of photosynthesis, is released into the air. When plants die and decompose, elements such as carbon are released back into the soil where they become available for other plants to use.

Plants buried deep in the earth for millions of years become carbon-rich fossil fuels such as coal and oil. When we burn these fossil fuels for energy, some of the carbon once stored in these ancient plants is released

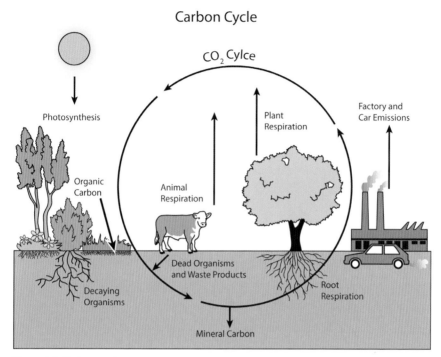

Figure 1.1. Carbon cycle.

into the atmosphere, where it becomes carbon dioxide. In addition, the incomplete burning of these fossil fuels adds prodigious amounts of methane, nitrous oxide, and other gases into the air. Collectively these compounds are called greenhouse gases. They form a gaseous blanket around the earth, preventing heat generated on the earth's surface from escaping into the upper atmosphere. As a result, the earth's temperature is rising. In fact, according to records kept by the National Oceanic and Atmospheric Administration (NOAA), there is about 30 percent more carbon dioxide in the air now than there was 150 years ago, at the beginning of the Industrial Revolution.

Water also travels through another critical biogeochemical cycle. The hydrologic cycle circulates water from the earth to the atmosphere and back again. Through evaporation and transpiration (release of water vapor from plant leaves into the atmosphere), water enters the atmosphere and forms clouds, falling to earth as precipitation. Rain and snowmelt return water to the earth's oceans, rivers, streams, and soil. A portion

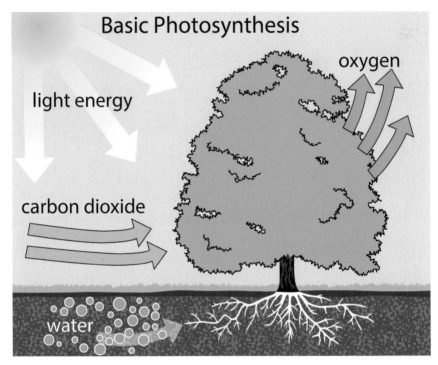

Figure 1.2. Photosynthesis.

of the precipitation also seeps into underground aquifers and recharges streams and rivers.

Humans have disrupted the hydrologic cycle, especially in urban areas, by paving over vast areas of land. Since rainwater cannot penetrate impervious hardscapes, such as parking lots, roads, and large expanses of roofs, water cannot soak into the soil to recharge the groundwater. Instead, the rainwater rushes off these surfaces, causing temporary surges, even flooding, in the rivers and streams. In the process, the rainwater also carries pollutants such as oil, pet waste, and gardening chemicals deposited on landscapes and hardscapes into storm drains and nearby rivers and streams.

The proper functioning of these and other biogeochemical cycles is vital to all life on the planet. These cycles provide a bounty of goods and services that we often take for granted. The production of goods such as food, fiber, fuel, and timber that support our comfortable, often sumptuous, lifestyles is intricately dependent on these cycles. More important, we

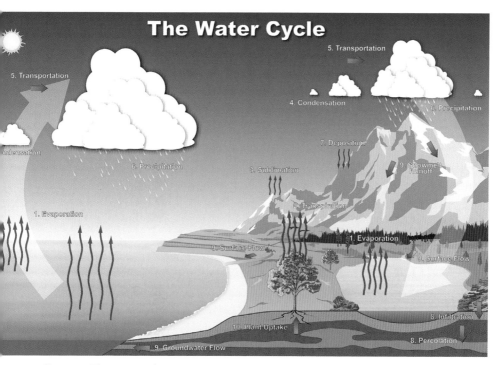

Figure 1.3. The water cycle.

cannot survive without nature's ecological services—water purification, waste management, climate and flood control, and pest management, to name a few. Plant roots and microbes purify water as it flows through the soil. Soil organisms degrade animal and plant waste into basic nutrients and minerals needed for new life. Trees and other plants slow rainwater as it strikes the earth and helps hold the soil in place, and their roots also absorb water from the soil, helping reduce flooding. A multitude of native trees, shrubs, flowers, and ground covers attracts a diverse array of insects, birds, and other animals that prey on pests, helping to keep infestations in check.

Nature's benefits to human health can be both obvious and obscure. For example, it is well-known that plants were used by ancient civilizations to cure illness and still serve today as the basis for many medicines such as aspirin, which was originally produced from willow, and digitalis, which is produced by foxgloves and is used to treat heart patients. More subtle are

Ecosystems provide many important benefits:

- Waste disposal and recycling
- Pollination
- Water purification
- Fresh drinking water
- Climate and temperature regulation
- Flood control
- Food
- Wood for construction, furniture, paper, and other everyday items
- Fiber for clothes and textiles
- Fuel such as coal, oil, natural gas, and radioactive material
- Pest control
- Medicines
- Aesthetics—natural beauty and feeling of well-being
- Spiritual

nature's psychological and spiritual benefits. Research reported (by Jolanda Maas and others) in the October 2009 *Journal of Epidemiology and Community Health,* for instance, confirms that the annual rates of fifteen out of twenty-four disease clusters were lower in environments that had more green space within a 1-kilometer radius. The relationship was the strongest for anxiety disorder and depression.

Cultivating a Sustainable Landscape

Gardeners can partner with Mother Nature and let her do the heavy lifting in maintaining cultivated landscapes. In other words, we can create landscapes that support the working of nature's cycles, reducing our workload. When designing a landscape or retrofitting an existing one, gardeners would be well-advised to cultivate the following concepts along with their plants.

Build Fertile Soil

Fertile soil is the foundation of most life on earth. In an undisturbed ecosystem, plants germinate, grow, reproduce, die, and decompose, releasing

Figure 1.4. Backyard compost bin.

minerals into the soil to become simple but essential nutrients for new life. A gardener can mimic this process by maintaining natural, undisturbed areas and by building soil fertility in the cultivated landscape with home-made compost.

Protect the soil with vegetation, and in the Southeast, preferably with trees, shrubs, flowers, and ground covers. In shaded areas where plants do not grow well, cover the soil with mulch. Bare soil exposed to the weather can wash into a nearby stream, river, or lake or may be blown by wind for long distances. It can also dry out, become compacted, and release carbon to the atmosphere. Fertile soil stores carbon, helping to mitigate climate change.

Action Tip: Make sure to include a compost pile in the landscape plan.

Plant for Biodiversity

Without human intervention, a natural landscape grows diverse plants that attract a multitude of animals, including birds, insects, and amphibians.

Figure 1.5. Many plant varieties create biodiversity in a landscape.

Each species has its own specialty or niche that helps maintain the delicate balance within a habitat and also contributes to the overall health of earth's cycles. For example, bees pollinate flowers, soil microorganisms decompose dead matter into nutrients plants can use, and insect predators help mitigate pest infestations.

Biodiversity is most easily restored by choosing a variety of native plants because natives are adapted to a particular region and its temperature ranges, soil, altitude, and rainfall patterns. Both research and practical experience confirm that insects that share an evolutionary history with native plants select those plants for food and in turn become food for many native birds, reptiles, amphibians, and mammals. Wildlife needs food, shelter, and water in the landscape, too. To attract a rich diversity of wildlife, include a selection of native trees and other plants that attract insects and birds, as well as a water source and areas where animals can forage, nest, and find shelter.

Action Tip: Select native plants when possible for their hardiness and contribution to the natural plant and animal community. Chapters 3 and 4 contain a list of native trees, shrubs, and flowers.

Conserve Water

This precious, life-giving resource must be shared by all living things—plants, humans, and other animals. With the burgeoning human population, the finite amount of water must be shared among increasing numbers of people, who often live in areas where limited freshwater resources are becoming increasingly inadequate for the community's needs. As a result, water restrictions and bans on outdoor watering are becoming commonplace in many areas of the country due to droughts and increased demand. Creating a water-wise landscape, or a xeriscape design, reduces the need for supplemental irrigation beyond what Mother Nature supplies. Xeriscape design, described at the end of this chapter, involves grouping plants according to water needs.

Action Tip: In regions of low rainfall and in times of drought, rain barrels and cisterns under downspouts may be a gardener's best watering tool. It's easy to collect rainfall from rooftops and use it to irrigate the landscape.

Manage Storm-Water Pollutants

There are no artificial pollutants in Mother Nature's scheme, where all naturally produced matter is recycled and reused through the biogeochemical cycles described earlier. Many human-made synthetic compounds, however, pose a challenge to nature's decomposers, which do not recognize novel chemical configurations and cannot degrade them easily. As a result, synthetic substances including pesticides and fertilizers may take a very long time to decompose in the natural environment. DDT (dichlorodiphenyltrichloroethane), an agricultural pesticide that was banned in 1972, is still found today in breast tissue of women exposed many years ago. Everything from gardening chemicals to pet waste and oil and grease from roads and parking lots may end up in water bodies.

Rain gardens, vegetated buffers, swales, and other similar landscape features collect storm water and allow it to seep slowly into the ground, where plant roots and soil microbes can begin to degrade contaminants. Minimizing walkways, driveways, and other paved surfaces allows rain to soak into the soil and helps prevent flooding in nearby streams and rivers.

Action Tip: Consider installing rain gardens and buffers to capture storm-water pollutants from your landscape. And when possible, use porous materials such as gravel, wood chips, bricks, or pavers for driveways, walkways, and patios.

Reduce and Remove Greenhouse Gas Emissions

As humans clear the land for such things as lumber, farms, subdivisions, and shopping malls and make other changes to the landscape, fewer trees and other plants are available to absorb carbon dioxide, and the excess accumulates in the atmosphere as a greenhouse gas. Planting the land with trees, shrubs, flowers, vines, and grass helps store or sequester excess carbon.

Action Tip: Strategically plant trees near the house to reduce heating costs in winter and cooling costs in summer, decreasing a homeowner's overall energy consumption. Using energy-efficient or solar outdoor lighting fixtures makes the garden even more sustainable.

Figure 1.6. A rain garden catches, filters, and helps degrade storm-water pollutants.

Figure 1.7. A vegetated buffer helps remove pollutants before they enter the stream.

Grow Food Locally

Today's food often travels great distances from farm to table. When a Virginian buys Florida strawberries, those berries may have traveled hundreds of miles, and when a New Yorker buys California iceberg lettuce, that produce has traveled more than three thousand miles from the farm to the table. Transporting food by fossil-fueled planes and trucks releases copious amounts of carbon dioxide and other greenhouse gases.

Action Tip: Make a low-emission decision: Grow some of your own vegetables, fruits, or even herbs for your table either in your own backyard or in a community garden. Also buy locally grown food.

Include a Safe Place to Live and Play

Grassy areas around the home provide a safe place to play ball, picnic, and enjoy the outdoors. Humans evolved on the grassy savannas of Africa because they could move about easily and had an unobstructed view of predators (Cerling et al., "Woody Cover and Hominin Environments"). Other studies show that children who play on well-maintained turf are less prone to injury than those who play on bare earth or paved surfaces.

Getting Started

Whether you've just moved into a new area or region or you've lived in the same place for years, the first step in planet-friendly gardening is to become better acquainted with the local environment. Find out about growing conditions, soils, and climate. Learn seasonal rainfall patterns—for example, is there a rainy season or a dry period during the year? Visit nature centers, parks, and botanical gardens to see what plants thrive in the local environment.

The zone hardiness map shown in figure 1.8 provides a bird's-eye view of the average minimum temperature in each region of the Southeast. Plants grow best within certain temperature ranges, so check the zone where you live to see what its limitations are.

Next, put on walking shoes and explore the landscape. Going through the following checklist will give you clues as to its diversity, health, and overall condition.

Walk the Land and Check It Out

- Are plants thriving, marginally successful, or downright dead?
- Are there any natural areas that can be preserved?
- What wildlife lives, roams, and flies in the area?
- Are most plants native to the area, or are they listed on the invasive list? (The state native plant society or Cooperative Extension office has a list.)
- Is there a variety of plants, or are there areas where one plant type, such as grass, dominates?
- Where are the high and low areas, slopes, and depressions?

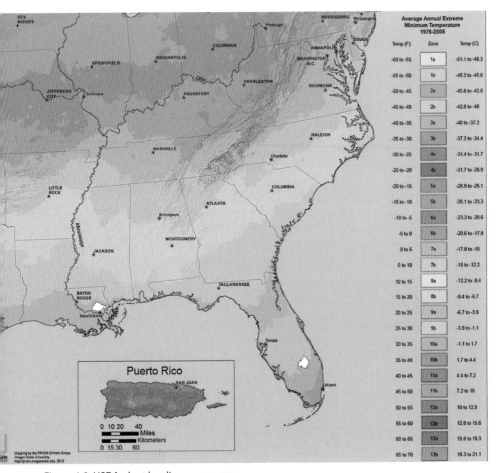

Figure 1.8. USDA plant hardiness zone map.

- What areas are in full sun, partial sun, or full shade? Note changes throughout the day and seasons.
- What areas are moist, and what areas are dry?
- How does rain flow off the rooftops, driveway, walkways and property? Are there gullies or signs of runoff?
- Is there a stream, river, lake, or pond nearby?
- Is it windy, and from what direction does the prevailing wind blow?
- Are there bare patches of grass and ground covers?
- Where are the underground pipes, cables, and drains?

Consider Available Resources

Gardening can be all-consuming, so design your landscape according to the time and resources available.

Time and Energy

Remember that an expanse of lawn is often labor-intensive and requires weekly mowing during the growing season and may also need regular applications of herbicides and fertilizer to maintain a relatively weed-free appearance. It is often said that perennials are perennial work, and annuals may need daily watering. Established trees, shrubs, and ground covers often require little water and maintenance.

Water

Is there sufficient rainfall to water the landscape, which may include a lawn, vegetable patch, and annual and perennial gardens? Do you live in an area with limited rainfall and that is prone to droughts? If rainfall is scarce, are alternate water sources close by? Are you willing to install barrels or a cistern to collect rainwater off the roof? Would a xeriscape landscape or one that conserves water be a good alternative to what is already planted?

Money

How you want to maintain the landscape—either as showplace or with a more natural look—determines the cost of gardening. Plants and seeds, equipment (mower, spreader, hoses, weed whacker, etc.), fertilizer, water, and mulches such as pine straw all have a price, which, collectively, can add up.

Develop a Land-Use Plan

How you plan the landscape begins with features closest to the house and extends outward to the property lines.

Close to Home

To save time and energy, put areas that need constant care, such as vegetable and herb gardens or annual and perennial beds near the house and the water supply. Keep in mind that vegetable and herb gardens need six to eight hours of sunlight every day. These gardens are not compatible with

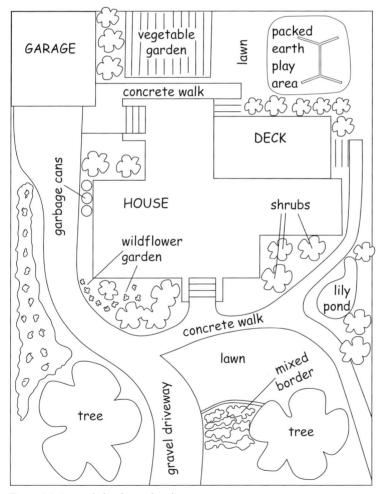

Figure 1.9. A sample land-use plan diagram.

deciduous trees planted on the south side of the house to shade it from the searing summer sun. Also note the location of outdoor faucets, decks, and patios, fenced areas for pets or urban livestock, such as chickens, and the utility area for garbage cans and air-conditioning units.

Farther Afield

Larger trees and shrubs that need little extra watering once they are established can be located farther away from the house. Swing sets, garden sheds, compost areas, and ponds should be within a short distance of the house and easily accessible.

Along the Property Line

If the land is sloped, install rain gardens and swales in the low-lying areas to manage storm water. If the landscape borders a stream, river, or lake, leave a strip of natural vegetation. Consult local ordinances to learn the correct buffer requirement. In windy areas, plant trees strategically along the property line or in other appropriate areas to serve as a windbreak. If your property borders a natural area, link up with it and create a wildlife habitat. This forms a wildlife corridor that gives birds and other animals a larger area in which to live and roam.

Think Ahead

Remember that seasons change and plants and trees grow taller and wider over the years. A sunny perennial garden may become shaded as young trees mature. The lawn may thin as the tree canopy increases. And the roots of mature trees may suck up the soil's moisture, leaving nearby flowers thirsty. Imagine how the landscape will look in five years.

Elements in a Land-Use Plan

Your lifestyle and the resources you want to devote to the landscape will factor into what it will look like. Here are some general elements you may want to consider. Planet-friendly gardeners will want to include natural areas to attract wildlife and a compost pile to renew the soil.

- Natural areas
- Trees and shrubs

- Foundation plants near the home
- Lawn, ground covers
- Annuals, perennials, and shrubs
- A grassy or mulch area for people and pets to play
- A swing set
- A deck or patio for outdoor entertaining
- Beds for vegetables, fruits, and herbs
- Walking paths
- Compost pile
- Irrigation system
- Rain barrels and cisterns
- Swales and rain gardens

Generate a Landscape Plan

The following step-by-step guide will help you create a plan for your landscape.

1. Begin by drawing the location of existing structures or hardscapes such as house, garage, driveway, walkways, deck, and patio.
2. Add existing landscape features that you will keep—lawn, natural areas, trees, shrubs, flower beds, fences, hedgerows.
3. Locate the compost pile away from drainage areas and at least 50 feet from streams, rivers, and ponds.
4. If the property is near a stream or river, include a vegetated buffer along the water.
5. If there are steep slopes, determine low-lying areas and incorporate swales and rain gardens in your plan.
6. Create wildlife habitats in natural areas.
7. In you live in a windy region, consider planting trees and shrubs as a windbreak.
8. Plan turf areas according to water availability and need. In planet-friendly gardening, the lawn will occupy no more than 40 percent of the landscape.
9. If considering a water garden, place it away from low-lying areas to prevent storm water from draining into it.
10. Create a water-wise landscape, as described next.

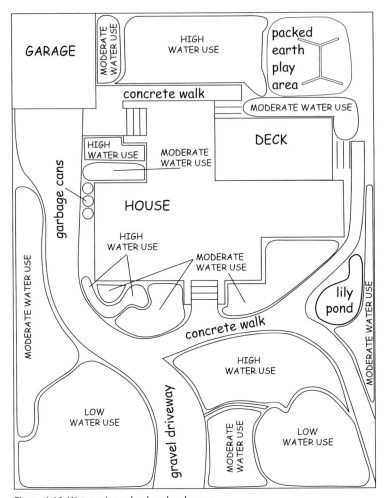

Figure 1.10. Water-wise suburban landscape.

What Is a Water-Wise Landscape?

A water-wise landscape, often referred to as xeriscape, minimizes the need for supplemental irrigation through design, plant selection, installation, and maintenance. Given the competing demands for drinking water and outdoor watering, which can double summertime residential water use, it is imperative to reduce landscape irrigation.

The term "xeriscape" (pronounced zera-scape) was coined in Colorado in 1981 in response to a prolonged drought. It derives from merging the Greek word *xeros*, meaning dry, with the word "landscape." A xeriscape-type landscape can reduce outdoor water consumption by as much as 50 percent without sacrificing the quality and beauty of the landscaped environment (Wade et al., *Xeriscape*). It also requires less fertilizer to maintain, and because it is low-maintenance, it saves a gardener time, effort, and money. Just about any landscape, whether newly installed or well-established, can be made more water-efficient.

A water-wise gardener divides the landscape into three water-use zones: *high* (regular watering), *moderate* (occasional watering), and *low* (natural rainfall). An individual landscape usually includes several of each of these zones.

High Water-Use Zones

These are small, highly visible areas such as seasonal annual beds of colorful flowers such as begonias, petunias, and pansies that require frequent watering. They are usually located in the front yard and surrounding the patio or deck. Avoid scattering a number of small colorful flower beds throughout the landscape that will be difficult to keep watered. To maximize water savings, concentrate seasonal flower beds in areas where they can be watered and maintained easily.

Moderate Water-Use Zones

These are areas where established plants are watered only when they turn a gray-green color, start to wilt, or show other symptoms of moisture stress. Plants for this zone may include azalea, dogwood, redbud, Japanese maple, and many herbaceous perennials.

Low Water-Use Zones

These contain plants that are watered only by natural rainfall and do not need additional irrigation. For greatest water conservation, design as much of your landscape as possible in low water-use zones. Most people are surprised to learn that the majority of our woody ornamental trees and shrubs, some herbaceous perennials, and even some annuals like vinca and verbena grow well in low water-use zones once they are established.

In gardening and farming, working in harmony with nature's cycles has been a well-understood dictum since the early days of human civilization. The Roman writer Marcus Seneca (54 BC–AD 39) wrote: "True wisdom consists in not departing from nature but molding our conduct according to her laws and models." Today's gardeners would do well to heed that advice and design their landscapes to connect with Mother Nature, thus benefiting from the ecological services she provides. Nature, which includes humans, is dynamic, so landscape plans can and should be adapted to changing ecological conditions such as warming temperatures or encroachment of shade as well as changing personal situations that may leave a gardener with less time, physical resilience, or money to pursue this hobby. The payback is an ecologically sensible symphony conducted by Mother Nature.

The Inside Scoop on Soil

The history of every nation is eventually written
in the way in which it cares for its soil.
Franklin D. Roosevelt

Farmers have a long tradition of believing that if you care for the land, it will care for you. That means that if you manage the soil well, your families—and successive generations who later cultivate the land—are likely to enjoy abundant harvests. Using this same approach, gardeners who protect and enhance their soil will be rewarded with a flourishing landscape. And the native wildlife and the earth itself will benefit as well.

Soil

All soils are various mixtures of the same basic ingredients: minerals, air, water, and organic and inorganic material. About 90 percent of the soil is inorganic and made of minute particles from rocks and minerals—sometimes worn down over millions of years. Fertile soil contains 4–10 percent organic material, which includes living and decomposed matter. The organic component not only stores energy, nutrients, and water needed by living plants and other organisms but also helps sustain a diverse plant and animal community above ground, regulates water flow, filters pollutants, recycles nutrients, and mitigates weather variations such as drought and temperature fluctuations.

While soil may appear lifeless and inert, in reality it teems with a diversity of microscopic life that contributes to essential physical, biological, and chemical soil-building processes. Bacteria, fungi, insects, worms, and a host of other micro- and macroorganisms inhabit rich soil, performing vital functions for all life forms that depend on soil. The most important role

Did you know? Just one shovelful of fertile soil contains more creatures than there are human beings on the planet, according to the Smithsonian National Museum of Natural History exhibit *Dig It! The Secrets of Soil.*

of these myriad soil organisms is to convert dead organic matter—leaves, vegetable scraps, and lawn clippings, to name a few—into dark, spongy, nutrient-rich material called humus.

Humus typically permeates the top few inches of soil and supplies much of soil's fertility and moisture-retaining qualities. In fact, each pound of humus can absorb as much as two pounds of water. Through the work of microorganisms such as bacteria and fungi, and macroorganisms such as beetles and slugs and earthworms, humus is continually replenished, revitalizing the soil with the nutrients necessary for plant growth. This natural cycle of life, death, decomposition, and rebirth is repeated throughout the seasons in forests great and small, in lawns and gardens, and in meadows and prairies.

Fertile soil also can store great quantities of carbon—an important offset for climate change. The 2007 Intergovernmental Panel on Climate Change report indicated that soil, high in organic matter, has the potential to mitigate a whopping 36 percent of greenhouse gas emissions.

When people alter natural landscapes to build cities and suburbs or create more farmland, they inadvertently but routinely remove ingredients vital to the creation of healthy soil. For instance, they haul away grass clippings, dead branches, and other debris instead of letting them decompose into soil and become humus. Even more detrimental than depleting the soil's humus, though, is leaving the soil bare and exposed to the harsh effects of sun, wind, and rain.

Gardeners who mimic nature's soil-building process are handsomely rewarded with rich soils that support lush plant growth. Composting is an easy, natural strategy to ensure a healthy, robust, fertile soil, rich in humus and nutrients. Composted organic material is easily made in the backyard using kitchen scraps, yard waste, and many other organic materials.

Soil Texture

Soil texture determines what kinds of plants will flourish in a landscape. For example, azaleas and blueberries thrive in well-drained acid soils; forsythia and hellebores prefer alkaline soils and tolerate higher levels of moisture-retaining clay. The three major soil types—sand, silt, and clay—influence soil texture, and, when combined in various proportions, they form the basis of soil classification. To get a better understanding of the soils in your garden setting, take samples throughout the landscape and examine them. Hold some soil in your hand and see how it feels. Compare your soil samples with the major soil types described here.

Clay Soils

Clay soils, often reddish-brown or gray, have small particles that clump together when wet. Water does not drain easily through clay soils. As the clay dries out, it becomes brick-hard. Clay is often nutrient-rich, but plant roots have a tough time penetrating the soil to reach the nutrients because the small soil particles are packed so tightly together.

Figure 2.1. Clay soil clumps in your hand.

Figure 2.2. Sandy soil feels gritty and has larger particles than clay.

Figure 2.3. Silty soil has fine particle size and feels silky.

Sandy Soils

Sandy soils feel gritty and are composed of large particles with large air spaces between them. Everything—including water and water-soluble nutrients—drains through sandy soils quickly, before plant roots can absorb them.

Silty Soils

Silty soils are made of fine- or intermediate-sized mineral particles that have a soapy, silky feeling and leave fingers dirty. Silty soils are reason-

Did you know? It is estimated that 1 inch of soil takes anywhere from hundreds to thousands of years to form under natural conditions. (Soil Science Society of America, *Soils Matter*)

ably moisture-retentive and nutrient-rich. They compact easily and can be heavy to work with.

Soil Structure

Soil structure refers to how the inorganic and organic portions are held together. Over time, roots, fungi, and bacteria clump the soil into crumbs and clods, which provide habitat for soil organisms and create channels for air and water. Good soil structure allows plant roots to penetrate deeply to absorb water and nutrients for growth.

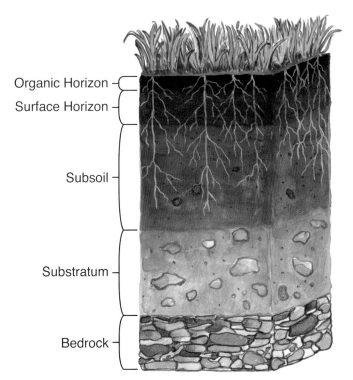

Organic Horizon

Surface Horizon

Subsoil

Substratum

Bedrock

Figure 2.4. Soil profile.

Figure 2.5. Standing water indicates poor drainage and soil structure.

Figure 2.6. Good soil structure.

Neither clay soils nor sandy soils have good soil structure. Clay soils are too tightly bound, and sandy soils are too loosely packed. Generous additions of humus can break up clay clods and can bind sandy soils to provide an environment more conducive for plant growth.

To figure out your soil structure, dig a hole, remove some soil, and inspect it. Can you roll it into a sausage, or does it crumble in your hands?

Is it loose and sandy? Enlarge the hole to 2 feet by 2 feet and fill it with water. Does the water drain within a few minutes, or does it collect for hours? The presence of water after one hour indicates poor drainage and most likely a heavy, clay soil—a better material for brick making than for gardening (see figure 2.5).

Indicators of good soil structure are a deep-brown color and a sweet, earthy smell. And earthworms can be found in abundance. Fertile soil is essential for a flourishing garden, is easy to dig, and crumbles in your hand. Because the soil is loosely compacted, plant roots are able to penetrate deeply and withstand droughts (see figure 2.6).

Life Underground

Gardening sustainably means ensuring that soil organisms have ample food, water, and air. In making fertile soil, microbes do the heavy lifting.

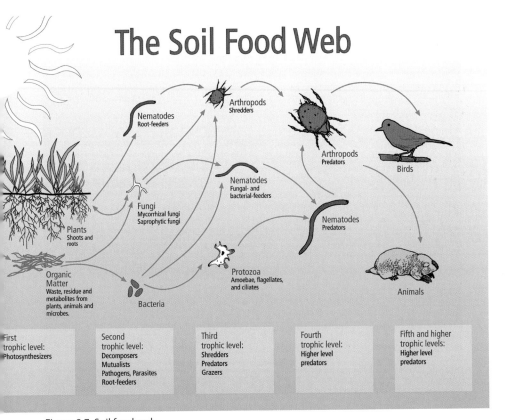

Figure 2.7. Soil food web.

Plants send chemical signals to nearby soil bacteria and fungi that indicate the plants' nutrient needs. The microbes respond by making these nutrients available in a soluble form that can be easily absorbed by the plant roots. Soil microbes also enhance soil structure and porosity, thus increasing infiltration of water. They also convert nitrogen, essential for plant growth, into a form that plants can use.

Mycorrhizae fungi are also important in soil fertility, In fact, they are soil superstars. They perform a very important role for plants. Some attach themselves to the cells inside a plant's roots; others form extensive networks between the outer surface of the roots and the soil. Both types help plants absorb more water and nutrients. In return, plants supply the fungi with food.

Since both fungi and plants benefit from their association, it is considered a symbiotic relationship. However, soil fungi are fragile. Repeatedly

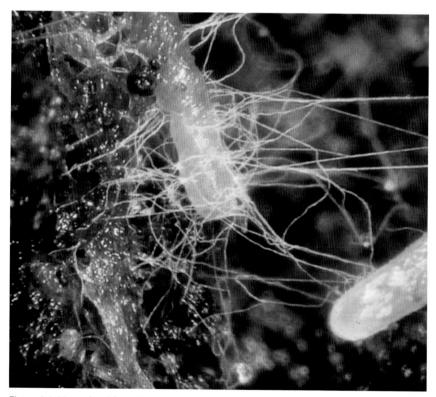

Figure 2.8. Mycorrhizal fungi form filaments to help plants absorb water and nutrients.

Figure 2.9. Earthworms, the "intestines of the earth."

digging the dirt disturbs their delicate network of filaments. They are also very sensitive to fungicides and prefer undisturbed, "no dig" gardens.

Earthworms, described by Darwin as "intestines of the earth," are important underground contributors to fertile soil. Their presence indicates soil health. They drag dead organic matter into the soil and eat and digest it, breaking it into smaller pieces for bacteria and fungi to feed on. When walking in a forest, you may have noticed leaf stems protruding from a small hole in the soil that is surrounded by casts. These are remnants of an earthworm's foraging. Their tunnels aerate the soil, and their nutrient-rich casts help form soil "crumbs." Only a few millimeters in diameter, soil crumbs are mineral particles of organic matter that form a network of pores to hold air and water. They provide the soil structure in which roots grow and soil creatures thrive.

It is important to note that above-ground diversity of plants and animals contributes to below-ground diversity of microbes, insects, and other organisms that contribute to soil fertility.

Nutrients Fuel Plant Growth

Like people, plants need a steady supply of nutrients and minerals to keep them healthy. Compost made in your backyard can provide most of the essential nutrients for your garden. They include macronutrients and micronutrients in trace amounts. Depending on what a gardener grows, some additional nutrients may be needed.

A plant's ability to use nutrients in the soil depends upon soil pH, or acidity or alkalinity. The pH ranges from 1, which is extremely acidic, to 14, which is very alkaline. Most soils have a pH range of about 4–8. The majority of plants grow in the range of pH 5.5–7.5. Figure 2.10 shows the range in which plants will grow well. Keeping the soil rich in organic matter prevents great pH fluctuations.

How you restore the soil—and, indeed, whether you need to—depends upon how it was managed in the past and what you expect to grow. No matter where you live in the Southeast, chances are good that the topsoil has been depleted at some time in the historic past. For example, in

Macronutrients—plants can't live without them.
- Nitrogen (N)—necessary for growth of leaves and shoots
- Phosphorus (P)—essential for root growth
- Potassium (K)—vital for flowering and fruiting
- Magnesium (Mg)—important in chlorophyll production
- Calcium (Ca)—integral part of the cell wall
- Sulfur (S)—central to root growth and seed production

Micronutrients—needed by plants in small but essential amounts to regulate various processes.
- Iron (Fe)—important for chlorophyll formation
- Manganese (Mn)—vital to enzyme systems involved in carbohydrate breakdown and nitrogen metabolism
- Copper (Cu)—important for reproductive growth
- Zinc (Zn)—essential for carbohydrate transformation
- Boron (B)—fundamental to seed and fruit development
- Molybdenum (Mb)—significant in nitrogen use
- Chloride (Cl)—valuable in plant metabolism

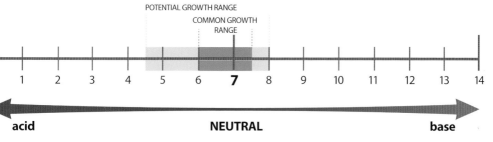

asparagus, spinach, lettuce, okra, onion, bluegrass, junipers, colver
6.0 - 7.5

melons, beans, peppers, tomatos
5.5 - 6.5

potatos, carrots, basil, camellias, tobacco, pine trees, centipede turf
5.5 - 6.25

blueberries, sweet potatos, azaleas, gardenias, hydrangeas
4.5 - 5.5

POTENTIAL GROWTH RANGE

COMMON GROWTH RANGE

1 2 3 4 5 6 **7** 8 9 10 11 12 13 14

acid   **NEUTRAL**   **base**

Figure 2.10. The pH requirements for various plants.

Figure 2.11. Massive gullies caused by poor farming practices.

the 1800s and early 1900s, much of the arable land in this region of the country—from the piedmont to the sea—was planted in cotton, which is notorious for its ability to deplete the soil of nutrients. In addition, the poor farming practices of the 1800s resulted in massive soil erosion. Providence Canyon State Park, or "Little Grand Canyon," in southwest Georgia is an extreme example of poor soil management. Gullies up to 150 feet deep were caused by soil erosion, and the canyon is now a tourist attraction (figure 2.11).

If you live in a newly built subdivision, chances are good that the soil is compacted from foot traffic, earth-moving equipment, and piled-up building materials on-site. Topsoil may even be exposed as a result of excavation or, worse, lacking entirely. Gardeners in these kinds of situations may have some serious soil building and amending to do before they can dazzle their friends with flourishing flower beds or vegetable gardens. But don't fret; soil can be improved one bed at a time.

Regardless of what you want to grow—grass, trees, shrubs, veggies, or flowers—soil improvements are best made according to recommendations provided by the local Cooperative Extension or other reliable sources of information after soil testing has been performed. The Cooperative Extension associated with each state land-grant university provides soil analysis, among other services. Sampling results will furnish the soil's nutrient content and pH and also will give recommendations on how to improve soil chemistry for intended uses—whether you plan to grow a lawn, create annual and perennial beds, or plant blueberry bushes. If you plan to grow drought-tolerant plants, they do not require a rich, fertile soil. However, if your garden includes a vegetable patch, you will need a good program to maintain soil fertility. The National Cooperative Extension website (www. csrees.usda.gov/Extension/) provides contact information for state offices. Contact your nearest office or a soil-testing laboratory to find out how to take and submit soil samples.

Become a Composting Connoisseur

The first thing a gardener can do to enhance the soil is to have a ready source of humus on hand. A backyard compost pile is a low-tech, low-cost way to make humus. Referred to as "black gold" by farmers, humus has

Figure 2.12. Turning vegetable scraps and yard debris to make compost.

been used to enrich farm and garden soils for thousands of years, long before synthetic fertilizers arrived on the scene in the 1950s.

Composting is a sustainable process in which organic waste from inside and outside the home is piled up for nature to decompose into the simple nutrients that plants require. The end product, humus, contains nitrogen, phosphorus, potassium, calcium, and other trace minerals essential to plant growth.

Homemade Compost Recipe

Since decomposition is a natural process, making humus is easy. Just toss kitchen scraps and yard waste in a heap on the bare earth and turn the pile from time to time. Don't be concerned about the "perfect" recipe or about arranging the pile in precise layers of greens (high-nitrogen material) and browns (high-carbon material). Gardeners can fast-track the decomposition process by locating their pile in the sun, keeping it moist, and turning it regularly, for example, weekly. If you prefer, you can opt for a cone-shaped composting bin that has a narrow neck to keep out curious neighborhood pets and wildlife. The following recommendations will help you understand the process and how to optimize it.

Ingredients for a Compost Pile

Nearly anything that once lived is a candidate for a backyard compost pile. Grass clippings, ground-up leaves, vegetable peelings, eggshells, pine needles, wood ashes, sawdust, nut shells, corn cobs, seaweed, hair clippings, coffee grounds, and tea bags are all excellent ingredients for your homemade compost. A variety of materials is best. A more diverse pile is likely to decompose faster, maintain a higher internal temperature, and contain a greater variety of needed nutrients.

"Green" and "Brown" Materials

Compost ingredients are organic materials that contain carbon and nitrogen and are classified as either "brown" (those high in carbon) or "green" (those high in nitrogen). Green materials decompose more quickly than brown materials. For best results, aim for a 3:1 brown-to-green ratio. Examples of each are listed in table 2.1.

Did you know? Yard waste makes up to 13 percent of the municipal solid waste collected, and compostable food scraps comprise nearly 14 percent of the garbage dumped in landfills. (U.S. Environmental Protection Agency, "Municipal Solid Waste Generation")

Composting Materials Needing Special Handling

- Meat, fish, and bones attract animals; if included, they should be buried deep in the pile.
- Dairy products make the compost smell bad if they are not covered well.
- Fats, oils, and grease may slow down the process.
- Waste from humans and pets may contain pathogens, which may not be killed if the pile temperature does not reach 131°F.
- Diseased and invasive plants and weeds gone to seed may not be killed if the compost temperature is lower than 131°F.
- Treated or painted wood may contain toxic chemicals. They should not be added to the compost pile.
- Wood ashes are strongly alkaline and can upset the desirable living conditions of microbes. However, ashes also contain phosphorus and potassium that plants need for growth, so small amounts—1 cup per a typical $4 \times 4 \times 4$–foot pile—can be added.

Table 2.1. Compost pile ingredients

Browns—Carbon sources	Greens—Nitrogen sources
Woody prunings, leaves	Grass clippings, discarded plants, including house plants
Straw, pine needles	Rotted farm animal manure
Cardboard egg cartons, tubes, paper bags	Fruit and vegetable scraps, eggshells, bread
Newspaper, wood shavings, sawdust	Hair, fur, feathers
Dryer lint, cotton fabric	Coffee grounds and filters, tea bags

Compost Pile Construction

Efficient decomposition depends on aeration, moisture content, particle size, temperature, and sufficient supplies of carbon and nitrogen. The following recommendations can enhance the process, prevent pollution problems, and keep you on good terms with your neighbors.

1. Choose a level, well-drained spot, preferably near your garden. If possible, locate the compost pile in partial sun to help heat the organic matter.

2. Locate the compost pile away from the neighbors' homes so any foul odors will not waft into nearby yards. Position your compost pile at least 50 feet from streams, rivers, and ponds to prevent compost nutrients from washing into the water during a rain-storm.

3. Build your pile directly on the ground or buy or build a con-tainer. Cone-shaped, rectangle, square, and round bins are all available to suit your personality type. The Cooperative Exten-sion in each state provides guidelines for composting. To ensure proper decomposition, the pile or container should be at least 3–4 feet by 3–4 feet. Smaller piles will not heat up enough to kill weed seeds and disease, and a pile much bigger is difficult to turn.

4. Place coarse material, such as twigs and short lengths of small tree limbs, at the bottom of the pile to provide good air circula-tion.

5. Chop and chip larger material if you want your pile to decay quickly. Take the time to chop up large fibrous materials such as woody stalks and small branches, and chip larger branches and tree trunks.

6. Layering "greens" and "browns" is often recommended but not necessary. For the layering approach, use 3–4 inches of "brown" material followed by 3–4 inches of "green" material. Cover with 1–2 inches of manure, and then top this off with 1 inch of soil. However, I toss material onto a pile in an approximate ratio of three parts "brown" and one part "green," and it works.

7. Water the pile periodically to keep it wet but not soggy.

8. Turn the pile at least once each month to move less decomposed matter into the middle of the heap and to keep offending odors down. As organisms start breaking down all the layers, you will notice that the center of the pile becomes very hot—130°–160°F. This is a sign that decomposition is happening!

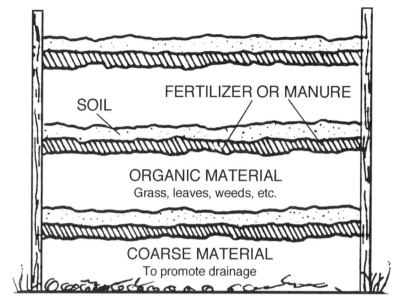

Figure 2.13. Diagram of compost pile construction.

9. Determine when the compost is ready for use. Humus is dark brown or black and resembles commercial potting soil, just lumpier. Worms should be burrowing through the soil.

Common Compost Questions

What If the Compost Pile Stinks?

If the compost pile smells bad, it is probably due to a lack of air or too much nitrogen-rich material such as grass. Increase the "browns," such as leaves and twigs, and turn the pile more frequently to introduce oxygen.

What If Animals Are Attracted to the Pile?

No doubt kitchen waste such as watermelon rinds and spoiled lettuce may entice the local turtles, raccoons, dogs, and cats to stop by for dinner. Bury kitchen waste in the pile or shovel soil over it to discourage hungry animals from scavenging.

Figure 2.14. Humus, the end product of decomposition.

Decomposition Process

Decomposition is nature's way of recycling nutrients from one generation to the next. There are two decomposition phases: anaerobic (without oxygen) and aerobic (with oxygen). Aerobic decomposition—where oxygen is in abundant supply—takes place on the surface of the forest floor and also in the outer regions of a compost pile. It occurs more quickly than anaerobic decomposition and produces no odors. Bacteria, fungi, and other microorganisms feed on the decaying matter in the early composting stages. In the later stages, mites, millipedes, beetles, and earthworms further break down the organic material. Anaerobic decomposition occurs slowly where no oxygen is available such as at the bottom of swamps, lakes, and the compost pile. The process of decomposition releases heat—between 130°F and 160°F in a compost pile—and these temperatures are high enough to kill weed seeds and plant pathogens. At these temperatures, organic matter putrefies and releases hydrogen sulfide, a foul-smelling odor (think rotten eggs). The end result of aerobic and anaerobic decomposition is humus.

How Long Does Composting Take?

It depends on many factors, including the composition of the original ingredients, whether the pile is in the sun or shade, temperature, and water. In summer, compost might be ready in three months if the pile is turned each week, watered, and fed the correct ratio of green material to brown material. Otherwise, it may take up to one year. When the compost looks like dark soil, has worms burrowing through it, and the original ingredients are not recognizable, it's ready. Once compost is ready, it can be used to improve clay and sandy soils and to act as a mulch for annual, perennial, and vegetable beds. Complete decomposition is not necessary when using compost as mulch. In time, the mulch will decompose and become part of the soil.

More Composting Methods

Leaf Mold

This foolproof compost can be made by putting raked leaves in a bin or pile and then turning them occasionally to make a low-nutrient soil additive and moisture-retaining mulch. The decomposition process is slower and fertility is lower than in a traditional compost heap of "greens" and "browns."

Worm Composting

High-fertility compost can be made by housing worms in a bin such as a garbage can or wooden crate and feeding them vegetable scraps. Good drainage is vital because worms can drown in wet conditions produced by kitchen waste. Worms process food slowly, so don't overfeed them; the excess food may rot, and the worms won't touch it. Then the container may smell foul. If this happens, mix in moisture-absorbing materials such as newspaper, cardboard tubes, and paper towels. Worm compost makes a great top dressing for vegetable gardens and house plants and can be used to enrich commercial potting mix. This is a good alternative to a traditional compost pile if kitchen scraps are the principal waste. It can be done in a small space such as the porch and has a higher nutrient value than compost.

Figure 2.15. Leaf mold is low-nutrient compost but easy to make.

Green Manure

Green manure is really just a cover crop that farmers and gardeners plant in fallow fields to regenerate the soil. Typically, the plants used are nitrogen-fixing, which means they increase or fix nitrogen in the soil. Green manure crops have dense foliage to suppress weeds and deep roots to improve soil

Figure 2.16. Worm compost is a high-nutrient compost that can be tricky to make.

Figure 2.17. Green manure such as this clover restores fertility to the soil.

structure. Good examples include winter rye and red clover. In gardening, green manure is used in areas such as vegetable patches, where the soil is left to rest and recover nutrients. Usually after fall harvest, seed for green manure, such as clover, is sown and left to grow during winter. In early spring, the plants are cultivated into the soil. Green manure improves fertility with little effort, but the land cannot be used during green-manure production.

Table 2.2. Common organic soil improvers

Material	Fertility Rating	Mulch	Dig in	Notes
Bark, fine	low	X		Good for mulch
Wood chips and coarse bark	low	X		Apply as mulch around trees, shrubs and perennials
Leaf mold	low	X	X	Made from composted fallen leaves
Straw	low	X		Obtain from an organic farm
Municipal compost	low	X		Yard waste recycled in large-scale facilities–not always composted
Municipal prunings: shredded, green, and woody	low to medium	X		Apply as mulch around trees, shrubs and flowers
Garden compost	medium	X	X	Composted yard trimmings, grass and kitchen food scraps
Animal manure	medium to high	X	X	High in nutrients; should be well-rotted
Worm compost	high	X	X	High in nutrients
Commercial products: composted manures, plant and food wastes	variable	X	X	An alternative to humus made in a backyard compost pile

Source: Adapted from Pears, *Rodale's Illustrated Encyclopedia of Organic Gardening*, p. 41.

Other organic ways to improve soil are listed in table 2.2, which compares and contrasts their nutrient value and how they can be used—either as an amendment or as mulch.

Steps to Restore Soil Fertility

Feed the Soil

If compaction is a problem or the soil is sandy, dig or till in 1–2 inches of humus directly into the top 6–8 inches of the soil. If the soil is heavy clay, till in the higher rate of compost as deeply in the soil as possible. Microbes will incorporate the organic material slowly into soil-providing nutrients at rates plant roots can absorb. Composted manures and plant wastes also can be purchased.

Avoid digging uncomposted pine bark nuggets, wood chips, or yard waste into the soil as an amendment. When soil microorganisms feed on these materials, they use nitrogen that plants need for growth. Incorporating uncomposted organic material into the soil can also cause the soil pH to drop dramatically below the desirable range. Use undecomposed organic material *only* if there is time for it to decompose before landscape planting or if it is used on top of the soil as a mulch to suppress weeds, retain moisture, and prevent erosion.

Trying to improve the soil with synthetic fertilizers is a losing proposition in the long run. This fast-food diet gives plants instant nutrition but adds nothing to soil structure and can be easily overapplied. Excess fertilizer that is not absorbed by the plants can run off the land and pollute nearby surface or ground water.

To Improve Fertility When Soil Is Not Compacted

If using high-fertility soil improvers, evenly spread manure and worm compost over the ground to a depth of ¼ inch. Apply in spring and summer only, when nutrients can be used by the growing plants.

Medium-Fertility Soil Improvers

When using medium-fertility soil improvers, such as garden compost, evenly spread the material 1 inch deep over the land. Also apply in spring and summer, when plant growth is maximal.

Low-Fertility Soil Improvers

Low-fertility soil improvers can be applied in greater quantities and used more frequently than the medium- and high-fertility soil improvers. Mulches like pine straw, bark, wood chips, and leaf mold can be spread over the land to a depth of 3–5 inches. To avoid disease problems on the mulched plants, do not place compost close to the stem or trunk. Replenish the mulch regularly to maintain the benefits. Avoid a mulch volcano, or piling up the mulch next to the tree trunk, which may kill the tree.

These materials can be applied at any time of the year because they add few nutrients but work well as a mulch to moderate soil temperature and soil moisture levels and to prevent weeds, especially in the spring.

Dig Only When Necessary

There are times when digging is necessary to break up badly compacted soil. However, in fertile soil with good structure, digging disturbs the soil creatures' habitat and their intricate web of activities such as decomposition and nutrient cycling. It also releases carbon stored in organic matter, brings weed seeds to the soil surface to germinate, and increases the risk of erosion. Some soil disturbance takes place when seeds are sowed, seedlings are planted, and food is harvested, but this can be kept to a minimum.

Assess the soil structure before tilling, plowing, or turning the soil with a shovel, and dig only if the soil is compacted. Otherwise, apply soil amendments directly to the soil surface to keep the underground creatures well-fed.

Figure 2.18. Ways to improve soil include (*top, from left*) shredded prunings, coarse bark, commercial cow manure, leaf mold, and (*bottom, from left*), fine bark, garden compost, straw, worm compost.

Walk with Care

Continually walking on the soil and driving heavy equipment over it will compact it and damage its structure. Compacted soil becomes devoid of air, making it difficult for roots and water to penetrate. It also becomes inhospitable for soil-living creatures. Walking on designated paths made with material such as wood chips, gravel, or porous pavers preserves the surrounding soil structure. When working in vegetable and flower beds, distribute your body weight by kneeling on a board or garden cushion.

Keep It Covered

To prevent erosion and protect soil structure, cover bare soil with plants or mulch. Since plants store carbon, keeping the land covered with plants helps reduce global warming and erosion and maintains soil structure.

Benefits of a No-Dig System

- Preserves soil structure
- Leaves soil organism habitat undisturbed
- Reduces dormant weed seeds from being brought to the surface to sprout
- Maintains soil moisture and organic matter
- Prevents the release of carbon from the soil into the atmosphere
- Reduces soil erosion

By making compost in the backyard, a gardener saves money and trips to the garden center to purchase fertilizer and mulch. Instead of releasing greenhouse gases by driving to a retail store to buy fertilizer, a gardener can help restore carbon to the soil with backyard composting. With so many good reasons to make compost, it is easy to see why backyard composting has increased in popularity in recent years.

Keep in mind the words of University of Washington geologist David Montgomery: "With 8 billion people, we're going to have to start getting interested in soil. We're simply not going to be able to keep treating it like dirt" (quoted in Mann, "Where Food Begins").

3

Plant Trees

Fight Climate Change

The true meaning of life is to plant trees,
under whose shade you do not expect to sit.

Nelson Henderson (1865–1943), pioneer farmer, Manitoba

Trees grace many southern landscapes and gardens with their beauty and majesty. Environmentalists—often referred to as "tree huggers"—value them for their bounty of ecological benefits. And you can have both aesthetics and environmental services by properly planting trees in your landscape. When trees are strategically placed, their shade cools us, our homes, and our communities. And more than that, trees control soil erosion, moderate their immediate climate, provide windbreaks, and purify both the air we breathe and the water we drink. Plus, trees provide habitat for a myriad of creatures from bugs to birds.

Acting as the earth's lungs, trees "inhale" air during photosynthesis, absorbing carbon dioxide and "exhaling" oxygen through their leaves. Trees and other plants with chlorophyll use the carbon to make sugar and build tissue, in effect "locking up" the carbon until the tree, or its leaves and branches, dies. This carbon-sequestering quality is becoming increasingly important because the carbon stored in trees is not available to bind with

Did you know? One tree can remove 26 pounds of carbon dioxide from the atmosphere annually, equaling 11,000 miles of car emissions. (Relf, *The Value of Landscaping*)

oxygen to form carbon dioxide, a greenhouse gas that contributes to global climate change. All vegetation stores carbon, but due to their size, trees store much more carbon than, say, a bed of petunias.

Considerable quantities of carbon are stored not just in the trunk and limbs but also in the roots. When land is cleared of vegetation, trees and other plants are no longer present to absorb the carbon dioxide released by burning fossil fuels and exhaled by humans and other animals.

Scientists first began tracking and documenting rising levels of atmospheric carbon dioxide in 1958 at the NOAA Mauna Loa Observatory in Hawaii. After five decades of tracking, carbon dioxide levels increased by 30 percent. Levels are expected to rise 180 percent by 2100 as the human population increases worldwide and as more people adopt a Western lifestyle.

The jagged line in figure 3.1 represents carbon dioxide's annual seasonal fluctuations. In the height of summer, when trees are leafed out and are

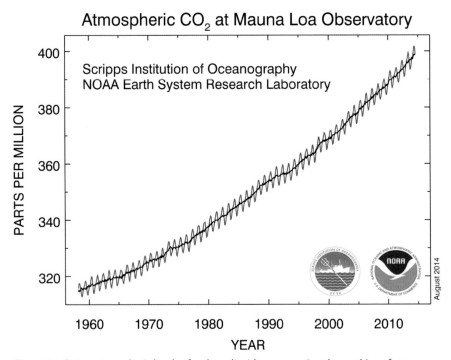

Figure 3.1. Rising atmospheric levels of carbon dioxide are warming the earth's surface.

Did you know? If every American family planted just one tree, the amount of CO_2 in the atmosphere would be reduced by 1 billion pounds annually. (American Forestry Association, *Tree Facts*)

"inhaling" greater amounts of carbon dioxide, atmospheric carbon dioxide levels are lower. In winter, after deciduous trees lose their leaves, carbon dioxide levels rise.

Ecological Benefits of Trees

In addition to removing the greenhouse gas carbon dioxide from the atmosphere, trees provide many additional environmental benefits that are described below in greater detail.

Secure the Soil

On average, tree roots penetrate 6–24 inches below the soil surface, depending on such factors as species, age, and growing conditions. They also radiate out two to four times beyond the diameter of the tree crown, anchoring the tree and holding the soil in place. Trees growing on hillsides, slopes, and ravines and along streams and rivers secure the banks so they don't erode and get washed away. People in just about every culture and civilization have learned the hard way how trees can help stabilize the soil. For example, during the nineteenth century in the United States, forests were clear-cut to farm. This practice led to massive erosion and eventually to the establishment of the Soil Conservation Service (SCS) in 1935, later renamed the National Resource Conservation Service, a permanent agency in the U.S. Department of Agriculture. The SCS recognized that "the wastage of soil and moisture resources on farm, grazing, and forest lands . . . is a menace to the national welfare."

Today's wise land managers plant trees along waterways. The trees not only form buffers that hold the soil in place but also purify the water of pesticides and fertilizers that run off the land. In 2003, a nine-year stream buffer study showed that a grass and forest buffer system reduced nitrogen and phosphorus runoff by 60 percent and herbicides to below detectable levels (Durham, "Designing the Best Possible Conservation Buffers"). Gardeners who live along waterways or lakes can enlist nature's help by planting a buffer of trees to cleanse water that runs off their property.

Mitigate Climate Change

A tree's ability to help reduce the effects of climate change depends on the amount of carbon it stores. And that amount depends on many factors—the tree's size and growth rate, the carbon dioxide concentrations in the air, the climate and the season, and the species of tree. The faster a tree grows, the more carbon it can store as carbon-rich carbohydrates and, eventually, as wood mass. Likewise, when a tree's growth rate slows because of such factors as advancing age or cold weather, the amount of carbon a tree can store begins to slow. The species of tree also affects its carbon-storing abilities. For example, dense-wood trees are the most effective carbon-storage units. A 2002 study (Nowak et al., "Effects of Urban Tree Management") identified some trees species that are more effective than others at storing carbon. The list of high carbon dioxide consumers includes silver maple (*Acer saccharinum*); American sweetgum (*Liquidambar styraciflua*); northern oak (*Quercus rubra*); white oak (*Quercus alba*); southern live oak (*Quercus virginiana*); black walnut (*Juglans nigra*); southern magnolia (*Magnolia grandiflora*); and flowering dogwood (*Cornus florida*).

Collect and Filter Storm Water

While a tree's roots are absorbing rain and reducing runoff and flooding, its leafy canopy is catching and also deflecting rain even before it reaches the ground, helping mitigate storm-water surges that increase erosion and cause rising creek and river levels. One effect of climate change in the Southeast is increased storms with higher-than-average rainfall.

Strategically planted trees in a landscape reduce the volume of storm water flowing from paved surfaces, such as roadways, driveways, and parking lots. As rainwater washes over these nonporous surfaces, it collects pollut-

Did you know? One hundred mature trees can intercept 100,000 gallons of rainfall per year in their crowns. (U.S. Department of Agriculture, Southern Region Forest Service, *Benefits of Urban Trees*)

ants such as pet waste, gasoline, and oil from cars. Tree roots and the soils around paved surfaces filter contaminants from storm water before it flows into sewers. Some water contaminants, such as pet waste, serve as nutrients that trees use to enhance growth.

Moderate the Climate, Especially in Cities

In summer, trees absorb and deflect radiant energy from the sun. A dense tree canopy can cool the temperature by as much as 10°F through shading and transpiration—the process by which trees release water vapor through their leaves (McPherson and Simpson, "Shade Trees as a Demand-Side Re-

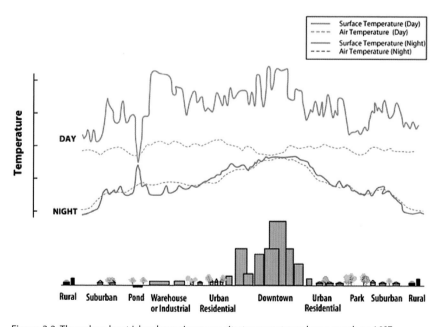

Figure 3.2. The urban heat island may increase city temperatures by as much as 10°F.

Did you know? Trees in urban areas of the United States remove an estimated 711,000 tons of toxic pollutants from the air each year. (Nowak, Crane, and Stevens, "Air Pollution Removal by Urban Trees and Shrubs")

source"). Planting trees in city parks and around homes cools the air, providing respite from the heat produced by the absorption of solar radiation by asphalt roads, parking lots, and rooftops. When these dark surfaces prevail, cities heat up in what is known as the heat-island effect.

The heat-island effect may cause city temperatures to rise as much as 22°F higher than the surrounding suburbs, particularly after dark (U.S. Environmental Protection Agency, "Heat Island Impacts"). Living in urban heat islands requires more air-conditioning to cool buildings and homes. Atlanta, in fact, has been nicknamed "Hotlanta" due to this condition.

Improve Air Quality

Leaves filter the air by removing dust and other small particles, which rain then washes into the ground for additional filtering by tree roots. As leaves absorb carbon dioxide from the air, they also absorb air pollutants, such as carbon monoxide, volatile organic compounds, nitrogen oxide, and particulate matter from car tailpipe emissions, creating better air quality in the tree's vicinity.

Cut Heating and Cooling Costs

Trees provide natural "low-tech" cooling. Depending on a tree's location, species, size, and condition in the landscape, its shade and transpiration can reduce home heating and cooling costs. By planting deciduous trees in the landscape, a homeowner can benefit from the shade provided in the summer and bask in the solar radiant heat in winter after the leaves fall.

Trees with compact or dense foliage are effective windbreaks and can absorb or deflect the initial impact of wind as well as rain, sleet, and hail, and they provide some protection for people, pets, and buildings.

Bring Wildlife to Your Doorstep

Planting mostly native trees will make a gardener's landscape teem with wildlife. Birds, insects, and small mammals will find suitable habitats among the leaves, branches, and crevices and also around the tree's base. Leaves, berries, and nuts provide seasonal food for these critters. Research by entomologist Douglas Tallamy, for example, has revealed that the oak tree ranks number one for attracting insects, birds, and mammals. The Southeast is particularly noted for its diverse plant communities, especially in the forested area of north Georgia and North Carolina and in the longleaf pine–wiregrass communities that occur from Virginia to Mississippi. Take advantage of the many native species of trees that thrive in the Southeast and select those that will attract the native wildlife. Pages 60–62 present a list of some large, medium, and small native trees that attract wildlife and are suitable for landscapes.

Things to Consider When Planting a Tree

Trees frame and define our landscapes. Because of their higher cost and larger size, they are usually the first plants to be installed in the landscape and the last to be removed from it. As a result, it is important to select and plant trees with care. Getting it right the first time will avoid the time-consuming task of transplanting later. To get a better understanding of what trees will be best for your landscape, answer the following questions:

What Purpose Will the Tree Serve?

Trees serve many functions. Some provide an abundance of shade, colorful flowers, fruits in season, or a splendid canopy of fall foliage when they mature. Some are perfect for screening the garbage can, a compost pile, or the neighbors' ongoing construction projects or cars under perpetual repair. Trees also create wildlife habitat and can be a great place for a swing or a tree house. What are your needs?

Is the Species Appropriate?

Select trees that are native or adapted to your area. See what native trees look like by visiting local botanical gardens, city parks, or a wildlife center.

Table 3.1. Southeastern native trees that attract wildlife

Common name, *Scientific name*	Hardiness zones	Evergreen(E), Deciduous(D)/ Growth rate	Sun	Ht. (ft)	Landscape uses
Red maple, *Acer rubrum*	6b, 7a, 7b, 8a, 8b	D/medium	F	50–75	Shade tree in moist well-drained soils; great fall color
Sugar maple, *Acer saccharum*	6b, 7a, 7b	D/medium to slow	F-P	50–75	Makes a fine specimen, street, or shade tree; prefers moist, well-drained soil; brilliant fall color
Yellow buckeye, *Aesculus flava*	7a, 7b	D/fast	F	70–90	Specimen tree that provides good shade and ornamental flowers; needs deep, moist, well-drained soils
River birch, *Betula nigra*	6b, 7a, 7b, 8a, 8b	D/fast	F	60–80	Shade or specimen tree, particularly in groupings; looks nice as multistemmed form
Mockernut hickory, *Carya tomentosa*	6b, 7a, 7b, 8a, 8b	D/medium	F	60–80	Beautiful fall yellow color; wildlife feed on the nuts
Sugarberry, *Celtis laevigata*	7a, 7b, 8a, 8b	D/medium	F	60–80	Long-lived shade tree that grows best in moist soils in the full sun
American beech, *Fagus grandifolia*	6b, 7a, 7b, 8a, 8b	D/slow	F-P	50–80	Shade or specimen tree that prefers moist, acidic, well-drained soil; full sun or partial shade
White ash, *Fraxinus americana*	6b, 7a, 7b, 8a, 8b	D/medium	F-P	50–80	Specimen or street tree for large areas; prefers well-drained soils and full sun
Green ash, *Fraxinus pennsylvanica*	6b, 7a, 7b, 8a, 8b	D/fast	F	50–100	Popular shade tree that transplants readily and grows in a variety of soils and sites
American holly, *Ilex opaca*	6b, 7a, 7b, 8a, 8b	E/medium	F-P	20–50	Use for screening or as a specimen tree; prefers deep, fertile soils and adequate moisture
Black walnut, *Juglans nigra*	6b, 7a, 7b, 8a, 8b	D/fast	F	75–100	Shade tree for stream banks and floodplains; needs moist, well-drained soils; high-value wildlife tree
Eastern red cedar, *Juniperus virginiana*	7a, 7b, 8a, 8b	E/medium	F	40–50	Excellent specimen tree or for windbreaks and hedges; tolerates adverse conditions and poor soils; provides refuge and cover for birds in winter

Tree	Zones	Type/rate	Light	Height	Notes
Sweetgum, *Liquidambar styraciflua*	6b, 7a, 7b, 8a, 8b	D/medium to fast	F	80–100	Shade or specimen tree that prefers moist, rich, and acid soils; moderate drought tolerance
Tulip poplar, *Liriodendron tulipifera*	6b, 7a, 7b, 8a, 8b	D/fast	F	80–100	Shade or specimen tree; large tulip-like yellow, green, and orange flowers appear in spring
Southern magnolia, *Magnolia grandiflora*	7a, 7b, 8a, 8b	E/medium to slow	F-S	60–100	Specimen tree or for screening; requires moist soils, full sun, or part shade; seeds are relished by wildlife and birds
Black gum or tupelo, *Nyssa sylvatica*	6b, 7a, 7b, 8a, 8b	D/medium	F	70–80	Use as a specimen tree; prefers moist, fertile soils; bees use tree for honey
Spruce pine, *Pinus glabra*	8a, 8b	E/medium to fast	F-P	70	Use for windbreak, screening, or specimen tree; performs best in moist, fertile soils
Longleaf pine, *Pinus palustris*	7a, 7b, 8a, 8b	E/slow	F	80–100	Canopy tree that provides filtered shade for understory plants like azaleas and dogwoods; needs well-drained, sandy, acidic soils in Coastal Plains
White oak, *Quercus alba*	6b, 7a, 7b, 8a, 8b	D/slow to medium	F	40–60	Beautiful, stately shade tree; prefers full sun, moist, acid, well-drained soil
Scarlet oak, *Quercus coccinea*	6b, 7a, 7b, 8a	D/medium to fast	S	60–80	Shade or specimen tree for dry sites; needs full sun, well-drained soil; drought-tolerant
Southern red oak, *Quercus falcata*	6b, 7a, 7b, 8a, 8b	D/fast	S	50+	Shade or specimen tree that grows on dry upland sites
Laurel oak, *Quercus hemisphaerica*	7b, 8a, 8b	E/slow	F-S	60–80	Shade or street tree that prefers well-drained sandy soils
Overcup oak, *Quercus lyrata*	7b-9a	D/medium	F	45–75	Good tree in difficult urban settings; tolerates most soil conditions, full sun to partial shade
Swamp chestnut oak, *Quercus michauxii*	7a, 7b, 8a, 8b	D/medium	S	50–100	Specimen or shade tree that originates from bottom-lands, floodplains in Piedmont and Coastal Plains
Water oak, *Quercus nigra*	7a, 7b, 8a, 8b	Semi-E/fast	S	50–80	Tolerates a wide variety of soils and site conditions; does well in full sun
Willow oak, *Quercus phellos*	7a, 7b, 8a 8b	D/medium	S	40–60	Shade or specimen tree that prefers moist, fertile soils; shallow roots; avoid using as street tree
Chestnut oak, *Quercus prinus*	6b, 7a, 7b, 8a, 8b	D/medium	S	60–70	Shade or specimen tree that likes well-drained soils and full sun; drought-tolerant.

continued

Common name, *Scientific name*	Hardiness zones	Evergreen(E), Deciduous(D)/ Growth rate	Sun	Ht. (ft)	Landscape uses
Northern red oak, *Quercus rubra*	6b, 7a, 7b, 8a	D/medium to fast	S	60–75	Large specimen or shade tree that needs acidic, sandy loam, well-drained soils, and full sun for best development
Shumard oak, *Quercus shumardii*	7a, 7b, 8a, 8b	D/fast	S	80–100	Shade or specimen tree for well-drained soils
Live oak, *Quercus virginiana*	7b, 8a, 8b	E/slow	S	40–80	Specimen tree in large places; prefers sandy, alkaline soils in coastal areas
Florida maple, *Acer barbatum*	7b, 8a, 8b	D/slow to medium	F–P	35–40	Use as a specimen, shade, or street tree for in moist upland sites with acid soils; moderately drought-tolerant.
Downy serviceberry, Amelanchier arborea	7a, 7b, 8a, 8b	D/medium	F–P	15–25	Flowering or specimen tree likes well-drained, acid soils with adequate moisture; fruit enjoyed by birds
Ironwood, *Carpinus caroliniana*	6b, 7a, 7b, 8a, 8b	D/slow to medium	P–S	20–30	Understory tree; tolerates excess moisture and drought; seeds eaten by birds
Flowering dogwood, *Cornus florida*	6b, 7a, 7b, 8a, 8b	D/medium	P	15–20	Understory hardwood tree; fruit favored by birds and other wildlife; deer browse leaves
Mayhaw, *Crataegus aestivalis*	7a, 7b, 8a, 8b	D/medium	F	15–30	Use in shrub borders or woodland edges; fruits are a favorite of songbirds
Parsley hawthorn, *Crataegus marshallii*	7a, 7b, 8a, 8b	D/slow	P–F	15–30	Understory tree that prefers moist soils; fleshy fruits eaten by songbirds and rodents
Washington hawthorn, *Crataegus phaenopyrum*	7a, 7b, 8a	D/medium	P–F	25–35	Excellent small specimen tree for screen or hedge near buildings; provides fruit and nesting sites for wildlife
Possumhaw, *Ilex decidua*	7a, 7b, 8a, 8b	D/medium to slow	F	12–15	Good specimen tree in shrub border or woodland edge; requires moist soil; small mammals and birds eat fruit
Yaupon holly, *Ilex vomitoria*	7a, 7b, 8a, 8b	E/fast	F–P	12–20	Specimen or hedge for screening; adapted to a wide variety of sites including sun or shade, wet or dry, and acidic or alkaline soils

Source: Wade, et al., "Native Plants for Georgia. Part I: Trees, Shrubs and Woody Vines," B 987.

A Disappearing Ecosystem—Longleaf Pine/Wiregrass Community

Shaped by thousands of years of natural fires, this ecosystem once covered 90 million acres in the southeastern United States and now stands at fewer than 2 million acres. Only scattered patches of the longleaf pine/wiregrass ecosystem remain on the coastal plains of the Carolinas, Georgia, Florida, Alabama, Mississippi, Louisiana, and Texas. The longleaf is hardy. Its wood is dense and strong; its long, straight trunks yield high-value wood products. It is resistant to many insects and diseases that attack other pines. Longleaf pine requires fire every two to four years to remove underbrush, allowing the seeds to germinate in the ash. The ecosystem ranks among the most diverse on the planet. In one 2010 study, 124 plant species were identified in a 100-square-foot plot of land (U.S. Department of Interior, Fish and Wildlife Service, Southeast Region, *Carolina National Wildlife Refuge Comprehensive Conservation Plan*). White-tailed deer, wild turkeys, northern bobwhite, and the nearly extinct red-cockaded woodpecker live here. Factors contributing to the demise of this ecosystem include fire suppression, clearing land for agriculture and development, and aggressive logging in the late 1800s and early 1900s for railroad ties, bridges, wharves, and factories. The U.S. Fish and Wildlife Service, Southeast Region, is working with Partners for Fish and Wildlife Program to locate private landowners who are interested in restoring this endangered ecosystem.

Figure 3.3. Southeastern longleaf pine/wiregrass ecosystem.

Did you know? Trees properly placed around buildings can reduce air-conditioning needs by 30 percent and can also save 20–50 percent in energy used for heating. (Nowak, Crane, and Stevens, "Air Pollution Removal by Urban Trees and Shrubs")

Native trees are resilient, tolerate local weather fluctuations and soil conditions, enhance natural biodiversity and beauty in your neighborhood, and provide food for wildlife. Avoid non-native invasive trees that have a tendency to spread quickly, crowding out native plants. Before selecting a specific ornamental tree or cultivar, check its hardiness zones—or the range of minimum temperatures it can withstand—to make sure it will thrive in your region. Consult the USDA cold hardiness map (figure 1.8) for the average annual minimum temperature for your geographic zone.

How Big Will the Tree Get?

Determine its mature height and spread. If you have a small lot, planting several big trees to shade the property will help conserve energy for your home. But if your plans call for a lawn or for a vegetable garden that needs six hours of sun a day, you will never eat salsa made from your homegrown tomatoes once those trees mature. Also, consider overhead utilities and safety in the street right-of-way when selecting trees.

Does It Have a Particular Insect Pest, Disease, or Other Problem?

Certain insects and diseases can cause serious problems on desirable tree species in some regions. Depending on the pest, some infestations may be difficult to control, or a pest may detract from the tree's attractiveness, if not its life expectancy. Some species such as the silver maple (*Acer saccharinum*) and Bradford pear (*Pyrus calleryana*) are known to have weak wood and are susceptible to damage in ice storms or heavy winds. If your area is prone to ice storms or high winds, then you may want to forgo these trees and select ones that better withstand these natural forces.

How Common Is This Species in Your Neighborhood or Town?

Let's face it, some species are overplanted. Avoiding these and opting for alternatives increases the neighborhood's natural diversity, provides more wildlife habitat, and helps prevent a specific disease or insect pest from destroying a whole species. The American elm (*Ulmus americana*) provides a good example of how a pest can alter a cityscape. This stately tree was planted widely on main streets throughout United States after the turn of the twentieth century. Dutch elm disease ravaged these trees, decimating the beauty of thousands of communities in only a few years.

Is the Tree Evergreen or Deciduous?

Evergreen trees provide cover and shade year-round. They may also be more effective as a barrier for wind and noise and as a visual screen. Deciduous trees, such as maple, provide summer shade but lose their leaves in winter and allow the winter sun to shine in. This may be a consideration for where to place the tree in your yard.

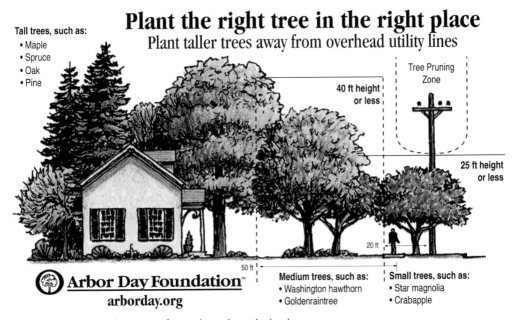

Figure 3.4. Best placement of trees throughout the landscape.

Best Placement of Trees

Best Time to Plant

The ideal time to plant trees is during the dormant season. In temperate climates, plant trees in the fall, after leaves have dropped. This allows all the energy produced during the previous growing season to be directed to root growth since there is little demand from the above-ground limbs and leaves. When spring arrives, a well-established root system is ready to provide the water and nutrients for optimum tree growth. Transplanting in spring or summer results in a competition between roots and shoots for water and nutrients. Often, if there are not enough roots to satisfy the demands of the canopy, then leaves wilt, and it may be necessary to prune the top to reduce the demand on the roots. In tropical and subtropical climates such as Florida, where trees grow year-round, any time is a good time to plant a tree, provided there is ample water.

Before deciding where to plant a tree, you may need to check with underground utility companies to mark the lines prior to digging. When using trees to shade homes, look at the sun's angle, the tree's mature height and canopy width, and the height of the home. Watch the position of the sun throughout the day and determine what windows receive sunlight at different times.

Shade Windows and Walls

Windows and glass doors are the most direct route for sunlight to enter the home, and trees should be positioned to shade them throughout the day in warm climates. Generally, trees planted on the southern and western elevations of a structure provide shade from the hot afternoon sun. Deciduous trees with high, spreading crowns can be planted to the south and west of the home to provide maximum summertime roof shading. After the leaves have shed, the trees' naked branches allow the winter sun to warm the home.

Trees with crowns that grow closer to the ground are more appropriate for western exposures, where shade is needed from lower angles of afternoon sun. A 6- to 8-foot-tall deciduous tree planted near the home will begin shading windows the first year; however, consider the tree's mature spread. Depending on the species of the tree and the size of the home, the tree could shade the first-story roof in five to ten years.

Create Windbreaks

A windbreak can be a single tree or multiple rows of trees and shrubs planted in a linear fashion that can significantly reduce both the wind and a home's heating fuel consumption. A windbreak alters the microclimate around a house, making the building more comfortable and saving on heating costs. Because they retain their foliage throughout the year, evergreen tree species are more effective than deciduous tree species as winter

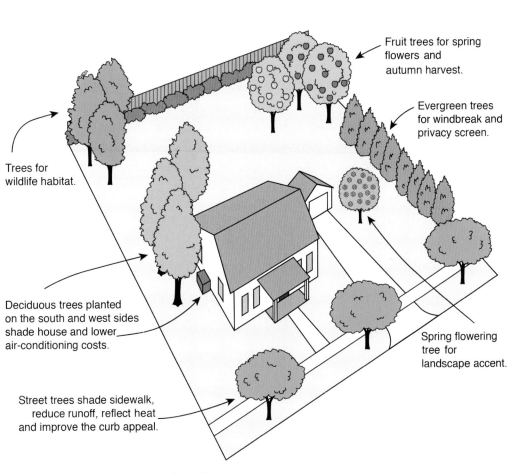

Fruit trees for spring flowers and autumn harvest.

Evergreen trees for windbreak and privacy screen.

Trees for wildlife habitat.

Deciduous trees planted on the south and west sides shade house and lower air-conditioning costs.

Spring flowering tree for landscape accent.

Street trees shade sidewalk, reduce runoff, reflect heat and improve the curb appeal.

Figure 3.5. Placement of trees for desired impact.

Did you know? In colder, windy climates, a windbreak planting can account for up to a 50 percent wind reduction. (Niemiera, *Conserving Energy with Landscaping*)

windbreaks. Consider planting evergreen trees on northern and western exposures to break winter winds. For maximum effect, windbreaks should be oriented perpendicular to the direction of the prevailing winter winds.

Living windbreaks will reduce speeds for a distance thirty times the height of the windbreak. For example, if the mature windbreak planting is 30 feet high, then the zone of maximum wind reduction occurs 150–210 feet downwind of the windbreak.

Choose relatively fast-growing, dense conifers or broadleaf species with stiff branches that will mature to a height of 1.5 times the height of the house. The species should retain its branches low to the ground at maturity. Many pines do not qualify since they lose their lower branches with age. Conifers and broadleaf evergreens suited for windbreaks in the Southeast are listed in table 3.2.

Shrubs planted about 5 feet from the house create an area of dead-air space that decreases heat loss from the exterior walls. Less air movement around the home prevents cold air from entering the home around windows and doors. As always, be sure the species you choose is adapted to the local climate, or plants may snap in an ice storm instead of breaking the wind.

Shade Air-Conditioning Units

By shading the air-conditioning system's outdoor compressor/condenser unit, you will use less energy. A tree can shade the unit when the sun is overhead, and nearby shrubs can provide protection during the early-morning and late-afternoon hours. Take care, however, not to block the conditioner's air flow. If the warm discharge air is prevented from escaping, the intake air temperature is raised, causing the unit to operate less efficiently.

Table 3.2. Southeastern native plants suited for windbreaks

Common name, *Scientific name*	Hardiness zone	Max. ht. (ft.)	Habitat
Eastern red cedar, *Juniperus virginiana*	7a, 7b, 8a, 8b	40–50	Dry, upland, rocky soils; also in moist flood plains
Slash pine, *Pinus elliotti*	8a, 8b	60–100	Moist to wet, sandy, poorly drained soils
Spruce pine, *Pinus glabra*	8a, 8b	50–60	Moist floodplains or hammocks with mixed hardwoods
White pine, *Pinus strobus*	6b, 7a, 7b	50–60	Dry, rocky ridges to wet, poorly drained areas
Virginia pine, *Pinus virginiana*	6b, 7a, 7b, 8a	40–70	Well-drained upland slopes, heavy clays, and dry rocky ridges
Eastern hemlock, *Tsuga canadensis*	6b, 7a, 7b	50–60	Hardwood forests, rocky bluffs
Southern magnolia, *Magnolia grandiflora*	7a, 7b, 8a, 8b	60–100	Moist hardwood forests and wet swampy coastal areas; seeds are relished by wildlife and birds
Devilwood, *Osmanthus americanus*	8a, 8b, 9a, 9b	50	In a mass, the trees' upright, oval form makes an excellent screen
Live oak, *Quercus virginiana*	7b, 8a, 8b	40–80	Sandy, alkaline soils, including coastal dunes

Shade Patios, Walkways, and Driveways

Paved areas retain heat from the sun's radiation. When planting trees near walkways, driveways, or patios, position the trees to provide shade and reduce the amount of the sun's heat transmitted to the surrounding surfaces.

Plant for Resilience

Choosing an appropriate, preferably native, tree and planting it properly gives it a good chance to adapt to the soils and live a healthy, long life. Haphazard planting, on the other hand, makes a tree more susceptible to environmental injury, including pests, drought, and cold. Always water plants thoroughly before removing them from their containers and planting them. A dry root ball is difficult to rewet after it is planted. Watering also helps prevent transplant shock.

Dig the hole to the root ball's depth, but no deeper, and make it two times wider than the root ball. A wide planting hole provides a favorable environment for early root growth and plant establishment. The right depth ensures that the top of the root ball is level with the soil surface and that the root ball will not settle over time and become too deeply set in the soil. If the planting hole is dug deeper than the root system, backfill with some native soil and tamp it firmly in the bottom of the hole.

Recent research at the University of Georgia and at other land-grant institutions in the Southeast has shown that it is best to place organic amendments on the soil surface and incorporate them uniformly into the top 12 inches of soil instead of placing them in planting holes. This provides a favorable environment for growth of the new roots, encouraging them to grow beyond the planting hole. It also helps the tree become established more quickly.

Trees may be purchased as container-grown plants; as balled-and-burlapped—"B&B" in the nursery trade—with their roots wrapped in burlap; or as bare-root plants. Container-grown trees are the easiest to plant and establish. They have well-established roots and suffer little transplant shock when planted in the landscape. Containers range in size from 1 gallon to several hundred gallons for really large trees. Balled-and-burlapped trees frequently are dug from a nursery, wrapped in burlap and kept in the nursery for an additional period of time to give the roots an opportunity to regenerate. The roots and soil of B&B plants can be quite heavy. Bare-root trees are usually small, 3–6 feet tall, and are usually offered in the early spring. They should be planted as soon as possible after they arrive, while still dormant. The roots also must be kept moist until planted. Frequently, bare-root trees are offered by seed and nursery mail-order catalogues or in the wholesale trade. Many state-operated forestry commissions have nurseries that sell bare-root stock in bulk quantities for only a few cents per plant.

Planting a Container-Grown Tree

Lay the tree on its side with the container near the planting hole. Gently pull on the lower trunk to remove the root system from the container. It may be necessary to lightly tamp the sides and bottom of the container to help free the roots. If the roots appear thick, dense, and matted or are circling the inside of the container, it may be necessary to use a knife to make several vertical slices, 1–2 inches deep, around the root ball. Although slicing the roots appears harmful, it actually encourages new root growth and allows water to move freely to penetrate the root mass (figure 3.6).

Planting a Balled-and-Burlapped Tree

Cut the nylon cord or wire securing the burlap around the trunk of the tree. If the root ball is small, it may be possible to remove the burlap entirely by gently rocking the root ball from side to side and pulling on the burlap. This may not be possible, or practical, on larger B&B stock. In that case, it is best to cut the wire and burlap and pull them away from at least

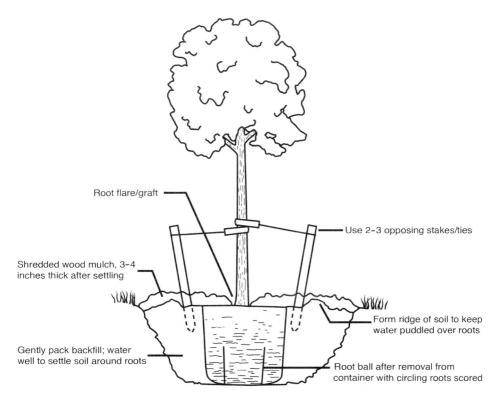

Figure 3.6. Planting a container-grown tree.

the top 12 inches of the root ball so they do not impede root growth. If roots are wrapped in plastic, be sure to remove plastic completely.

Planting a Bare-Root Tree

Mound the soil in the middle of the hole and spread the roots out evenly over the mound. Bare roots can dry out quickly, so cover them with soil immediately and water the area as soon as possible (figure 3.8).

Backfill with the Soil and Then Water

Break apart clods and remove any stones, sticks, or other debris from the soil removed from the hole. Backfill with enough soil to cover about one-third of the root ball, then water the soil to settle it and remove air pockets.

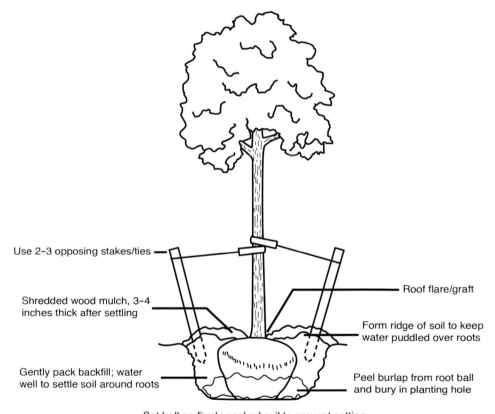

Use 2–3 opposing stakes/ties

Shredded wood mulch, 3–4 inches thick after settling

Gently pack backfill; water well to settle soil around roots

Roof flare/graft

Form ridge of soil to keep water puddled over roots

Peel burlap from root ball and bury in planting hole

Set ball on firmly packed soil to prevent setting

Figure 3.7. Planting a balled-and-burlapped tree.

Repeat this process when the hole is two-thirds full, then again when it is completely filled.

To help direct water to the roots of the tree during establishment, build a soil ring 3–4 inches high along the perimeter of the planting hole. However, the ring needs to be pulled out and away from the hole about eight weeks after planting to prevent it from eroding over the planting hole and possibly suffocating the tree's roots.

Stake the Tree, If Needed

On exposed, windy sites, stakes or guy wires are sometimes used on trees and large evergreen shrubs to hold them in place while they become established. The goal is to keep the tree from blowing over and becoming

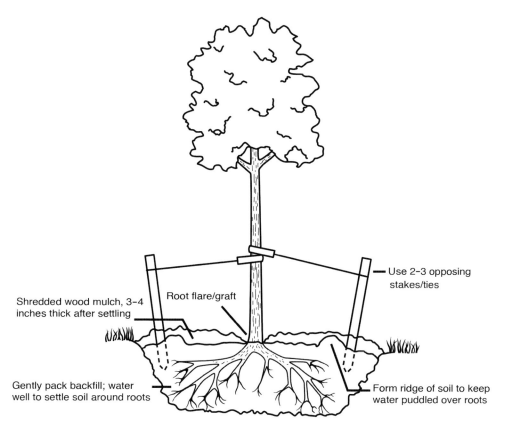

Figure 3.8. Planting a bare-root tree.

Figure 3.9. Mulch mounded around a tree to help retain water.

uprooted during the establishment phase. Allow for a little flexing; trees allowed to move slightly with breezes develop a larger root system and a stronger trunk. Once trees are established, remove all support wires.

Apply Mulch to the Soil Surface

Apply 3–5 inches of mulch over and beyond the planting hole, if possible. Mulch helps maintain soil moisture and insulates roots from extreme summer heat and winter freezes. It prevents weed growth and certain soil-borne diseases. It also protects tree trunks from damage by mowers, string trimmers, and other lawn equipment. In the Southeast, it is difficult and frustrating to grow turfgrass under trees because of shading and root competition; mulch provides an alternative to a living ground cover.

Organic mulches are best because they gradually decompose and return nutrients to the soil. Use fine-textured, nonmatting mulches such as pine straw, pine bark mininuggets, hardwood chips, and cypress mulch.

Shredded bark and limbs work well, too. Many municipalities and power companies chip discarded brush and provide it for free to keep it out of the landfill. Fall leaves also make excellent, economical mulch. Shredded leaves stay seated better and do not blow around as readily as whole leaves.

Inorganic mulches, such as rock, may be used in the Midwest, but they are not recommended for southeastern landscapes unless they are used in shaded areas. Rock mulches absorb radiant heat from the sun then reradiate that heat into the landscape, increasing water loss from foliage and possibly causing heat stress on trees. Wilting, yellowing, or leaf scorching are common symptoms of heat stress.

As trees become established and their roots penetrate the soil beyond the planting hole, the mulch area should be gradually expanded, if possible. Researchers at the University of Florida found in one study that roots of newly planted trees grow to three times the branch spread within two or three years after planting (Gilman, *Dispelling Misperceptions about Trees*).

Water Again and as Necessary during Establishment

After planting the tree, water thoroughly one more time. After that, water as necessary to maintain soil moisture during establishment. There are no precise guidelines as to how much water to apply because it depends on soil type, time of year, amount of recent precipitation, and size of tree planted. Sticking your finger in the soil or using a soil moisture sensor to see if it is moist are often the best gauges for determining water needs. Water slowly so that the water penetrates the soil and does not run off.

Don't Fertilize the Tree after Planting

Trees have enough stored energy in their roots to get established, so it is best to wait until the tree is established before fertilizing it.

If you want to make an environmentally friendly gardening statement, you can begin by planting an oak tree. Oak trees sequester great quantities of carbon and help in the fight to reduce global climate change. Native oaks attract great biodiversity. Their acorns nourish birds, squirrels, deer, and raccoons, and their leaves provide nutrients for moths, butterflies, and caterpillars. Songbirds forage among their branches, and owls and woodpeckers nest in their cavities. Oaks shade our homes and us. They purify the air, hold the soil in place, and prevent erosion. And their splendor graces our lives. Choose from a plethora of native species growing in the Southeast in various habitats.

4

Restore Biodiversity with Native Plants

The radical reduction of the world's biodiversity is the folly our descendants
will least likely forgive us. . . . At the current rate of habitat destruction and the
spread of alien species, we could lose half the species of plants and animals
on earth before the end of the 21st century.

E. O. Wilson, ecologist and Pulitzer Prize–winning author

Most every gardener has heard the dire news about the planet-wide decline in biodiversity. From the tropics to the poles, populations of many beloved wildlife and plant species are diminishing, some at alarming rates. Among animals rapidly losing ground are eastern meadowlarks, leatherback turtles, and chorus frogs; southeastern plants listed as threatened or endangered include Virginia spiraea and the beautiful pawpaw.

Over the span of millions of years, most species eventually become extinct as the climate changes and other species better adapted to a changed environment emerge and take their place. Extinction occurs at a natural "background" rate of about one to five species per year. We're now losing species at one thousand to ten thousand times the background rate, with literally dozens going extinct every day (Chivian and Berstein, *Sustaining Life*).

Overpopulation, overharvesting, habitat destruction, invasive species, and pollution are all taking their toll on natural systems. For example, the Carolina parakeet (*Conuropsis carolinensis*) once inhabited old-growth wetland forests along rivers and in swamps, especially in the Mississippi-Missouri drainage basin. The birds used the large hollow trees including cypress and sycamore as roosting and nesting sites. The last known Carolina parakeet sighting occurred in Okeechobee County, Florida, in 1918. Deforestation combined with hunting the birds for their colorful yellow

> *Did you know?* Landscape ecologists estimate that a mere 3–5 percent of U.S. land remains undisturbed by humans; that is, remains in its natural state. (Tallamy, *Bringing Nature Home*)

and green feathers—once used to adorn women's hats—led to the extinction of this beautiful bird.

As hopeless and inevitable as these population declines may seem, gardeners and landscapers can make a difference. Native plant communities sustain a diversity of wildlife (Flanders et al., "Effects of Invasive Exotic Grasses"). During the 2000 and 2001 breeding seasons, for example, scientists examined two south Texas rangeland habitats: one that remained in native vegetation and the second that was overrun with invasive exotic grasses introduced in the 1940s to "restore" overgrazed rangeland. The first parcel supported vigorous wildlife diversity; the second one, however, lost 60 percent of native insects and spiders, and 32 percent of native bird species. That's why it is important for gardeners and others who care about species diversity to do all they can to improve and restore natural diversity to a parcel of land.

It turns out that gardens and landscapes rich in biodiversity are easier to manage than those planted mostly in non-native and horticultural varieties. That's because Mother Nature takes charge of native landscapes. Biodiversity gives stability to an ecosystem or a natural area. Native plant and animal species perform various tasks that in the end contribute to recycling nutrients, converting energy from sunlight into plants, then into animals, then into fungi, bacteria, and other macro- and microorganisms, and then back into plants again. An intricate food web of native flora and fauna prevents one species from dominating the landscape.

If gardeners intentionally plant monocultures or choose to cultivate only one species—for example, creating large beds of one kind of flower or planting great swaths of lawn—then the landscape becomes more vulnerable to attack from diseases and harmful insects that thrive on these specific plants; in effect, the landscape provides a bountiful food supply for certain pests.

A 2012 University of Maryland study illustrates this point well (Shrewsbury and Leather, *Using Biodiversity for Pest Suppression*). Researchers found that a garden of diverse plants kept pest populations in check without pesticide use because a balance existed between pests and their predators.

Gardeners who are also birders reap an additional benefit when they enhance their landscapes with an assortment of native plants. Ninety percent of birds, for instance, eat insects at some time during their life cycle, according to the Xerces Society. So the greater the diversity of native trees, shrubs, and other vegetation, the greater the assortment of insects for birds and other animals. Birds, bees, butterflies, and other animals can find a wider selection of foods, shelter, and places to lay eggs and start a new generation in landscapes that are rich in plant diversity.

We also depend on a variety of insects to pollinate 30 percent of our plant-derived food (Klein et al., "Importance of Pollinators"). If insect pollinators were to disappear from our world, grocery shelves would be empty of many southern favorites: okra, watermelon, cantaloupe, peaches, strawberries, cucumber, squash, and the list goes on.

When humans attempt to alter nature's delicate web, the results can be catastrophic. Examples abound. In the 1860s, for instance, the federal government conducted a campaign to exterminate the wolf because it preyed upon livestock, which resulted in economic loss for farmers. By the middle of the twentieth century, the U.S. Forest Service had succeeded in eliminating most of wolves in the lower forty-eight states except in small patches of northeastern Minnesota and Michigan. An unintended consequence of wolf extermination, however, was the multiplication of deer populations across the country. Wolves are predators of deer. Today, in the Southeast, deer are plentiful and have become a nuisance in many areas. They roam freely in suburbia, dining on ornamental flowers and prized azaleas, sipping water from koi ponds, and darting across highways, sometimes colliding with oncoming vehicles.

Since many studies show that habitat destruction is often the main reason for population declines, gardeners are in a strong position to provide much-needed help. For these reasons, I devote an entire chapter to earth-friendly gardening practices and ways gardeners and landscapers can help increase biodiversity in their urban and rural landscapes.

Restoring Biodiversity Begins with Native Plants

When it comes to landscapes, native plants offer many advantages over introduced species. Natives are adapted to their indigenous region and can survive weather fluctuations in everything from the usual temperature changes to rainfall variations. Natives also recover quickly from more extreme weather fluctuations such as droughts, unseasonal cold snaps, and hail, wind, or heavy thunderstorms. Native plants typically are also much easier to grow and maintain than non-native plants.

Insects dine on plants they choose for appealing leaf chemistry, flowers, and timing of seed set. In fact, insects can be quite specific in their food choices. The monarch butterfly, for example, lays her eggs only on species of milkweed plants. Insects, in turn, become food for native birds and other animals that know which insects are available on what plants throughout the year.

Long-term studies have shown that native insects find most non-native or alien plants unappetizing. Douglas Tallamy stated in his book *Bringing Nature Home* that most plant-eating insect species should be able to eat only vegetation from plants with which they share a common evolutionary history. Therefore, a garden of alien plants attracts far fewer native birds, amphibians, reptiles, and mammals because the cupboard is empty.

Some kinds of native trees, shrubs, and other vegetation support a greater diversity of wildlife than other native species. If greater varieties of insects feed on leaves of a particular kind of plant, and if that same plant also produces appetizing nuts, berries, or other fruits, then that plant has the potential to attract an even wider array of birds and mammals. A University of Delaware study ranks plants according to their ability to support common moths and butterflies (order *Lepidopterans*) (study results in Tallamy, *Bringing Nature Home*). This order of insects represents 11,500 species and 50 percent of all insects that eat vegetation. The chart on page 82 provides details about these findings.

Trees That Attract Abundant Biodiversity

This section provides a more detailed description of some trees listed in table 4.1 and why they attract great quantities of wildlife. Using the

Did you know? Big bluestem (*Andropogon gerardii*), a warm-season prairie grass native to the mid-South and midwestern prairies, can have roots extending 12 feet into the soil. It has no known pests and provides excellent wildlife habitat. (U.S. Department of Agriculture, Natural Resources Conservation Service, Plants Database)

Figure 4.1. Big bluestem (*Andropogon gerardii*).

Table 4.1. Twenty most valuable woody and perennial native plants that support butterfly and moth biodiversity in the mid-Atlantic region

Trees		Perennials	
Common name, *Plant genus*	Number of Lepidoptera species supported	Common Name, *Plant genus*	Number of Lepidoptera species supported
Oak, *Quercus*	534	Goldenrod, *Solidago*	115
Black cherry, *Prunus*	456	Aster, *Aster*	112
Willow, *Salix*	455	Sunflower, *Helianthus*	73
Birch, *Betula*	413	Joe-Pye weed, *Eupatorium*	42
Poplar, *Populus*	368	Morning glory, *Ipomoea*	39
Crab apple, *Malus*	311	Sedges, *Carex*	36
Blueberry, *Vaccinium*	288	Honeysuckle, *Lonicera*	36
Maple, *Acer*	285	Lupine, *Lupinus*	33
Elm, *Ulmus*	213	Violet, *Viola*	29
Pine, *Pinus*	203	Geranium, *Geranium*	23
Hickory, *Carya*	200	Black-eyed Susan, *Rudbeckia*	17
Hawthorn, *Crataegus*	159	Iris, *Iris*	17
Alder, *Alnus*	156	Milkweed, *Asclepias*	12
Ash, *Fraxinus*	150	Verbena, *Verbena*	11
Rose, *Rosa*	139	Beardtongue, *Penstemon*	8
Filbert, *Corylus*	131	Phlox, *Phlox*	8
Walnut, *Juglans*	130	Bee balm, *Monarda*	7
Beech, *Fagus*	126	Veronica, *Veronica*	6
Chestnut, *Castanea*	125	Little bluestem, *Schizachyrium*	6
		Cardinal flower, *Lobelia*	4

Source: Tallamy, *Bringing Nature Home.*

U.S. Department of Agriculture Plants Database (http://plants.usda.gov), choose the tree species that are native to your region.

Oaks (Genus *Quercus*)

The mighty oak, our national tree, stands supreme in its ability to support diverse wildlife, from insects to birds to mammals. Approximately fifty native oak species are native to the Southeast. Many are deciduous, some are evergreen, and they are classified as either white oaks or red oaks. White

Figure 4.2. Southern red oak (*Quercus falcata*).

oaks have acorns maturing at the end of the first season; red oaks have acorns developing in the second season. Planting oak trees in urban and suburban neighborhoods that are traditionally light on wildlife can transform the neighborhoods into wildlife sanctuaries. Here is why.

Caterpillars of some moths and butterflies, for example, polyphemus moths and branded and striped hairstreak butterflies, eat oak leaves. Acorns feed raccoons, turkeys, mice, deer, squirrels, and wood ducks. Cavities in living and dead trees serve as nesting sites for birds, such as owls, downy woodpeckers, bluebirds, and wrens. Oak logs are the preferred lodging for certain beetles that live where they construct their tunnels. Several mammals also use logs for shelter.

Cherries and Plums (Genus *Prunus*)

Native black cherries, chokecherries, pin cherries, and plums are excellent food sources for humans and wildlife. They make beautiful ornamental trees with their spring flowers. They can be planted as part of the understory or as transitional plants from the lawn to the woods. The leaves feed

Figure 4.3. Common chokecherry (*Prunus virginiana).*

Figure 4.4. River birch (*Betula nigra*).

Figure 4.5. Loblolly pine (*Pinus taeda* L.).

numerous insect species—at least ten species of giant silk moths, five butterfly species including the eastern tiger swallowtail, and sixty-three worm species. And berries sustain birds in late summer.

Birches (Genus *Betula*)

Six birch species are native to the southeastern United States and include yellow birch, black birch, white birch, and the river birch, which is particularly common along streams, rivers, and floodplains. Birches attract 411 species of moths and butterflies including luna moth, eastern tiger swallowtail, cecropia moth, and polyphemus moth.

Pines (Genus *Pinus*)

Pines are a predominant part of the landscape in the southern United States. Depending upon the species, they may grow deep in the forest or along coastal areas. Their seeds nourish turkeys, grouse, quail, squirrels, chipmunks, mice, voles, and dozens of species of songbirds. Pine needles support at least 203 species of moth and butterfly larvae as well as saw fly larvae.

The Comeback Tree: American Chestnut

The American chestnut, once considered the most important tree in the eastern United States, supported an immense diversity of wildlife. Great quantities of chestnuts nourished many animals, including squirrels, chipmunks, deer, elk, black bears, turkeys, doves, blue jays, and mice. Equally important were the number of insects that dined on the trees' leaves and that also attracted huge populations of songbirds. A Japanese chestnut tree introduced into the United States in 1904 contained a fungus that spread to the American chestnut and in just a few decades wiped out up to 3 billion trees from Maine to Mississippi along with the wildlife diversity these stately trees attracted. The American Chestnut Foundation, dedicated to restoring the tree to its rightful niche in the Appalachian Mountains, has developed a blight-resistant hybrid tree using the Asian chestnut.

Figure 4.6. The American chestnut, which supports great biodiversity, was wiped out by fungus and is now on the rebound.

What Is a Non-Native Plant?

Non-native plants (also called aliens, nonindigenous plants, or exotic species) have been introduced into an environment in which they did not evolve or occur naturally. Invasive non-native plants often grow prolifically and overtake natives because they have no natural enemies and often outcompete the native flora (think kudzu).

The introduction of non-native plants to American landscapes has been both accidental and deliberate. They spread by seed, roots, or spores and compete with native plants for nutrients and water. Nurseries intentionally introduced many of these species for their appealing qualities, such as fragrant flowers, leaf appearance, and ability to reproduce quickly. They include the camellia, a native of Japan prized for its beautiful flowers and shiny leaves, and the gardenia, a native of Africa and southern Asia that has fragrant flowers. Both grace many southern gardens with their beauty but contribute little to the health of a garden community, much less the greater ecosystem.

Non-native plants can be either noninvasive or invasive. Noninvasive non-native plants do not grow or reproduce quickly so they will not overtake and replace native plants like invasive species do. Examples include the weeping willow, Japanese cherry, many azaleas, and cultivars of hydrangea.

Invasive non-native plants pose a serious threat to a native habitat. They are fast-growing and have no enemies or controls to limit their spread so they can ravage a landscape and engulf a forest. They are capable of converting complex native plant communities with hundreds of different wildlife-supporting plant species into a monoculture, essentially creating a dead wildlife zone.

Three of the more notorious invasive plants in the Southeast are kudzu, mimosa, and privet.

Did you know? Some fifty thousand alien plant and animal species have colonized North America since colonial times. (U.S. Fish and Wildlife Service, "Frequently Asked Questions about Invasive Species")

Figure 4.7. Kudzu vine may engulf forests in the U.S. Southeast.

Kudzu (*Pueraria lobata*)

Kudzu was introduced in the United State at the 1876 Centennial Exposition in Philadelphia as a fragrant flowering vine from Japan. In the early 1900s, it was planted as livestock feed in the southern United States because it has the nutritive equivalent of alfalfa and produces ten times more biomass. In the 1930s, the U.S. Soil Conservation Service encouraged farmers to plant kudzu for erosion control. It was also planted along rights-of-way for this same purpose, which is why you often see it growing along highways. The near-perfect growing conditions in parts of the Southeast allow

Figure 4.8. Glossy privet (*Ligustrum lucidum* W. T. Aiton), an invasive non-native.

this perennial vine to grow as much as 12 inches a day. It destroys southern forests by creeping over trees and shading them.

Chinese Privet (*Ligustrum sinense*) and Japanese Privet (*Ligustrum japonicum*)

These are shrubs or trees that can grow as tall as 30 feet high and have invaded southern floodplain forests and woodlands. They grow just about anywhere because they are hardy and can tolerate air pollution and other detrimental environmental conditions. Privet was introduced into the United States in 1852 as an ornamental shrub and is still being used for hedges. Privet spreads by seeds, root, and stump sprouts. Cut it down, and it pops back up. Pull it out by the roots or repeatedly chop it back to get rid of it.

Figure 4.9. Mimosa tree (*Albizia julibrissin*).

Mimosa Tree (*Albizia julibrissin*)

Originally from China, the mimosa, or silk, tree was introduced to the United States in 1745 and was cultivated primarily as an ornamental. Mimosa remains popular because of its fragrant and showy flowers. Because of its ability to grow and reproduce along roadways and disturbed areas and because of its tendency to readily establish after escaping from cultivation, mimosa is considered highly invasive by Florida's Exotic Pest Plant Council. Mimosa is a strong competitor in open areas or forest edges because it grows well in various soil types, produces large amounts of seed, and regenerates when cut back or damaged. Mimosa reduces sunlight and nutrients available to desired species because of the denseness of the stand.

Restoring Biodiversity without an Extreme Makeover

Renovating the yard by tearing out non-natives and grass and replacing them with natives is costly in time and money. Using a slow, commonsense ap-

Table 4.2. Invasive exotic plants to avoid in the Southeast

Common name	Scientific name
TREES	
Tree-of-heaven	*Ailanthus altissima*
Mimosa	*Albizia julibrissin*
Australian pine	*Casuarina equisetifolia* L.
Chinaberry	*Melia azedarach*
Princess tree	*Paulownia tomentosa*
Callery 'Bradford' pear	*Pyrus calleryana*
Chinese tallow tree	*Sapium sebiferum*
Brazilian pepper tree	*Schinus terebinthifolius* Raddi
Portia tree	*Thespesia populnea* (L.) Soland. ex Correa
SHRUBS	
Japanese barberry	*Berberis thunbergii*
Russian olive	*Eleagnus angustifolia*
Thorny olive	*Eleagnus pungens*
Autumn olive	*Eleagnus umbellata*
Bicolor lespedeza	*Lespedeza bicolor*
Japanese privet	*Ligustrum japonicum*
Glossy privet	*Ligustrum lucidum* W. T. Aiton
Chinese privet	*Ligustrum sinense*
Common privet	*Ligustrum vulgare*
Oregon grape	*Mahonia bealei*
Japanese knotweed	*Reynoutria japonica*
Multiflora rose	*Rosa multiflora*
VINES	
Porcelain-berry	*Ampelopsis brevipedunculata*
Oriental bittersweet	*Celastrus orbiculatus*
Sweet autumn virginsbower	*Clematis cuspidatum*
Winter creeper	*Euonymus fortunei*
English ivy	*Hedera helix*
Cypressvine morning glory	*Ipomoea quamoclit*
Japanese honeysuckle	*Lonicera japonica*
Kudzu	*Pueraria lobata*
Chinese wisteria	*Wisteria sinensis*
Japanese wisteria	*Wisteria floribunda*
AQUATIC PLANTS	
Alligator weed	*Alternanthera philoxeroides*
Water hyacinth	*Eichhornia crassipes*
Hydrilla	*Hydrilla verticillata*
Water lettuce	*Pistia stratiotes* L.

Source: "Going Native: Urban Landscaping for Wildlife with Native Plants."

proach to eliminate undesirable invasives can be easy on your pocketbook and your energy.

Essentially, emulating nature or re-creating food webs will restore biodiversity. It may sound overwhelming, but it isn't. Take a walk in the woods, meadow, or in a nature preserve near your home and observe the plants within it.

If you walk in the woods, check out the forest structure: notice the tall tree canopy of oaks, maples, beech, pine, and tulip trees with their branches reaching for the sun. Beneath the canopy are understory trees and shrubs like American holly, dogwood, rhododendron, and sumac. Closer to the ground are perennials and ground covers like Christmas fern and ground pine and spring wildflowers such as blood root, jack-in-the-pulpit, trout lily, and dwarf crested iris.

This succession of plants can be re-created in the backyard, front islands, hedgerows, and border plantings of your landscape.

Remember to choose native plants that are adapted to your growing conditions. If they are installed in environments that are marginal for their growth requirements, they will not achieve their full potential size, health, and beauty, much less their potential value to the ecosystem. For example, planting an understory native shrub, like the oakleaf hydrangea, in full sun will weaken it and make it susceptible to disease and insect pests.

Once you've decided what plants to include, arrange them according to nature's plan—a canopy to shade the area, an understory below, and annual and perennial plants and ground covers closest to the soil. Lightly spread mulch or leaf litter around newly installed plants to protect them. If you already have moss, it also works fine as a ground cover.

Here is a step-by-step approach to renovating the landscape.

Take an Inventory of Landscape Plants

Identify both the natives and the non-natives in your landscape. A good clue is to look at the plant's leaves. Do they have insect holes or are they unblemished? If they are perfect, chances are they are non-natives because the local insects find them unpalatable. State-based native plant societies and local Cooperative Extension offices have comprehensive lists of recommended native plants.

Remove Invasive Aliens

The Southeastern Exotic Pest Plant Council maintains an updated, comprehensive list of invasive species for each region. However, the most comprehensive national record with photos of invasive plants, animals, insects, and pathogens is found at the University of Georgia Center for Invasive Species and Ecosystem Health website (www.invasive.org). The site also hosts a blog where gardeners can discuss their particular situation with specialists. Table 4.2 lists some of the Southeast's most destructive invasive plants.

Replace Invasive Non-Natives with Natives Adapted to the Site

If aliens are removed from a hill or stream bank, install natives that will hold the soil in place. If the area is wooded, it might be fun to let wildlife do the planting. Squirrels and blue jays prefer to bury their nuts and seeds in bare soil. Seeds may be blown by the wind or contained in the soil. A gardener may also use the slow-restoration method and plant an acorn and watch it grow. The shrubs listed in table 4.3 and the perennials found in table 4.4 are suited for either sunny or shady areas in southeastern gardens. Most shade-loving plants prefer dappled shade. Native wildflowers bloom in profusion in the early spring when the deciduous trees have not yet leafed out.

Replace Ailing Non-Natives with Natives

This is a slow, simple way to bring back biodiversity. Many non-native plants will become fodder for pests or succumb to the latest drought or snap in the wind. However, some invasive plants like kudzu and privet have few enemies and can take over the landscape and the nearby forest if they are left unconstrained.

Plant Native Trees for a Big Biodiversity Draw

Because of their larger size, native shade trees support more diversity than most native shrubs, perennial plants, or ground covers. A suburban yard usually has room to add a few more trees. Consider planting trees that are biodiversity attractors, listed in table 4.1. Also, be aware that planting trees

Table 4.3. Native shrubs

Sun-loving		Shade-loving	
Common name	Scientific name	Common name	Scientific name
Adam's needle	*Yucca filamentosa*	Bottlebrush buckeye	*Aesculus parviflora*
American beautyberry	*Callicarpa americana*	Oakleaf hydrangea	*Hydrangea quercifolia*
Witchhazel (part shade)	*Hamamelis virginiana*	Alabama azalea	*Rhododendron alabamense*
Dwarf palmetto	*Sabal minor*	Sweet azalea	*Rhododendron arborescens*
Virginia sweetspire	*Itea virginica*	Florida azalea	*Rhododendron austrinum*
Dwarf fothergilla	*Fothergilla gardenii*	Flame azalea	*Rhododendron calendulaceum*
Summersweet clethra	*Clethra alnifolia*	Piedmont azalea	*Rhododendron canescens*
Rabbiteye blueberry	*Vaccinium virgatum*	Plumleaf azalea	*Rhododendron prunifolium*
Georgia basil	*Clinopodium georgianum*	Catawba rosebay	*Rhododendron catawbiense*

that offer dense shade, over the long run, will alter the ground cover. If you have a lawn, be aware that most turf grasses have minimum requirements for full sun.

Replace Some Lawn with a Native Garden

Rethink the need for large swaths of lawns that require considerable time, money, and energy to maintain but attract little biodiversity. Replacing sections of a single-species lawn with islands of native plants not only decreases maintenance but also increases plant and animal diversity. Converting some lawn to a native garden allows a gardener to design and plant a small parcel from scratch.

Redesign Small Patches of Existing Garden

Creating wildlife habitat in small areas in the garden can be fun, instructive for children, and beneficial to biodiversity. Chapter 10 provides instructions for diversity theme gardens to attract bees, butterflies, birds, and amphibians.

Table 4.4. Native perennials

Sun-loving		Shade-loving	
Common name	Scientific name	Common name	Scientific name
Bee balm	*Monarda didyma*	American alumroot	*Heuchera americana*
Black-eyed Susan	*Rudbeckia hirta*	Bleeding heart	*Dicentra eximia*
Blue wild indigo	*Baptisia australis*	Bloodroot	*Sanguinaria canadensis*
Butterfly milkweed	*Asclepias tuberosa*	Cardinal flower	*Lobelia cardinalis*
Creeping phlox	*Phlox stolonifera*	Christmas fern	*Polystichum acrostichoides*
Goldenrod	*Solidago rugosa*	Cinnamon fern	*Osmunda cinnamomea*
Hairgrass	*Muhlenbergia capillaris*	Dwarf crested iris	*Iris cristata*
Purple coneflower	*Echinacea purpurea*	Eastern blue phlox	*Phlox divaricata*
Purple Joe-Pye weed	*Eutrochium fistulosum*	Eastern columbine	*Aquilegia canadensis*
Red hibiscus	*Hibiscus coccineus*	Foamflower	*Tiarella cordifolia* var. *collina*
Seashore mallow	*Kosteletzkya virginica*	Foxglove beardtongue	*Penstemon digitalis*
Sessile blazing star	*Liatris spicata*	Green-and-gold	*Chrysogonum virginianum*
Stokes' aster	*Stokesia laevis*	Hairy-stem spiderwort	*Tradescantia hirsuticaulis*
Summer phlox	*Phlox paniculata* 'David' and 'Robert Poore'	Southern shield fern	*Thelypteris kunthii*
Swamp sunflower	*Helianthus angustifolius*	Wild ginger	*Asarum canadense*
Virginia blueflag	*Iris virginica*	Woodland phlox	*Phlox divaricata*

Use Border Gardens

Transitional native gardens can be planted between a cultivated landscape and the woods or the neighbor's yard. For example, a border garden can offer an attractive visual barrier and sound buffer. A rain garden of native plants may be needed along the property line to collect storm water and filter pollutants. Chapter 7 gives planting instructions for rain gardens.

Finding native plants for the landscape is easier now than ever before.

Figure 4.10. Native island garden brings diversity to the lawn.

Nearly every state, for example, has a native plant society that may have a database of nursery vendors. Nurseries nowadays stock more native plants than in the past. Tags identifying the plant tell gardeners its name, its growth patterns and living requirements, and whether it is a native.

Plant rescues provide another source. When land is slated for development, native plant enthusiasts may come from all over, fanning out in woods and natural landscapes in search of native plants to rescue before bulldozers level the land for homes and shopping centers. These gardeners don't mind getting down and dirty to dig up native flowers, ferns, moss, shrubs, and small trees to relocate to their yards, a nursery, or a holding facility. This is a messy and time-consuming way to get free plants, but if a gardener has the time and inclination, it can be fun and rewarding.

Most states have native plant societies whose members are only too happy to help repopulate the earth with native plants. They may be very

Caution: Never dig native plants on public property, and dig them on private property only with the owner's permission—and even then, only if the plants will be lost to development.

pleased to share offspring from their plants. They also may extend an invitation to attend a plant rescue.

The question of how much of the garden should be planted in natives comes up often at Master Gardener and garden club meetings. Native plant purists believe that only native plants should sink roots into their soil, in much the same way that local foodies think that only food produced within 100 miles of their homes should grace their plates. However, being rigid on either of these important environmental issues is out of sync with Mother

Figure 4.11. Border gardens of native plants make a good transition between homes.

Nature, who is flexible and ever-changing. Using native trees, particularly oaks, goes a long way toward enhancing the biodiversity needed in urban and suburban landscapes. Native plants should predominate among the understory trees, shrubs, and ground covers whenever possible and practical. Some species of butterflies, moths, bees, and hummingbirds need nectar-producing native plants. However, if you use some noninvasive, nonnative plants that are adapted to the climate and are prized for qualities like beautiful flowers (camellias and azaleas) and shapes (Japanese maple), they will not wreak havoc on the landscape's ecological balance. In much the same way that we may savor the occasional chocolate bar or cup of espresso, we also anticipate the colorful show of nonindigenous flowering camellias and cultivated azaleas each spring.

Plant a Resilient Landscape

Love the land as those who have gone before you have loved it. Care for it as they have cared for it. . . . And with all your strength, with all your mind, and with all your heart, preserve it for your children.

Chief Seattle, 1854

Plants need certain conditions to thrive, and the good news is that gardeners can control or at least influence many of them. The health of a plant depends on multiple factors, including soil conditions, temperature, sunlight, fertility, water availability, and vulnerability to and protection from harmful pests and diseases.

By choosing plants adapted to the local climate and soils, by preparing the soil with required nutrients, and by placing plants in the right sun exposure, gardeners can satisfy many of a plant's environmental needs. Water, too, is essential in the right amounts and at the right times. And by keeping a watchful eye for diseases and insect pests, gardeners can minimize infestations. Maintaining balance in the landscape may seem overwhelming, but with careful thought, preparation, and some work at the onset, it's not all that daunting. And the ultimate reward is that plants will flourish, the landscape will be attractive and inviting, and your efforts will contribute to a healthier world.

Creating a resilient landscape will help your plants withstand today's changing climate, which includes increased temperatures and periods of prolonged drought and rainfall. Geological history shows us that native habitats can survive and rebound even after serious climate disruptions. Climate change wreaked havoc on the earth's first rainforests, which existed 300 million years ago, but these natural communities bounced back over time (Falcon-Lang et al., "Incised Channel Fills"). During the ice ages, the rainforests were pushed to the brink of extinction, but they managed to recover and return to their former glory.

It is important to manage environmental conditions so that plants thrive and grow into sustaining members of the landscape and the surrounding plant community. Although providing good growing conditions requires effort and plant nurturing, especially during the early stages of a plant's adjustment to its new home, gardeners are rewarded with health and harmony in the garden. Conversely, when plants live in a poor or marginal environment, they weaken, become vulnerable to disease and harmful environmental factors, and require much more gardening effort. For example, native azaleas planted under shade trees—their preferred environment—may bloom for years. However, if they are placed in the full sun, bugs and disease may weaken and kill them, making them fodder for the compost pile.

Environments change over time as landscapes grow and mature. It's disheartening to watch flowering plants like roses, crepe myrtles, and forsythia, which all require at least a half day of full sun to bloom abundantly, decline in flowering profusion as nearby trees grow and shade them. Gardeners then have to readjust their expectations or do some transplanting or tree trimming.

General Plant Groups

To better understand the needs of landscape plants and their uses in a garden setting, it helps to know that plants in the landscape are generally grouped according to their growth habits: annuals, biennials, herbaceous perennials, and woody ornamentals. Below is a quick overview of each category.

Annuals

Annuals complete their life cycle—they germinate, flower, and die—in one growing season, and typically they are shallow-rooted. Common annuals suited for the South include marigolds, pansies, gerbera daisies, vincas, petunias, and begonias. Annuals provide continuous color for one season only and must be replanted the following growing season. However, many plants such as cleome, pansies, and marigolds drop their seeds, which may germinate the next year, reducing or eliminating the need to replant. Since many annuals need frequent watering, they should be planted close to a water source.

Figure 5.1. Annuals work well for seasonal color. *Top, left to right*: petunias ('Peppy Lavender'), marigolds ('Alumia Red'); *bottom, left to right*: gerbera daisies, pansies.

Biennials

Biennials require two growing seasons to complete their life cycle. In the first season they germinate and grow leaves, and in the second growing season they flower, produce seeds, and then die. Foxglove, Sweet William,

Figure 5.2. Biennials. *Top, left to right*: foxglove, parsley; *bottom, left to right*: money plant, dianthus.

parsley, and money plant are good examples of biennials. Like annuals, they are typically shallow-rooted and may need frequent watering.

Herbaceous Perennials

Herbaceous perennials often live for many years and offer a variety of bloom times, from early spring through fall. These soft-tissue plants typically die back to ground level at the end of the growing season and regrow year after

Figure 5.3. Perennials. *Top, left to right*: hosta, purple coneflower; *bottom, left to right*: old roadside daylily, black-eyed Susan (*Rudbeckia* 'Viette's Little Suzy').

year from roots as well as tubers and bulbs. Perennials are more deeply rooted than annuals and therefore usually require less watering. Common herbaceous perennials that work well in many southern landscapes and are very easy to grow include yarrow, lenten rose, hosta, purple coneflower, black-eyed Susan, roadside daylily, autumn sedum, and some bulbs such as daffodils, crocus, and hyacinth.

Woody Ornamentals

Woody ornamentals are usually perennials that produce above-ground woody stems and branches. They include trees such as oaks and maple; shrubs such as hydrangea, rhododendron, and azalea; and vines such as clematis. Once they are established, native woody ornamentals usually require little maintenance.

Figure 5.4. Woody ornamentals, all native to the Southeast. *Left*: Oakleaf hydrangea (*Hydrangea quercifolia*); *top right*: rhododendron (*Rhododendron catawbiense*); *bottom right*: flame azalea (*Rhododendron calendulaceum*).

Selecting Plants

Local Climate Conditions

Seek out native or adapted plants that are adjusted to the region's temperatures, rainfall, and other climate factors (see chapter 4). Visit your local botanical garden and nursery for ideas also, and contact the local Cooperative Extension office for a list of plants that grow well in your area.

The Garden Site

Consider your landscape's environmental conditions and the plant's range of needs, including the sun and shade exposure, soil nutrients, pH, drainage, and wind when purchasing plants. Also match the size of the mature plant with the space designated for it. Well-meaning gardeners with sustainability on their minds may choose a lovely plant that may grow to cover their windows or doors over time if they don't consider its ultimate size.

Ability to Attract Beneficial Insects

Choose nectar- and pollen-producing plants that will entice beneficial insects to pollinate your flowers and vegetables and to prey upon pests. Plants with small flowers such as sweet alyssum, dill, fennel, garlic chives, lavender, citrus, and Queen Anne's lace are great beneficial-insect attractors for southern gardens. Other popular plants include asters, coneflowers, coreopsis, cosmos, yarrow, goldenrod, sunflowers, milkweeds, yellow alyssum, sweet clover, buckwheat, and hairy vetch.

Pest Resistance and Pest-Free Plants

Take care in selecting individual plants for your landscape so you don't end up planting problems. Plants that are vulnerable to pests or those purchased from the nursery that are loaded with bugs will cause you grief in trying to manage infestations later. Be careful in choosing pest-resistant varieties to incorporate into your landscape. Look carefully on the undersides of leaves for signs of disease and insects and inspect plants for weak or broken stems or branches. Also, check plant tags for information about pest resistance or contact your Extension office for their recommendations.

Drought Tolerance

If you live in an area of the Southeast where potable water is limited (for instance, in some areas of Florida), or if the area is prone to drought (such as parts of Alabama, Tennessee, Florida, and Georgia), then select plants that don't consume much water. Table 5.1 on page 108 can help guide your plant selections.

Avoid Invasive Plants

Become familiar with invasive species in your area. Table 4.2 contains a list of common invasive species found in the Southeast. For a list of invasive species in your state, check the Southeast Exotic Pest Plant Council website. If you find that your landscape already contains invasive plants, such as mimosa, nandina, and kudzu, contact your Extension Office for advice on how to remove these plants and ask for recommendations of noninvasive alternatives.

Avoid Too Many Plants of the Same Species

Resist the urge to purchase and plant dozens of one favorite-colored perennial to provide a swath of color in your landscape. Large groupings of a single species may inadvertently provide an all-you-can-eat buffet for bugs. To create large areas of one color, select various flowering species in that hue to create a similar colorful effect.

Buy Plants in Biodegradable Pots

Nurseries often stock plants in pots made of peat moss, pressed paper pulp, biodegradable plastic, rice hulls, or composted cow manure. These containers are biodegradable and can be put directly in the ground, which eliminates root disturbance and the need to recycle pots.

Did you know? The underlying cause of many disease problems in home gardens is water—either overwatering plants, poor site selection, or poor water drainage, according to University of Georgia plant pathologist Elizabeth Little.

Prepare the Planting Bed

The foundation of the garden is the planting bed, so prepare it with great care. Grade the site according to the following recommendations.

If you're planting on a slope, grade the site, if possible, with a 1–2 percent slope (1- to 2-foot drop per 100 linear feet) to prevent rainfall from creating puddles and collecting water. If that is not practical, try forming gentle sloped terraces to improve drainage. Few ornamental plants, with the exception of aquatic plants, can tolerate long periods of standing water. Slope the plant beds away from buildings and adjacent plants.

Test the Soil

Two to three weeks before planting, take soil samples to see if the pH and nutrient levels are correct for the plants you intend to put there. If new soil is brought onto the site, or if soil is redistributed during the final grading, sample the soil when the grading is completed. Soil sampling is available through local Cooperative Extension offices.

Reduce Compaction and Improve Drainage

Most urban and suburban landscapes have high-traffic areas where people gather to play, barbecue, or relax, and the ground in these areas usually becomes compacted. If you are starting a new bed in a compacted area, first add 4 inches of organic amendments to the soil surface and then till the soil to a 12-inch depth. This treatment is equivalent to adding approximately 1 cubic yard per 100 square feet, or nine 3-cubic-foot bags to the soil. Deeply prepared soil promotes a vigorous root system and helps plants tolerate temperature and moisture extremes. Some poorly drained soils may also require subsurface drain pipes or French drains to carry the water away from plants.

Raised Beds Improve Soil Drainage

Raised beds work well for vegetables, fruits, and herbs, and they offer the advantage that the soil can be tailored to meet specific plants' needs.

There are also some minuses to raised beds. The soil dries out more easily; a good soil mix must be brought in for planting; and the bed will most

Table 5.1. Drought-tolerant perennials for the Southeast

Common name *Botanical Name*	Height Width	Growing conditions	Comments
Yarrow *Achillea* species	2–3' 2–3'	Sun; well-drained soil; Piedmont	*A. millefolium* is a native; numerous cultivars
Southernwood *Artemisia abrotanum*	3–5' 4–6'	Sun; well-drained, low-fertility soil	Pleasantly scented foliage
'Powis Castle' wormwood *Artemisia* 'Powis Castle'	2½–3' 4–6'	Sun; well-drained soil; tolerates humidity; Piedmont	One of the best silver-gray plants for the South
Butterfly weed *Asclepias tuberosa*	2–3' 2'	Sun; well-drained soil	Native; attracts butterflies
False indigo *Baptisia* species	3–6' 2–5'	Sun; well-drained soil	Several native species; does not transplant well
Tickseed *Coreopsis* species	1–2' 1–2'	Sun; well-drained soil	Many native species; trim or deadhead after bloom
Montbretia *Crocosmia* hybrids	3–4' 1'	Sun to part shade on coast; well-drained soil	Vivid orange, yellow, or red flowers
Cheddar pinks *Dianthus gratianopolitanus*	1' 1–2'	Sun; well-drained soil; heat- and humidity-tolerant; Piedmont	'Bath's Pink,' 'Firewitch,' and 'Tiny Rubys'
Coneflower *Echinacea* species	1–3' 1–3'	Sun; well-drained, low-fertility soil; heat tolerant	Native; new colors in yellow, gold, white, apricot, and rose
Globe thistle *Echinops ritro*	2–4' 3'	sun; prefers moist, well-drained soil; Piedmont	Flowers dry well and keep blue color
Barrenwort *Epimedium* species	8–15" 12"	Shade to heavy shade; high organic matter soil; Piedmont only	One of best for dry shade
Hardy ageratum *Eupatorium coelestinum*	2–3' 3'	Sun or light shade; spreads rapidly in fertile soil	Native; blue flowers late summer until frost
Indian blanket *Gaillardia* × *grandiflora*	2–3' 2'	Sun; well-drained soil; very adaptable	Can be short-lived but easy to grow from seed
Sunflower *Heliopsis helianthoides*	3–5' 2–3'	Sun; well-drained soil	Blooms July until frost; 'Summer Sun'
Daylily *Hemerocallis* cultivars	1½–3' 18–24"	Sun or light shade; highly adaptable	Thousands of cultivars in every color but blue
Red yucca *Hesperaloe parviflora*	3–4' 3'	Sun; well-drained soil; very adaptable	Slender pink to rose flowers, narrow foliage
Bearded iris *Iris* hybrids	8–36" 10–24"	Sun or light shade; well-drained soil; Piedmont	Thousands of cultivars
Red hot poker *Kniphofia uvaria*	3–5' 4'	Sun; very well-drained soil	Long-lived plants
Lantana *Lantana camara*	5–6' 5–8'	Sun; tolerates heat, salt, and infertile soil	'Miss Huff' and 'Mozelle' are hardiest cultivars

Common name _Botanical Name_	Height Width	Growing conditions	Comments
Lavender _Lavandula_ species	1–3' 2–3'	Sun; well-drained, low-fertility soil	_L. × intermedia, L. dentata, L. stoechas_ best in Southeast
Blazing star _Liatris spicata_	2–3' 2'	Sun; tolerates heat and low-fertility soil	Native
Sea lavender _Limonium latifolium_	24–30" 30"	Sun; well-drained soil; good air circulation	Small lavender flowers in large clusters dry well
Evening primrose _Oenothera_ species	1–3' 1–2'	Sun; very adaptable; best in Piedmont	Several of the species are native
Prickly pear cactus _Opuntia_ species	2–5' Variable	Sun; excellent soil drainage	_O. humifusa_ is native
Russian sage _Perovskia atriplicifolia_	4–5' 4'	Sun; well-drained soil; tolerates heat	Trim after flowering to encourage rebloom
Creeping phlox _Phlox subulata_	6–9" 12"	Sun; well-drained soil; do not fertilize	Shear lightly after flowering to encourage tight growth
Brazilian blue sage _Salvia guaranitica_	5–6' 4–5'	Sun or part shade; well-drained soil	Attracts hummingbirds
Little leaf sage _Salvia microphylla_	3–4' 3–4'	Sun; needs excellent drainage	Very similar to _S. greggii_
Lavender cotton _Santolina_ species	1–2' 2'	Sun; well-drained soil; prune hard after flowering; Piedmont only	_S. chamaecyparissus_ is gray; _S. virens_ is green; evergreen
Stonecrop _Sedum_ species	3–24" 18–24"	Sun or light shade; well-drained soil; adaptable	Numerous species; some evergreen, some deciduous
Hens & chicks _Sempervivum tectorum_	8–12" 9"	Sun; well-drained soil	Cultivars with a variety of shapes and leaf colors
Goldenrod _Solidago_ species	2–6' 2–4'	Sun or light shade; tolerates heat and low fertility soil.	Many species are native; 'Fireworks,' 'Golden Fleece'
Lamb's ear _Stachys byzantina_	12–15" 12"	Sun to light shade; well-drained soil; Piedmont	'Big Ears' is best cultivar for Southeast
Thyme _Thymus_ species	2–12" 1–2'	Sun; well-drained, light soil	Culinary herb with colorful flowers
Purple heart _Tradescantia pallida_	12–18" 18–24"	Sun or light shade; prefers moist, well-drained soil	Lavender pink blooms above purple foliage
Verbena _Verbena_ species	8–24" 18–36"	Sun; well-drained soil; good air circulation	Several species are native; _V. bonariensis_ grows 3–6' tall

Source: Home and Garden Information Center, Clemson Cooperative Extension, Clemson University.

Advantages of raised beds include:

- Soil warms more quickly in the spring.
- Soil remains loose and not compacted.
- Soil can be custom-made for a specific plant's needs.
- They offer a defined planting area for adding seasonal color to the landscape or for high-traffic areas.
- They offer an area easy to fence, and later to electrify, to keep out the marauding deer herd!

Figure 5.5. Raised beds make sense where drainage is an issue.

Figure 5.6. Raised bed schematic.

likely need to be rebuilt after several years of use because the wood will deteriorate.

Choose a flat area for a raised bed. You don't need to remove grass from the area. The bed can be constructed on top of the turf, which will break down and feed the soil, but you will need plenty of soil to cover the grass well. The bed can be framed in 2 × 6-inch rot-resistant lumber such as cedar or recycled plastic lumber. Treated lumber is not a good idea for vegetable beds since it may have chemicals that can leach from the wood and be absorbed by the food.

Avoid using railroad ties treated with creosote for vegetable gardens. Creosote is a toxic wood preservative that can leach into the soil. The U.S. Environmental Protection Agency reports that creosote is a possible human carcinogen and does not recommend it for residential use.

Stones and bricks can be piled up to outline a bed, and, simpler still, you can mound the dirt to form a planting area. The bed should not exceed 4 feet in width. Anything wider makes it difficult to reach across to the center of the bed and tend the plants.

It's best to raise the bed 8–12 inches above the current soil grade, particularly if you are trying to get the plant roots out of an area of standing water. Use native or well-drained soil. When making the final grade, avoid leaving swales or low areas where water can collect.

Improve Soil Nutrients and Water-Holding Capacity

Use organic amendments such as peat moss, rotted animal manure, or compost. Uncomposted wood chips or bark won't work well since they require soil nitrogen for decomposition, depleting the soil and resulting in nitrogen-deficient plants.

Adjust the pH as Necessary

In general, southeastern soils tend to be acidic with high clay content. Adding compost to break up the clay will help raise the pH. The majority of ornamental plants prefer an acidic soil with a pH in the range of 6.0 to 6.5 for the optimum absorption of nutrients. If the pH is less than 6, the soil is too acidic, and if the pH is more than 7.5, the soil is too alkaline. For highly acidic soils, ground limestone can be added to raise the pH, and if the soil is too alkaline, sulfur can be mixed in to lower the pH. Soil test recommendations also come with suggestions for raising or lowering the pH. It is always best and easiest to select plants that thrive in the native soil pH.

Planting: Getting It Right the First Time

Avoid "a survival of the fittest" mentality when planning and planting the landscape. It's akin to throwing away time, money, and plants. Like people, plants have certain requirements for good living, and if these are met, the plants thrive. Before you purchase and install plants, do your homework and learn what these requirements are. Outlined below are various elements to consider when placing plants.

Use the Recommended Spacing, Size, Sun, and Soil Requirements

Planting ornamentals correctly helps them develop a rigorous root system and increases their chances for survival. Plant tags usually give spacing recommendations, the plant's ultimate height and width, the sun and soil requirements, and watering needs. By following these recommendations, you maximize success and prevent problems later.

Fall is the optimum season to plant trees, shrubs, vines, ground covers, and herbaceous perennials. (Annuals are planted seasonally according to local recommendations.) In most parts of the Southeast, cool fall temperatures are less stressful to plants than the heat of late spring and summer. Most important, the above-ground portions of most plants stop growing and go dormant in the fall. So plants are less likely to suffer transplant shock at this time. Foliage also loses less water to evaporation in the fall,

Figure 5.7. Plants tags give a wealth of planting information.

so plants require less watering to become established. In winter, the roots grow slowly, so plants installed in the fall will be ready for spring growth.

After you remove container-grown plants from their pots, inspect the roots to see if they are pot-bound. If so, before planting, open the root mass by hand or cut into the root ball with a knife as illustrated in figure 5.8. This encourages root growth, allows water to move freely into the root ball, and helps roots branch out into nearby soil.

Just before planting, water both the root ball and the soil in the hole to minimize the transplant shock and maximize the transport of water and nutrients to the plant roots.

Planting depth is critical. Prepare the hole and the soil to allow the top of the root ball to be level with the soil surface. Planting too deeply restricts the movement of oxygen to the roots, which results in root suffocation. Planting too shallowly exposes the roots to the sun and wind and causes them to dry out.

Figure 5.8. Cutting root mass to encourage root growth.

Remember to create a shallow berm along the perimeter of the planting hole to help direct water to the roots. Once the plant is established, remove the berm with a rake.

Stake up perennials with natural fibers, which are less likely to strangle the plant and can be composted afterward.

Go Slow with Fertilizer

Slow-release, or natural organic, fertilizers are preferred over conventional chemical fertilizers because the former release nutrients slowly over an extended period of time as nature does with decomposed organic matter.

Timing Is Everything

Incorporate slow-release fertilizer or mix compost directly into the soil of annual or herbaceous perennial beds. Apply fertilizer only when plants are actively growing. Fertilize woody ornamentals four to six weeks after planting. After they are established, many woody ornamentals do not need supplemental fertilizer. Water in fertilizers after every application. Use a gentle spray to dissolve the fertilizer and to avoid runoff.

Fertilizer Faux Pas

Avoid being heavy-handed with fertilizer on the theory that if a little is good, more must be better. Fertilizer should be applied at a rate the plant can absorb. Overfertilizing, even when using organic ones like manure, can result in nutrients running off the landscape and into the storm drains or nearby lakes and streams after a heavy rain.

Don't fertilize during periods of drought because it encourages growth that requires watering.

Resist the temptation to fertilize prior to a rain, expecting the rain to water-in the fertilizer. Rainfall amounts are unpredictable, and a heavy rain can wash the fertilizer off the land.

Near landscape ornamentals, refrain from using weed-and-feed lawn fertilizers that contain herbicides; the herbicide component contains broadleaf weed killer that may injure or kill ornamental plants.

Keep fertilizer away from paved surfaces. If granules fall on these surfaces, sweep them onto lawns or beds with a broom; otherwise they may end up as stream pollutants.

Marvels of Mulch

Mimic Mother Nature by mulching the plants with organic material. Mulch has tremendous ecological benefits, including:

- Suppressing weeds, thereby reducing the need for herbicides or hand weeding
- Retaining soil moisture, reducing the need for watering
- Moderating soil temperature and reducing plant stress

Did you know? In summer, a 3- to 4-inch layer of organic mulch can cut water needs in half. (Thomas and Wade, "Mulching Helps Plants Retain Valuable Moisture")

- Increasing soil organic matter that feeds beneficial organisms
- Improving soil fertility and porosity
- Increasing disease and pest resistance, thus reducing chemical use
- Preventing soil erosion
- Protecting roots from injury

Organic Mulches

Organic mulches, such as wood chips, pine straw, pine bark nuggets, and shredded hardwood mulch, add organic matter and nutrients to the soil as they decompose. Most organic mulches must be replenished yearly to maintain their effectiveness. Fine-textured mulches, such as pine bark mininuggets, pine straw, and shredded hardwood mulch do a much better job of retaining moisture than coarse-textured mulches like large pine bark nuggets.

Inorganic Mulches

Inorganic mulches, such as brick, marble chips, rock, or stone, won't decompose and enrich the soil. They are not recommended for warmer climates since they absorb solar radiation, which heats the landscape, increases water loss, and causes heat stress.

How to Apply Mulch

- Remove weeds and water the soil before applying mulch.
- Keep mulch from contacting the plant stem to avoid disease problems.
- Spread mulch to a depth of 3–5 inches.
- Keep mulch on top of the soil surface to prevent it from robbing the soil of nitrogen, which plants need for growth.
- Top dress yearly by applying 1–2 inches of compost on the flowerbed soil surface in early spring before planting or in fall when the garden is put to bed.

Before mulching, spread newspaper over the cleaned soil surface to keep weeds at bay. Newspaper is biodegradable and will decompose, but for a period of time, it provides a good weed barrier.

Black or clear plastic placed under mulches to prevent weeds is not recommended. Plastic prevents water, nutrients and oxygen from penetrating the soil and reaching the roots. It also traps excess moisture in the soil and encourages root-rot diseases.

Where to Find Mulch

Green Waste

Gardeners with wood chippers can shred their own tree prunings, brush, and leaves.

Wood Chips and Shavings

Power utilities and tree companies usually offer free wood chips to gardeners who can transport them. Some companies may be willing to unload their chips in your driveway if they are working in the vicinity. Avoid using chipped treated lumber, which can be toxic.

Chipped Bark

Local nurseries and gardening retail stores sell chipped bark by the bag or truckload. A thin layer of uniform-sized chipped bark spread over green waste makes an attractive landscaping material.

Pine Straw

Nurseries and retail gardening stores sell pine straw by the bale.

Compost

Sustainable gardeners can make compost in their backyards or purchase it by the truckload from a reputable business.

Water Wisely

The amount of water that plants need depends on several factors, including their size, the time of day, soil conditions, and recent rainfall. When plants are watered determines how much water reaches their roots and how much water is lost to evaporation. For example, watering at noon with an overhead sprinkler on a hot, sunny day is a waste of time, money, and water.

Much of the water is lost to evaporation. A general rule of thumb is that annuals require more frequent watering than herbaceous perennials, and herbaceous perennials need more water than established woody ornamentals. Plants growing in porous sandy soils generally must be watered more often than those in clay or humus-enriched soils.

During drought conditions, many states regulate outdoor watering. In these areas especially, gardeners must make every water drop count. If permitted, rain barrels and cisterns can capture rainwater to use during dry periods. For extensive information on landscape irrigation, see chapter 7.

A hand-held hose or watering can works well for annuals and perennials. Direct the spray onto the soil and roots and avoid wetting the leaves. Wet leaves make the plant susceptible to disease. Ooze hose or drip tubing is recommended for ornamentals in areas where outdoor watering is allowed.

Watering Tips

- Wait until plants turn a gray-green color or start to wilt before irrigating.
- Water between 9:00 p.m. and 9:00 a.m. to minimize evaporative loss. Early morning is preferred over evening watering; plants don't like to go to bed with "wet feet" because this makes them more susceptible to fungal diseases.
- Water after the dew forms and before the dew dries to minimize the period of moisture on the leaves, which can increase the possibility of disease.
- In the absence of rainfall, water flowering annuals two to three times a week or as needed. To determine if it is time to irrigate, use your finger to check soil moisture to a 6-inch depth. For newly planted herbaceous perennials and shrubs, irrigate the root zone thoroughly.
- During the establishment of newly planted trees and shrubs, concentrate irrigation on the planting hole and its periphery to encourage root growth and expansion.
- Halt irrigation when water runs off the landscape. If water is applied faster than the soil can absorb it, irrigate in a different loca-

tion while allowing the water to soak in. Consider soil aeration or subsurface drainage if water infiltration is sluggish.

- Water deeply. Frequent and light watering encourages shallow roots and can make the plants susceptible to drought.

Practice Natural Pest Control

Weeds, insect pests, and diseases are all classified as pests, and most can be managed naturally using integrated pest management (IPM). IPM is a simple, multistep program that reduces weed, insect, and disease pests in the landscape and uses the least-toxic means possible. It involves monitoring plants for pests, controlling pests only when they impair plant health, and then using the most environmentally friendly treatment possible. Chapter 8 provides a thorough discussion of the subject. Included here are some basic principles and practices, beginning with pest prevention.

- Build fertile soil with compost so water and nutrients flow unimpeded to the roots. Hard, impervious soils obstruct the flow of water to the plants and endanger their health.
- Put the "right plant in the right place" so it will adapt to the site and be less prone to pest infestations.
- Include native plants in the landscape to attract beneficial insects, birds, amphibians, and reptiles that keep pests in check.
- Avoid planting large beds with only one or two plant species that give pests an expansive food source.
- Hand-watering or drip irrigation is preferred to overhead watering to minimize periods of moisture on the leaves, which increases the possibility of disease.
- Remove weeds that harbor pests.
- Tolerate imperfection. Plants can tolerate a few holes in their leaves just as humans can tolerate scrapes and bruises to their skin without needing major surgery. This is part of the wear and tear of living. In fact, plants can tolerate up to 20 percent leaf damage before they experience any decline.

Before the advent of integrated pest management, landscapers sprayed the entire landscape to prevent pest problems. Today, scientists have

Figure 5.9. Plant leaves with insect holes.

shown that using this approach kills plants' natural defenders, such as beneficial insects, birds, amphibians, and other wildlife that prey on pests.

Implement Integrated Pest Management

The program basics are straightforward. Just follow these guidelines:

- Check your plants frequently for insect damage and insects. By catching the problem early, infestations can be averted.
- Use good cultural practices, such as correct mowing, and avoid improper pruning and overwatering. Allowing plants to become stressed makes them more vulnerable to insect pests and disease.
- Don't plant problems. If certain plants seem to attract pests, get rid of them.
- Correctly identify pests, diseases, and beneficial insects. (Check reliable online resources or contact your local Cooperative Extension Service for help.)

- Monitor for established thresholds of pest populations before taking further action.
- Select and correctly use appropriate control tactics.

A sustainable garden stirs our senses and gives us the satisfaction of helping maintain a healthy functioning ecosystem. Singing birds, chirping crickets, and chattering and scattering squirrels indicate the garden is alive with wildlife. Spiders spinning webs, honeybees gathering pollen, and butterflies flitting about and sipping nectar demonstrate that ecosystem services are under way. When pest problems are few and when watering, mowing, and pruning do not occupy your entire weekend, chances are good that nature is quietly weaving its magic in your landscape.

Sustainable Lawn Care

I enjoy mowing the lawn, it relaxes me. It gets me outdoors, it's good exercise, the freshly cut grass smells great, and the engine is loud enough that I'm sure no one else can hear my thoughts—or intrude upon them.

Astrid Alauda, writer

A lawn is nature under totalitarian rule.

Michael Pollan, *Second Nature*

Lawns and Turfgrass

The American lawn stirs passion on both sides of the hedge. There are those who feel caring for their grass connects them to nature and is a worthwhile expenditure of time and money. They love welcoming family and friends to their home with a living green carpet and value the lawn as a safe surface where their kids can play soccer or toss a football. Then there are those who prefer other weekend activities instead of mowing, blowing, edging, fertilizing, and dethatching their grass. They see little environmental, aesthetic, or recreational value to lawns. Some extreme environmentalists believe lawns are nature's nemesis and should be obliterated from the earth.

There is a middle ground that can perhaps satisfy both the lawn enthusiasts and the tree huggers. Lawns, when well-maintained, can provide important environmental benefits, especially if they don't occupy the entire land-

Did you know? There are three times more acres of lawns in the U.S. than irrigated corn. (Milesi et al., "Mapping and Modeling")

History of American Lawns

Lawns haven't always been an American obsession. In fact, in our nation's early years, vegetation surrounding homes was removed since it provided habitat for vermin such as snakes. Farm animals grazed on native grasses—a distance from the house. Louis XIV (1638–1715) is credited with inventing the *tapis vert*, or green carpet, that was a precursor of the first lawn. His gardeners planted a grass monoculture for his Versailles palace and kept it cut short. And from there the idea of manicured lawns spread to other European palaces and estates. In the late 1800s, Frederick Law Olmsted and other American landscape architects visiting Europe became enamored with the vast English lawns surrounding grand estates. These influential designers incorporated the concept of a green expanse into American city parks such as New York City's Central Park. As suburbs extended outside cities, lawns became part of homeowners' landscapes. In the late nineteenth century, the emerging garden club movement championed lawns to beautify cities and suburbs. Seizing an economic opportunity, in 1900, the U.S. Department of Agriculture began breeding programs for grasses other than forage that could grow in various soils and climates throughout the country. After World War II, a whole industry evolved around lawn care. Today, homeowners can buy a panoply of equipment such as spreaders, lawn mowers, string trimmers, blowers, rubber hoses, and sprinklers to seed, fertilize, water, apply pesticides to, trim, and edge their lawns. (Jenkins, *The Lawn: A History of an American Obsession*)

scape. This chapter discusses how gardeners can cultivate an eco-friendly lawn and still have time to play ball with their children.

Research shows that lawns can be an ecological asset or liability, depending on how gardeners care for them. Sizing the lawn according to a gardener's needs and willingness to maintain it avoids great expanses of unkempt lawns. Following is a discussion of the advantages and disadvantages of planting and maintaining a lawn.

Benefits of Well-Maintained Lawns

With consideration to factors such as grass variety, watering, fertilizing, pest management, and mowing, lawns offer the following environmental benefits:

1. Grass plants add diversity to a garden of trees, shrubs, and flowers.
2. Grass absorbs air pollutants, such as dust and soot.
3. In combination with trees and shrubs, lawns lower air temperatures 7–14°F through shading and evapotranspiration (Leslie, *Handbook of Integrated Pest Management*).
4. Lawns cut noise levels by absorbing, deflecting, reflecting, and refracting sounds.
5. Sod holds soil in place and prevents erosion.
6. Grass absorbs water during rainstorms and helps prevent flooding.
7. Turf allows rain to penetrate the soil and fill underlying aquifers.
8. Lawns filter storm-water pollutants and prevent them from running into nearby streams, rivers, and lakes.
9. Grass reduces the effects of global climate change by absorbing carbon dioxide from the atmosphere.
10. Turf reduces injuries for people who play on grass versus dirt lots or hard surfaces.

Problems from Poorly Maintained Lawns

When lawns are not managed with sustainable practices, they become environmental liabilities. Enthusiastic gardeners may overapply chemicals in their quest for the perfect turf, or they may apply them before a storm. In both cases, these chemicals can pollute nearby streams, rivers, and lakes.

Another homeowner approach to lawn care is neglect, which usually

Did you know? Eight hundred pounds of carbon is stored in one acre of grass. The roots accumulate most of the carbon. (Qian and Follett, "Assessing Soil Carbon Sequestration")

Figure 6.1. Thinning zoysiagrass resulting from poor management practices.

results in thinning grass and exposing bare soil. A thin stand of grass is less effective than a lush one at preventing erosion, mitigating floods, and filtering storm-water pollutants. Less carbon is stored in its blades, roots, and soils, reducing its ability to mitigate climate change.

On any given suburban weekend, the cacophony of gasoline-powered mowers, blowers, string trimmers, hedge trimmers, chippers, and power saws can drown out the delightful sounds of birdsong and rustling leaves. These noisy machines also release a toxic brew of compounds, such as carbon monoxide and nitrogen oxides, into the air, which contributes to climate change and ground-level ozone. Ground-level ozone impairs lung function in animals and inhibits growth in plants. To protect human health and the environment, the U.S. EPA issued new standards for small engines used in outdoor garden equipment that took effect in 2011.

Did you know? The U.S. Environmental Protection Agency estimates that more than 127 million pounds of pesticides were applied to American lawns and gardens in 2007, some of which ended up in streams and rivers. (Grube et al., "Pesticide Industry Sales and Usage 2006–2007 Market Estimates")

A Sustainable Approach to Lawn Care

University of Georgia scientists recommend devoting not more than one-quarter to one-third of the landscape to grass, leaving plenty of space for trees, shrubs, flowers, and ground covers that add diversity and attract wildlife. Before planting or renovating the lawn, take time to answer these few questions to help you determine how much land you want to devote to lawn.

How Will the Lawn Be Used?

Lawns work well for the home entrance, and for walking, sitting, recreational, and picnic areas. Grass makes a safe playing field for children's sports activities and play because it cushions their fall. If the lawn is used for sports activities where it takes a pounding, then a tough turf species is essential. However, sports turf is high-maintenance. Various options are discussed later in this chapter. On steep slopes, ground covers that don't need mowing are better alternatives to grass because mowing grass on an incline may topple the mower and the driver.

How Much Time and How Many Resources Are Available for Lawn Care?

Cultivating grass, like growing any plant, requires some effort to keep it healthy. Grass may need weekly mowing during the growing season except during drought times, plus fertilizing (usually twice yearly), weed control as needed, and watering in the absence of rain. Will you do this work, or will you hire a landscape professional? Lawn care costs money, too. Even a do-it-yourselfer needs a minimum of tools—usually a lawn mower. Seed and fertilizer are other expenses, and water can be pricey, depending on the region where you live.

Figure 6.2. Grass makes a soft surface on which young children can play safely.

Did you know? Japanese beetle larvae develop primarily on grass roots. By limiting the lawn size, a gardener can mitigate the larvae's food supply and a Japanese beetle outbreak.

Is There Sufficient Sunlight?

Most grasses require six hours of sunlight between the hours of 8:00 a.m. and 4:00 p.m. Some grasses can tolerate some shade, but full shade—fewer than four hours of sun per day—won't produce a robust lawn. If there are trees on the property—and hopefully there are—their canopies will increase with age, and so will the shade. Adjust the lawn size to match the available sunlight. Ground covers other than grass work well in dense shade.

Does the Region Have Sufficient Water for Irrigation?

Watering lawns may be difficult in regions where outdoor irrigation is restricted or banned during periods of drought, such as in Durham, North Carolina, and Atlanta, Georgia. Even without water restrictions and bans, it is becoming less acceptable throughout many areas of the United States to use potable water to irrigate lawns. Even golf courses are switching from potable water to wastewater to irrigate their greens.

Do Other Ground Covers Make More Sense for Certain Areas?

For areas of dense shade and steep slopes, homeowners who have neither the inclination nor the time and money to devote to lawn care should consider using ground covers other than grass. They offer the same environmental benefits—such as carbon storage, erosion control, and filtration of pollutants—but without the expense and time required to maintain a lawn. If moss is already growing naturally and well in the shade, it can make a beautiful ground cover. Be aware, however, that moss does not hold up well with a lot of foot traffic. Figure 6.3 shows some lawn alternatives.

Sustainable Lawn Care Practices

Environmentally friendly, sustainable lawn care requires a holistic approach. Greater sustainability of turfgrass systems can be achieved by reducing or replacing the use of minerals with organic fertilizers, replacing the use of chemical pesticides with biological pesticides, mowing less often, and returning the clippings to the soil (Singh, "Soil Organic Carbon Pools").

Figure 6.3. *From left*: Moss under trees in dense shade; mondo grass holds soil on steep slope (not to be confused with Liriope, a.k.a. monkeygrass, which can be invasive); *right:* and pachysandra growing in light shade.

A sustainable gardener must be able to tolerate a few weeds, insect pests, and diseases to avoid overapplying pesticides that may damage the environment including wildlife and pets. Healthy, well-maintained grass can resist infestations. Outlined in the following sections are the steps needed to cultivate grass that is earth-friendly.

Choose a Grass Type Adapted to the Environment

Selecting the right turfgrass for your southern landscape is the most important factor in developing and maintaining an attractive and problem-free lawn. Base your grass selection on environmental conditions, desired appearance, intended use, and maintenance requirements. The environmental conditions include temperature and moisture, shade adaptation, soil pH, and fertility. If the grass will be used for a ball field rather than for visual beauty, select a tougher turfgrass. All turfgrasses have good as well as potentially undesirable features. Thus, selection should be based on which grass meets your needs.

Planting and maintaining grass is a big investment of time and money. Changing to a different variety is costly and disruptive. Take time to learn which grasses will work best for the environment and your needs. The local Cooperative Extension is the best information source for finding out which grasses grow well in each area's climate and soils. Fact sheets often are available on Extension websites. Visit the local garden center to see what the various grasses look like.

Here is a quick overview of grasses that grow well in the Southeast. They are classified as either cool-season or warm-season grasses.

Cool-Season Grasses

Cool-season grasses grow well during the cool months of spring and fall when temperatures average 60–75°F. They may become dormant, or stressed and injured during the hot summer months and may require more water than the warm-season grasses. Cool-season grasses include:

Tall Fescue (*Festuca arundinacea*)

Adapted to a wide range of soil conditions but grows best on fertile, well-drained soils with a soil pH of 5.5–6.5. It may need watering to remain attractive during the summer; however, excessive water and overfertilizing can lead to disease problems.

Kentucky Bluegrass (*Poa pratensis*)

Kentucky bluegrass has a fine- to medium-leaf texture and bright color. A major attribute of Kentucky bluegrass is its creeping growth habit. Kentucky bluegrass can become semi-dormant during hot weather and grows best in a fertile soil with a pH of 5.5–6.5. While it does best in partial shade, it will grow in open sun if adequate moisture is present.

Figure 6.4. Tall fescue.

Figure 6.5. Kentucky bluegrass.

Figure 6.6. Perennial ryegrass (*left*) and annual ryegrass (*right*).

Ryegrasses: Perennial ryegrass (*Lolium perenne*);
annual ryegrass (*Lolium multiflorum*)

In the Southeast, they can be used as a winter cover on new lawns where
the permanent grass has not been established or to provide a green cover
on a warm-season grass during winter.

Warm-Season Grasses

Warm-season grasses grow best when temperatures reach 80–95°F in the
spring, summer, and early fall. They grow vigorously during this time and
become brown and dormant in winter. Below are the most common warm-
season grasses in the Southeast.

Figure 6.7. Bermudagrass.

Common Bermudagrass (*Cynodon dactylon*)

Also called "Arizona Common," bermudagrass is adapted to many soil conditions and makes a good turf if fertilized and mowed correctly. It is popular for home lawns since it can be easily established by seeding. The vegetative hybrids are susceptible to more disease but also have weed resistance, greater turf density, finer and softer texture, and more favorable color.

Bermudagrass

Bermudagrass varieties work well for sports activities. They typically produce no viable seed and must be planted as sprigs, stolons, or sod. Commonly used bermudagrasses include:

'Tifway'

With its dark-green color and frost resistance, this well-liked hybrid makes an ideal turfgrass for lawns. It usually begins growing earlier in the spring and remains green later in the fall than other bermudagrasses.

'TifSport'

This grass looks similar to 'Tifway,' but compared with 'Tifway,' 'TifSport' is slightly more cold-tolerant, has greater density, and tolerates lower mowing levels. In addition, it is more drought-tolerant, and it's also not on the mole cricket's list of favorite foods.

'Tifton 10'

With a coarse leaf texture similar to common bermudagrass, 'Tifton 10' has natural dark-bluish–green color. It establishes rapidly from stolons and performs well in low-maintenance conditions. Since this grass requires little mowing, your lawn mower will spend most of its time in the shed.

'TifGrand'

It shares many of the same characteristics as 'Tifway' and 'TifSport,' but 'TifGrand' has a darker-green color. It was also bred for shade tolerance.

Centipedegrass (*Eremochloa ophiuroides*)

This eco-friendly grass is adapted to soils with low fertility but grows best, like most turfgrasses, at a soil pH of 5.0–6.0. It is resistant to most

Figure 6.8. Centipedegrass.

insects and diseases and ideal for the gardener who wants a low-maintenance lawn. This slow-growing but aggressive grass can produce a dense, attractive, weed-free turf. It is more shade-tolerant than bermudagrass but less shade-tolerant than St. Augustinegrass and zoysiagrass. It can be established by either seed or vegetative parts and does not require much fertilizer.

Carpetgrass (*Axonopus affinis*)

This coarse-leafed, creeping grass grows throughout the Southeast in either sun or shade, but is less shade-tolerant than St. Augustinegrass. Carpetgrass is recommended only for lawns on wet, low-fertility, acid (pH 4.5–5.5), sandy soils where ease of establishment and care is more important than quality.

Zoysiagrass (*Zoysia* Spp.)

It forms an excellent turf when properly established and managed.

Zoysiagrass makes a dense, attractive turf in full sun and partial shade but often thins in dense shade. It may need periodic thinning or dethatching. In general, zoysiagrasses are slow to cover completely, thus more costly to establish; less drought-tolerant than bermudagrass; and recommended

Figure 6.9. Carpetgrass.

Figure 6.10. Zeon zoysiagrass.

for people willing to provide the required maintenance. It is established by sodding or plugging, but there also are seeded types.

Following are several varieties of zoysiagrass:

Zoysia japonica

Zoysia japonica is sometimes called Japanese or Korean lawngrass or commonly just zoysiagrass. It has coarse leaf texture, excellent cold tolerance, and some cultivars (e.g., 'Zenith' and 'Compadre') can be seeded.

'Emerald' Zoysiagrass

'Emerald' zoysiagrass is well-suited for top-quality lawns where a good maintenance program is provided. It has a dark-green color, very fine leaf texture, good shade tolerance, high density, and a low-growth habit. 'Emerald' will develop excess thatch if overfertilized and is prone to winter injury from the Atlanta area and north.

Figure 6.11. St. Augustinegrass.

'Meyer' Zoysiagrass

'Meyer' zoysiagrass, also called 'Z 52' and 'Amazoy,' is an improved selection of *Zoysia japonica*. It has medium leaf texture, good cold tolerance, and spreads more rapidly than many other zoysiagrasses.

'El Toro'

'El Toro' looks like 'Meyer' zoysiagrass but has a coarser leaf texture. It is a relatively fast-growing zoysiagrass, tolerates mowing with a rotary mower, and produces less thatch than 'Meyer.' It performs well in drought conditions.

St. Augustinegrass (*Stenotaphrum secundatum*)

Similar to centipedegrass, this grass has large, flat stems and broad, coarse leaves. It has an attractive blue-green color and forms a deep, fairly dense turf. It is shade-tolerant and spreads by above-ground runners. St. Augustinegrass can be susceptible to winter injury. It is planted only by vegeta-

Table 6.1. Qualities of common southeastern turfgrasses

Grass Type	Centipede-grass *Eremochloa ophiuroides*	St. Augustine-grass *Stenotaphrum secundatum*	Zoysiagrass Various species	Perennial rye grass *Lolium perenne*	Bermuda-grass *Cynodon spp.*	Tall fescu *Festuca arundinae*
Spreading habit	Stolons	Stolons	Stolons and rhizomes	Bunch type	Stolons and rhizomes	Bunch ty
Leaf texture	Medium	Coarse	Fine to medium	Fine to medium	Fine to medium	Coarse t medium
Shoot density	Medium	Medium	Medium to high	Medium	High	Low to medium
Soil Type Required	Wide range; grows well on sandy, acidic, infertile soils	Wide range	Wide range	Wide range; moist, fertile best	Wide range; fertile best	Wide ran
Establishment Rate	Moderate	Fast	Very slow	Fast	Very fast	Medium-f
Recuperative ability	Poor	Fair	Poor; will recover but slowly	Poor to fair	Excellent	Poor to f
Wear resistance	Poor	Fair	Good	Fair to good	Very good to excellent	Good
Cold tolerance	Poor	Least tolerant	Fair to good	Good	Fair to good	Fair
Heat tolerance	Excellent	Excellent	Excellent	Poor to fair	Excellent	Good
Drought tolerance	Fair	Fair	Good	Fair	Excellent for common; good for hybrids	Good
Shade tolerance	Fair to good	Excellent	Good	Fair to good	Very poor	Fair to go
Salt tolerance	Poor	Good	Good	Fair	Good	Good
Submersion tolerance	Poor	Fair	Poor	Fair	Poor	Good
Maintenance Level	Low	Medium	Medium to high	Medium	Medium to high	Low to medium
Fertility Requirement	Low	Medium	Medium	Medium	High for hybrid; medium for common	Medium
Mowing height (inches)	1–2	1.5–3	1.0–1.5	1–3	1.0–1.5	1.5–3

ass Type	Centipede-grass *Eremochloa ophiuroides*	St. Augustine-grass *Stenotaphrum secundatum*	Zoysiagrass Various species	Perennial rye grass *Lolium perenne*	Bermuda-grass *Cynodon spp.*	Tall fescue *Festuca arundinacea*
atching ndency	Low to medium	Moderate	Medium to high	Low	High for hybrids; low for common	Low
sease tential	Low	High	Medium	Medium	Moderate	Low
matode oblems	Severe	—	Severe	—	Severe	—

rce: Adapted from "Georgia Turfgrasses—Selection and Adaptation." www.commodities.caes.uga.edu/turfgrass/
orgiaturf/Turfgras/1150_Selection.htm.

tive means. Perhaps the greatest disadvantage of this species is its sensitivity to the chinch bug and to gray leaf spot disease.

Assess the Lawn

If a desirable grass variety dominates the lawn—50 percent or more—and weeds represent the minority faction, renovate the existing lawn. If weeds make up the majority, destroying the lawn and starting all over may be the easiest solution. This option also gives a gardener the chance to select a drought-tolerant and pest-resistant grass species and a chance to enrich the soil with organic material and correct nutrient deficiencies. For some, it may be acceptable to kill the existing lawn with a systemic herbicide such as Roundup-Pro or Finale since they leave no residues in the soil, according to some researchers. An alternative is to deep-till the remnants of grass and weeds into the soil.

Establishing a New Lawn

Establishing a lawn is a three-step process. The first and most important step is preparing the soil. The second step is planting, which involves seeding, sprigging, or sodding. The final step is the care of the grass during the establishment period of two to four weeks after it is planted.

Step 1. Prepare the Soil

In cultivated, healthy soil, grass plants are able to grow deep roots and secure the nutrients and water they need as well as anchor themselves. A
deeply rooted, thick stand of grass is resilient. It can withstand changes
in environmental conditions such as periods of heavy rains and droughts,
changes in temperatures, and pest infestations. Whether you are seeding,
sprigging, or sodding, the soil should be prepared as described here.

Take Soil Samples

This procedure is described in chapter 2. Include a test for organic matter.
There may be an additional cost, but gardeners need to know if the soil
has sufficient organic material to germinate and sustain a lawn. The soil-
test results come with recommendations to improve the nutrient content,
also.

Clean the Planting Site

Remove all debris from the planting area including rocks, broken glass,
metal fragments, and tree stumps. Care should be taken not to destroy or
damage existing trees. Tilling under a tree may cut tree roots and damage
or kill the tree. Trees can also be suffocated by deeply covering the roots
with soil.

   If a subsurface drainage pipe is needed or if you are interested in an irrigation system, now is the best time to install either. The subgrade may
become compacted by machinery during rough grading, especially if the
ground is wet. Break up this compacted layer by tilling before proceeding.

Replace Topsoil

Once the subgrade is established, spread the topsoil over the subgrade. On
steep slopes or where rock outcrops exist, cover with at least 12 inches of
topsoil.

Add Organic Matter If Needed

The organic content of the soil should be 2–4 percent. If it is lower, organic
materials such as compost, peat moss, well-rotted sawdust (at least six to
eight years old) or leaf litter can be added. Add 1–3 cubic yards of organic

matter per 1,000 square feet of lawn area. All these materials should be mixed thoroughly with the native soil to a depth of 6–8 inches. If great amounts of soil have been moved, lightly wet the area with water to help firm the seedbed and fill any low areas before planting.

Add Fertilizer and Lime

Once the topsoil is spread and graded, add fertilizer and lime as recommended by the soil test report. Lime and fertilizer should be thoroughly mixed with the top 4–6 inches of topsoil. To avoid runoff, lightly water in fertilizer prior to planting the grass.

If the soil-test report shows a calcium deficiency, then sulfur or gypsum (calcium sulfate) can be added to the soil at the required amounts. Unlike

Using Organic vs. Inorganic Fertilizer

Organic fertilizer is becoming increasingly popular with home gardeners who want to reduce their carbon footprint. Answering the call for eco-friendly fertilizer are companies that manufacture it from plant, animal, and human waste. Examples include cotton seed meal, bone meal, animal manure, and sewage sludge. Organic fertilizer may improve the soil's structure, water-holding capacity, and bacterial and fungal activity. However, organic fertilizers work more slowly than inorganic fertilizers because they must be decomposed by soil microbes before plants can use the nutrients. Organic fertilizers are more expensive than inorganic fertilizers, are voluminous, and have varying nutrient contents.

Inorganic fertilizers, on the other hand, are manufactured from nonliving materials, including fossil fuels such as natural gas and coal. They are produced in a form—either granular or liquid—that can be directly absorbed by the grass roots. Inorganic fertilizers do little to improve soil structure. They contain chemical salts, which if applied improperly, can easily "burn" roots or create a toxic concentration of salts.

lime, gypsum does not affect soil pH, and gypsum applications have been shown to reduce soil crusting and increase water infiltration. Gypsum also improves the overall soil structure. Scrap wallboard left over from construction can be ground up as a good source of calcium sulfate. For more information on using scrap wallboard, refer to University of Georgia Extension Special Bulletin #1223.

Final Grading

Complete the final grading and fertilizer application right before planting. If this is done too far in advance, some fertilizer may leach out of the soil, and the soil may become crusted. On sandy soils, the seedbed should be firmed. This will help prevent the soil from drying out.

Step 2. Seed, Sod, and Sprig the Grass

Cool-Season Grasses

Most cool-season grasses are established by seeding. In addition to being sold as an individual cultivar, grass seed is sold as either blends or mixtures. A blend contains two or more varieties/cultivars of the same species. Mixtures, however, contain two or more turfgrass species. Blends and mixtures are preferred since they add some plant diversity. For the proper seeding rate and procedure, follow the instructions provided by the local Cooperative Extension office. Always purchase quality seed, that is, certified seed with a high percentage of germination and purity. Inexpensive seed often ends up being expensive due to its low germination rate and the presence of weeds.

After seeding, rake ¼ inch of soil over the bed. This contact between the seed and the soil increases the chance of germination. Then roll the seedbed lightly to firm the soil. Finally, spread a thin layer of mulch, such as wheat straw, over the soil. Mulch helps prevent soil erosion and holds moisture for the seeds to germinate. If straw is used, find a weed-free source. One bale of straw (60–80 pounds) will cover approximately 1,000 square feet.

Warm-Season Grasses

Planting vegetative parts such as sprigs, stolons, or sod is the best way to launch lawns comprised of warm-season grasses. Weeds may infest newly planted grass. Remove them by hand or cut them with frequent mowing.

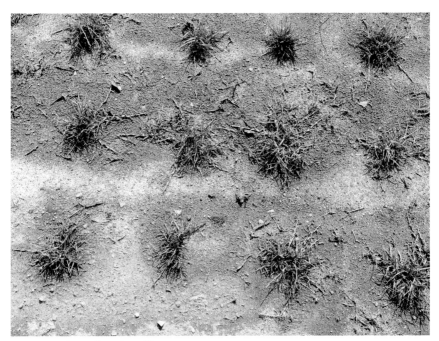

Figure 6.12. Recently sprigged lawn.

Sprigging

Sprigging is the placing of grass plants, runners, rhizomes, stolons, or small sod pieces (2–4-inch plugs) in small holes or furrows on the soil surface. To plant sprigs, dig furrows 8–12 inches apart and place the sprigs 1–2 inches deep every 4–6 inches in from the furrows. After placing the sprigs in the furrow, cover part of the sprig with soil and roll or step on the soil around the sprig. Apply water immediately.

Stolonizing

Stolons are above-ground grass stems. Broadcast them by hand or by a mechanical spreader over the prepared seedbed. Then top-dress with ¼ inch of soil. After topdressing, roll the soil surrounding the stolons. Water the grass immediately.

Sodding

Sodding produces an instant lawn. Use quality sod that is free of weeds, diseases, and insects. It should be freshly harvested and stored in the shade and kept slightly damp or moist until ready to use. For sodding instructions, contact the Cooperative Extension. After installing sod, roll the area to improve sod-to-soil contact. Apply ¼–½ inch of water within 30 minutes of installation. Lightly irrigate daily to keep the sod moist until it has firmly rooted (about two weeks).

Plugging

Plugging is planting 2–4 inch squares or sod pieces into similar-sized holes every 6–12 inches in a row. Space rows 6–12 inches apart. Tamp plugs firmly into the soil. Keep the soil moist until the grass is well-rooted and spreading vigorously.

Figure 6.13. Laying sod.

Figure 6.14. Grass plug.

Step 3. Maintain the Lawn with Sustainable Practices

After establishing the lawn, it needs fertilizer, water, mowing, and occasional renovating. No one practice is more important than another. They are interrelated and necessary.

Fertilize with Essential Nutrients

Fertilize the lawn based on the grass requirements, soil-test results, maintenance practices, and desired appearance. By using organic fertilizers, a gardener improves the organic content of the soil as well as adds the necessary nitrogen, phosphorus, and potassium needed by the grass. Often an organic fertilizer does not supply the specific nitrogen, phosphorus, and potassium ratio required. Use the nitrogen value on the bag as the basis for fertilizer selection. Apply no more than 1 pound of nitrogen per 1,000 square feet at one time. Generally a lawn needs no more than 4 pounds of nitrogen per year. However, centipedegrass is an exception. One pound of nitrogen per 1,000 square feet per year is ample for most established centipedegrass lawns. When gardeners grass-cycle, or let the grass clippings stay on the lawn after mowing, the average lawn may need only 2 pounds of nitrogen per year. Applying fertilizer at the right time is as important as knowing how much to apply.

Cool-season grasses such as tall fescue and Kentucky bluegrass should be fertilized in the fall. Warm-season grasses should be fertilized in spring and late summer with a complete fertilizer (one containing nitrogen, phosphorus, and potassium). The spring fertilizer application should be made once the last frost date has passed, and soil temperatures at the 4-inch depth are consistently above 65°F. The fall application should be made about six weeks before the average first-frost date.

Fertilizing Tips

1. Read the label directions before spreading fertilizer.
2. Water in fertilizer slowly and thoroughly with ½ inch of water to prevent it from running off the landscape during a storm.
3. Use a mechanical spreader to distribute the fertilizer. Calibrate it to make sure fertilizer is applied at the correct amount.
4. Use a drop-style spreader rather than a rotary spreader near water bodies—including ornamental ponds—to avoid contamination.

Figure 6.15. Using a drop-style spreader for better broadcast control near a pond.

5. Close the spreader when passing over driveways and sidewalks. Fertilizer on hard surfaces can wash into storm drains and nearby streams and ponds with the first downpour.
6. Sweep any fertilizer that has landed onto driveways, walkways, and roadways back onto the lawn to minimize contamination of storm sewers or other water systems.
7. Fill and wash spreaders on the lawn and not on hard surfaces.

AVOID Fertilizing

- When the lawn is wet. It may burn the grass blades.
- When lawns are dormant. The grass won't use it, so it can become a water pollutant.
- During a drought. It increases the lawn's need for water.
- In shaded areas. Shaded areas need 20–50 percent less fertilizer than sunny areas.

DO NOT fertilize the lawn within 25 feet of a lake, pond, river, or stream. Rain can wash the fertilizer into the water. High levels of fertilizer or nutrients in water bodies causes eutrophication, the process by which dissolved nutrients lead to excessive plant growth and the depletion of dissolved oxygen, sometimes causing the death of a pond or the growth of unsightly "green scum" on the water's surface. This process eventually robs aquatic wildlife of oxygen and can kill fish and reduce biodiversity.

Figure 6.16. Eutrophication is caused by excess fertilizer washing off the land during rain.

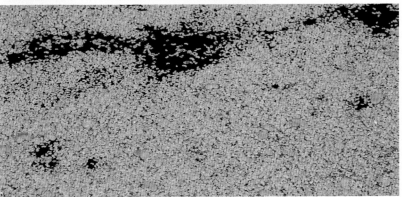

Add Lime to Soil to Raise the pH

Another important factor in growing healthy plants is the soil acidity level. Most lawn grasses grow best at a pH of 5.5–6.5. A pH either too low or too high reduces the grasses' ability to absorb nutrients. Broadcasting lime on the soil will raise the pH. Use a dolomitic source of limestone, which supplies magnesium as well as calcium. Base any lime applications on soil-test results.

Make Every Drop Count

Many factors influence how much and how often you water the lawn. Soil type, grass variety, soil fertility level, frequency of rain, temperature, wind, and humidity all affect the amount of water needed. Both highly fertilized lawns and hot, windy days tend to increase water demand, while lawns lightly fertilized and cool, cloudy days tend to decrease water needs. The key to success is to condition the grass to require as little extra water as possible.

Irrigation is a maintenance practice often done incorrectly. Light, frequent irrigations produce shallow, weak root systems. A shallow root system prevents efficient use of plant nutrients and soil moisture. If the soil becomes compacted or crusted, loosen it by core aeration so that water can penetrate the surface and move into the root zone. Follow these recommendations for a deep-rooted system of grass that can withstand rainfall and temperature fluctuations and resist disease and pest pressure.

- *Water when grass shows stress and not on a set schedule.* Most stressed grasses appear dark and dull, the leaf blades begin to fold or roll and footprint indentations remain after walking over the area.
- *Moisten the soil several inches deep* to produce a deep-rooted lawn that can withstand drought. Shallow-rooted grass dries out quickly during rainless periods. Daily watering produces short roots incapable of tolerating periodic stresses.
- *Water during the early-morning hours* (3:00 a.m. to 10:00 a.m.) to minimize evaporative losses and maximize water infiltration. Irrigate during the early-morning hours to reduce disease problems that can arise if grass stays wet for a prolonged period of time.

> *Did you know?* Watering during the middle of the day may result in 50 percent evaporation. (Waltz, *Water Lawns Wisely*)

- *Apply only the amount of water the soil can hold*; otherwise it runs off the lawn.

Cut Grass and Emissions

After California politicians raised concerns over spills and emissions from gasoline-powered lawn equipment, the U.S. EPA enacted stricter national standards for gasoline-powered lawn mowers built in 2011 or later. The new standards are expected to reduce emissions by 35 percent annually to comply with California's air-quality regulations.

Manufacturers are answering gardeners' call for noiseless, nonpolluting lawn mowers that pack the same power as gasoline mowers. For small lawns of less than 3,000 square feet, an easy-to-operate, hand-powered reel mower is making a comeback. Some reel mowers run on rechargeable batteries. Corded electric mowers have been around for years, but their range is limited to the cord length. For bigger lawns, consider a cordless electric mower. They run on rechargeable batteries that can be charged overnight in a standard outlet costing only pennies. For the serious eco-minded gardener, a solar-powered mower is now on the market. There are also lines of garden tools that have interchangeable batteries. Whatever lawn mower or energy-efficient garden tools you select, make sure to cut, blow, mulch, and edge the grass according to best environmental practices.

Skip the Gym; Work Out with Hand Tools

Cross-train with various hand tools to keep your body and lawn in shape. Power walk behind your hand-powered mower. Exercise your forearms by sweeping grass clippings off paved surfaces onto the lawn. Go for the burn by hauling wheelbarrows of compost to top-dress the lawn.

Mow Grass to the Recommended Height

As always, the state Cooperative Extension office knows the best way to mow locally grown grasses. Scalping the lawn or mowing it too low stresses the grass plants and creates an entrée for pests and weeds. Thick grass has more surface area to convert nutrients to food. Lush grass crowds out weeds, resists diseases, and is more drought-tolerant. Increase the mowing height by ½ inch during the summer to help grasses tolerate stress and drought. Sharpen mower blades at least once a year to maintain a smooth cut. Dull blades shred leaf tips, causing grass to use more water and become susceptible to infection. Create mulched beds around trees to avoid injuring the trees with the mower.

Figure 6.17. Shredded grass tip from dull mower blades.

Grass-Cycle Clippings

Until recently, bagging clippings was standard practice. Research shows that letting grass clippings fall onto the lawn adds nitrogen to the soil. University of Connecticut turfgrass specialist William Diest compared lawns where clippings were bagged with lawns where clippings were grass-cycled. Grass-cycled lawns showed:

- 45 percent less crabgrass
- Up to 66 percent less disease
- Up to 45 percent more earthworms
- 60 percent more water reaching plant roots
- 50 percent less fertilizer needed

Lawn clippings will not increase thatch buildup. Excess fertilizer does. Clippings decompose quickly and add nitrogen to the soil. A light layer of fallen leaves can also be chopped up with the mower and left on the lawn to add nutrients. However, if leaf cover is thick, bag the clippings and toss them onto the compost pile. If clippings fall onto walkways or driveways, sweep them back onto the lawn, or they may contribute to stream pollution.

Aerate to Manage Thatch

Thatch is a layer of undecomposed or partially decomposed organic residues situated above the soil surface. If it is more than ½ inch thick, then water, air, and fertilizer cannot enter the soil easily. Thatch can also harbor harmful insects and invite diseases. Thatch buildup happens when grass is overfertilized and not from grass cycling.

Soils with sufficient organic matter attract earthworms and soil microbes that decompose grass clippings quickly. The best way to reduce thatch is

Did you know? If gardeners would recycle grass clippings, U.S. lawn area could store about 37 billion pounds of carbon—the weight of about 147,000 blue whales. (Milesi et al., "Mapping and Modeling")

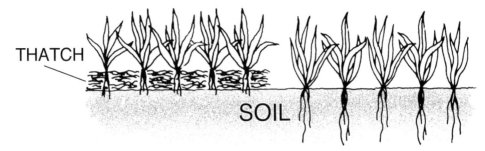

Figure 6.18. The thatch layer pictured may prevent air, water, and fertilizer from reaching soil.

to aerate the lawn. Core aeration mechanically removes soil cores from the lawn and reduces compaction by allowing air and water to penetrate it more easily. Gardeners can rent an aerator or hire a lawn-care professional to aerate. Core aeration is a good annual practice best done in the fall.

Top-Dress with Compost to Build Soil

Spreading a thin layer of compost over the lawn or garden restores organic matter to the soil. This practice works well in combination with soil aeration. It can be done either before or after aeration. Use a spreader or the "dump and rake method" to put ¼ inch of compost on the lawn. Compost can be bought by the bag, by the truckload, or it can come from a gardener's backyard pile. Approximately 21 cubic feet of compost is recommended for 1,000 square feet of lawn. (A 30-gallon garbage can holds about 4 cubic feet.) Top-dressing with compost helps in the thatch decomposition.

Overseed to Improve Lawn Quality

If the lawn thins and the soil is exposed, reseed or overseed it to restore the lawn's vitality. Overseeding is not necessary every year, but when it is done, the best order of operations is as follows.

1. Match species and cultivars to the current grass.
2. Mow the lawn short: 1–1.5 inches.
3. Aerate the lawn.

4. Apply seed with a mechanical spreader at recommended rates.

5. Top-dress the lawn with compost to cover seed.

6. Water well.

7. Keep seed moist until it germinates.

8. Stay off the grass until it is established.

9. Mow at normal heights after the grass is established.

Prevent Lawn Problems

Most home lawn problems—approximately 70 percent—are caused by peo-ple, pets, poor management practices, and climate conditions. A common pet problem is animal urine—the "dog-on-it" problem. The remaining 30 percent are attributed to fungal disease, weeds, and insects, which are dis-cussed in chapter 8. Here are examples of problems attributed to nonliving causes, even though some are brought about by people.

Abiotic or Nonliving Causes

- Poorly applied pesticides
- Too much fertilizer
- Nutrient deficiencies
- Chemical spills—fuel, cleaners, or soaps
- Soil compaction
- Excess thatch
- Shade and tree root competition
- Scalping and mower injury
- Abrasive injury from heavy use—ball fields and dog runs
- Septic tank drainage fields
- Water stress—drought, flooding, and ice cover
- Temperature—heat stress and winter kill

Figure 6.19 illustrates some of these.

Gardeners can control most of these situations with the exception of the weather-related ones. Keeping Fido off the lawn (or policing the lawn be-hind Fido), planting ground covers, or using mulched beds over the septic field and under trees, and following best environmental practices outlined

Figure 6.19. *Top*: Dog urine spots; *middle*: soil compaction and root competition; *bottom*: thin grass under trees.

in this chapter will minimize lawn problems. Growing dense, deeply rooted grass can ward off many weeds, diseases, and insects, and the lawn becomes an asset to the home as well as the environment.

Guidelines for Choosing a Lawn-Care Service

Not everyone with a yard has the time or interest to maintain a lawn, but they may still want one as part of their landscape. If you are not a hands-on gardener, then turning to a professional lawn-care service may be a good decision. Choose carefully, however, and find one that will likely use sustainable practices. Here are few questions to consider before you make your selection.

Is the Company Licensed?

Nearly all states require lawn-care companies to be licensed if they apply pesticides. Having a license means they are operating legally.

Does the Company Have a Good Track Record?

Call the Better Business Bureau or the state pesticide regulatory agency to see if the company is on record as having committed any violations.

Is the Company Affiliated with a Professional Lawn-Care Association?

Professional associations often work with universities to learn the latest researched-based best practices.

Does the Company Use Integrated Pest Management (IPM)?

This holistic approach to pest management uses a system of nontoxic pest controls on an as-needed basis only. If the company offers IPM, find out exactly what they mean by it.

Is the Company Willing to Tell You What Pesticides It Applies and Why, and to Explain the Health and Environmental Risks?

You have a right to this information. The U.S. EPA requires products labeled as pesticides to be registered. The packaging will contain this information.

Since nature constantly strives for biodiversity, don't fret when weeds and other plants pop up in your grass. Nuts falling from the trees and seeds blown by the wind or carried by birds and animals are a few of the many ways nature tries to diversify a lawn. By tolerating some weeds and limiting your lawn size to an area you can manage, you will minimize your frustration, time, and expense in striving for the picture-perfect lawn. And most important, you will do right by the environment.

7

Water Wisely

Water promises to be to the 21st century what oil was to the 20th century:
The precious commodity that determines the wealth of nations.

Shawn Tully, *Fortune Magazine*, May 15, 2000

Water is fast becoming the new crude. Only 1 percent of the earth's water is fresh and available for farming, gardening, industry, and human use. The remainder is either salty seawater or frozen in glaciers. As the world's population now exceeds 7 billion, we must share our finite water supply among greater numbers of people. But it's not easy. In the Southeast, for instance, a contentious, nearly two-decade-long dispute among Georgia, Alabama, and Florida has yet to produce a plan to equitably allocate water in the interstate rivers.

According to the U.S. Environmental Protection Agency, Americans use, on average, a third of their household water outdoors for such things as washing cars and running sprinklers (see table 7.1). However, the majority of outdoor water goes to irrigating residential and commercial landscapes.

With frequent droughts plaguing the Southeast, state and municipal governments are restricting or banning potable water for irrigating lawns, flowers, trees, and shrubs. Gardeners with an eye to the future are conserving water and, increasingly, are gathering and storing rainwater in barrels and cisterns to use on landscapes during dry times. By designing a water-wise landscape or renovating an existing one to include water-wise features, a gardener can cut outdoor watering in half.

Another water issue bubbling to the surface is the contamination of rivers, streams, and lakes by gardening chemicals. After a rainstorm, improperly applied fertilizers and pesticides can wash into nearby drains, lakes, and streams. To make matters worse, large areas of impervious surfaces

Table 7.1. Average American household water use

Source	Amount (gallons per day)
Toilet	18.5
Clothes washer	15
Shower, bath	12.8
Sinks, faucets	10.9
Leaks	9.5
Dishwasher	1
Other sources	1.6
Total indoor use	**69.3**
Total outdoor use	**30–40**

Source: U.S. Environmental Protection Agency, "Water Sense," www.epa.gov/
WaterSense/pubs/indoor.html.

such as roofs, roads, parking lots, walkways, and driveways collect vehicle
oil, grease, chemicals, pet waste, and other contaminants that are then carried off by the rain into storm drains, which eventually empty into streams
and rivers. Often rivers that run through cities supply drinking water, as the
Chattahoochee River does for metro Atlanta.

According to the U.S. Census Bureau, more than 80 percent of Americans live in urban areas. Maintaining good-quality water is necessary for
the health of both humans and aquatic ecosystems. Research confirms that
as the percentage of impervious surface increases, the health of the nearby
streams and rivers decreases, as shown in figure 7.1.

Degradation of Watershed as Impervious Surface Area Increases

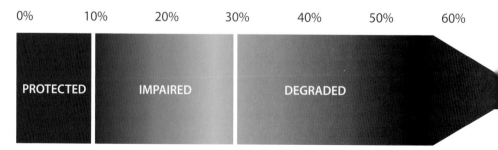

Figure 7.1. As the amount of urban land increases, along with the number of roofs and parking
lots, the health of adjacent waterways deceases.

Seven Steps to Water-Wise Gardening

The fundamentals of conserving water and managing storm water in the landscape are outlined below in seven steps. This water-wise approach not only safeguards natural resources but also saves gardeners time, water, and even money. Many of these steps are presented in more detail in other chapters, but they are arranged here to emphasize the necessary elements of water-wise gardening.

1. Group Plants According to Water Needs

Conserving water in the garden begins by arranging plants into three water zones—low, medium, and high. This highly efficient system minimizes watering because the only areas you need to monitor on a regular basis are the small high-water zones. Keep an eye on plant leaves—they are a good indicator of when supplemental watering may be needed. Don't forget to incorporate shade into the plan, too. It cools the landscape and reduces water evaporation from the soil. Below is a review of the various water zones.

Low

Except during extreme drought, this area needs little supplemental water beyond what nature provides. At least 60 percent of the landscape—established trees, shrubs, and ground covers—should be incorporated into the low water-use zone, which typically is a dry area of the landscape.

Medium

Plants in this section—no more than 30 percent of the landscape—require supplemental water during prolonged rainless periods. Highly visible or functional plants like perennial beds and lawns are medium water users.

High

Since plants in this zone require frequent watering, dedicate 10 percent or less to this section, which is usually small but placed in high-impact areas. These areas are often naturally moist, but not soggy, and are located near a water source. Examples of plants needing frequent watering include colorful annuals arranged in beds and containers near the home's entrance or on the deck to give high visual impact.

2. Build Soil Fertility

Soil rich in organic matter holds water in its air spaces, similar to the way a sponge holds water. These tiny underground reservoirs supply water to plant roots. When the soil is saturated, the excess water slowly seeps into the groundwater and replenishes underground aquifers. Determine the soil's organic content by testing it through the state Cooperative Extension or a reputable soil laboratory.

3. Choose the Right Plant for the Right Place

Follow the eco-gardener's mantra by selecting climate-appropriate, drought-tolerant, and native/adapted plant species for the garden. Examples include blue-green grasses, lamb's ear, lavender, yarrow, sedum, purple coneflower, black-eyed Susan, salvia, rosemary, santolina, and daylilies. Check with your local Cooperative Extension office for a list of local plants that are resilient

Figure 7.2. A water-wise landscape offers beauty and conserves water. Plants used: *Echinacea purpurea, Ratibida pinnata, Lobelia cardinalis, Panicum virgatum, Phlox paniculata.*

and require less water. Place plants in their preferred environment, considering the soils, sun and shades patterns, water needs, and other factors.

4. Downsize the Irrigated Lawn

Minimize water use by shrinking the lawn area to represent no more than 40 percent of the landscape. Also, choose drought-tolerant grasses such as centipede, bermudagrass, and zoysia that can go for weeks without rain. For more information on lawn care, see chapter 6. Your local Cooperative Extension office knows which turfgrasses are adapted to your area's soils and climate. Contact them for more information.

5. Water Efficiently

Water-wise gardeners understand the advantages of various watering systems, including the best time of day and the preferred ways to water plants.

Figure 7.3. A small lawn is easy to irrigate and manage.

Figure 7.4. Rain gauge measures rainfall.

Figure 7.5. Soil moisture sensor.

Having a rain gauge and a soil moisture meter on hand helps determine how much water to give the landscape when rainfall is scarce.

A **rain gauge** measures rainfall and is an easy way to monitor the output of sprinklers.

Soil moisture sensors help gardeners know when the soil is dry or saturated and whether it needs water.

6. Much Ado about Mulch

Mulch reduces both water loss from soils and the need for supplemental irrigation during dry times. It insulates the plant's roots from summer heat and winter cold. Mulch also prevents the soil surface from crusting and allows water to penetrate the soil easily. In addition, mulch decomposes and returns organic matter to the soil, enhancing both soil fertility and its capacity to hold water.

7. Keep the Landscape Healthy

Let the plants tell you when they need water. When leaves and entire plants droop, turfgrass turns blue-green, and trees start shedding their

Figure 7.6. Pine straw mulch prevents water loss and controls weeds.

leaves prematurely, it's time to water. Water slowly and deeply to a depth of about 4–6 inches.

Fertilize infrequently and as recommended, using organic or slow-release formulas. Once plants are established, reduce the amount of nitrogen you apply. Leave clippings on the lawn to reduce fertilizer needs. Heavily fertilized plants and lawns grow more than unfertilized ones and therefore require more water.

Every one to two years, retest the soil's organic content, nutrient levels, and pH, and adjust fertilizer and other soil amendments as needed. Top-dress the soil yearly with compost to keep soil porous and nutrient rich. Water cannot penetrate compacted soil.

Mow turfgrass at its recommended height. Mow no more than ⅓ of the grass blade with each cutting. Keep the mower blade sharp—dull blades shred the grass and cause water loss. Raise the mower blade during dry weather to cut the grass higher. Tall grass shades the soil and helps conserve soil moisture.

To reduce or relieve compaction and to increase water and air flow though the soil, aerate the lawn every few years. In areas where there is heavy foot traffic, such as from sports activities, aerate it yearly.

Maintain mulched beds. Before applying mulch, thoroughly water the area you want to cover. Then spread 3 inches of mulch under plants and trees. When possible, extend the mulched area two to three times beyond the canopy spread of the tree. Pull back the mulch 2–3 inches from the tree trunk to prevent wood-rotting diseases.

Prune at suggested times and according to guidelines recommended by the Cooperative Extension. Pruning stimulates new succulent growth, which needs adequate watering. So prune carefully and infrequently.

Choosing a Watering System

Match the water demands of the plants with the best technique to irrigate them. For example, you wouldn't attempt to water your lawn with a watering can, except maybe around the dry edges. Nor would you use an overhead sprinkler to water pots of petunias. Following are various ways to irrigate the landscape and their pros and cons. Choose the method that best fits each area of your garden.

Hand-Watering

Watering with a hand-held hose, portable sprinkler, or watering can is the simplest and most efficient way to water certain plants. This method permits gardeners to direct water where it is needed. It works particularly well for small annual beds and containers and for plants that are not drought-tolerant. Rainwater collected in rain barrels or saved from baths, showers, cooking, air conditioners, and dehumidifiers is usually applied by hand.

Did you know? Households that manually water with a hose typically use 33 percent less water outdoors than those that use an automatic irrigation system. (U.S. Environmental Protection Agency, "Conserving Water")

Drip Irrigation

Also called trickle or microirrigation, drip irrigation applies water slowly and directly to the plant's roots through perforated or porous flexible pipes or tubing. It minimizes evaporative loss and runoff. It also avoids wetting foliage, which can encourage plant diseases. Drip irrigation is suitable for perennial and annual beds that need occasional watering. There are many types of drip irrigation systems, so choose a simple one that saturates the soil where it will reach the plant's roots. For best results, space perforated or porous pipe and tubing 12–18 inches apart under mulch in beds of flowers and shrubs.

Overhead Sprinkler Systems

This automated system of in-ground pipes with sprinkler heads sprays water overhead, usually in wide circles. Typically, overhead sprinklers are used to irrigate large areas, such as lawns. Automated systems turn on and off at preset times, saving you time and water. However, when water is sprayed through the air, like Old Faithful, during the heat of the day or when it is windy, evaporative loss is high. Direct the sprinkler heads onto the landscape so driveways and roads don't get soaked too. Leaky pipes happen frequently. Since they are buried and not easy to find and fix, gardeners usually discover they have a leak when their water bills exceed their food bills.

The following tips can help you make these systems more efficient.

- To reduce evaporative losses, operate sprinklers between 9:00 p.m. and 9:00 a.m., when temperatures are lower and there is little or no wind.
- Attach a rainfall sensor to the irrigation controller so you don't automatically water the lawn during a downpour.
- Connect a soil moisture sensor to the system to turn on the irrigation system when soil moisture levels fall below a certain minimum.
- Closely monitor and reprogram the automatic controller throughout the growing season as irrigation needs change.
- Direct sprinkler heads to areas that need water. Irrigating driveways, walkways, and roads wastes a precious resource.
- Retrofit old rotors and sprayers with newer, more efficient ones.
- Check pipes and heads regularly for leaks.

Figure 7.7. Drip irrigation is an efficient way to irrigate a vegetable patch or flower garden.

Did you know? A well-designed drip irrigation can reach nearly 100 percent efficiency. (Alliance for Water Efficiency, "Promoting the Efficient Use of Water")

Figure 7.8. Overhead sprinklers must be carefully calibrated to irrigate only the landscape.

Watering Guidelines

Some plants, such as hydrangea and other herbaceous perennials, may wilt after a long, hot, sunny day but recover fully at night. Monitor plants daily during hot periods to learn their water needs. The following general instructions serve as guidelines only.

Annuals

Annuals have a shallow root system and may need daily watering during hot summer months. Saturate the soil to the root depth—usually several inches. Hand-watering works best since you can water as needed.

Perennials

Perennials have deeper roots than annuals and may require twice-a-week watering in the absence of rain. Look for signs of plant stress before watering.

Trees and Shrubs

Trees and shrubs have deeper and more mature root systems. The roots of a mature tree may also extend two to three times farther than the canopy spread. As discussed in chapter 5, newly planted shrubs and trees need frequent watering as they adapt to the site, but once they are established (generally 8–10 weeks after planting), rain should provide sufficient water, except in times of severe drought.

Lawns

Lawns usually need 1 inch of water weekly during hot weather if the rain is infrequent. However, some drought-tolerant grasses can go for weeks without water. Check with the local Cooperative Extension office to see how much water your turfgrass needs. Deep watering encourages a deep-rooted and resilient lawn.

Best Time of Day to Water

The most efficient time to irrigate is after dew develops (after 9:00 p.m.) and before it dries in the morning (before 9:00 a.m.) to minimize evaporation and to avoid extending the period when the plants' leaves are wet. Leaves that are wet for prolonged periods make plants more susceptible

Measuring an Inch of Water

Insert a rain gauge or place an empty can on the lawn and run the sprinkler. (The container needs to have vertically straight sides, such as a tuna can.) Note the time when the sprinkler is turned on. When the gauge or can fills with 1 inch of water (use a ruler to measure), check the time again. The amount of time it took to fill the gauge or can with 1 inch of water is the time needed to irrigate the lawn. If the rain gauge fills with ½ inch of rain, then the lawn needs only an additional ½ inch of water from the sprinkler weekly. When watering the lawn, it is best to provide ½ inch twice a week rather than 1 inch once a week.

Did you know? Each year a typical suburban lawn consumes 10,000 gallons of water above and beyond the natural rainfall. (U.S. Environmental Protection Agency, "Conserving Water")

to disease. Since drip irrigation systems are buried, there is no evaporative loss. Check the local water regulations to see if there are watering restrictions or bans.

Surviving Extreme Drought or Watering Restrictions

The Southeast has experienced several severe droughts recently (2000–2002, 2006–8, 2010–12) that have strained drinking water reservoirs and even underground aquifers. As a result, some states and regions implemented outdoor watering bans. To keep the landscape alive in times of severe droughts and water restrictions sometimes requires drastic measures that begin by saving the most valuable plants in a landscape with buckets of bath and cooking water and preparing the rest to tough it out. To help you manage the landscape during those trying times, use this strategy until it rains.

Consider the cost of replacing plants and save those that are most valuable. Annuals can be replaced more readily than shrubs and trees, which are long-term landscape features that should be preserved. Neglect the annuals; water the shrubs and trees deeply when they show signs of stress.

Deeply rooted drought-tolerant turfgrasses and perennials go into a dormant state under moisture stress. They will recover when rain returns. Maintain mulched beds around annuals, perennials, shrubs, and trees.

If outdoor watering restrictions continue for a period of time, thin the canopy of trees and shrubs by one-third to one-half if they begin shedding their leaves. For perennials, it may mean cutting the plants to ground level to increase their chances of surviving.

Use water from alternative sources such as rain barrels, cisterns, water pillows, air-conditioning condensate, and even cooking and bath water. The various possibilities are discussed in the following section.

Tapping into Alternative Water Sources

Today's gardeners are finding creative ways to water their landscapes during droughts. Some ideas come to us from the ancient practice of capturing rainwater with cisterns, and others are inspired by the modern era, such as collecting air-conditioning condensate in barrels and recycling gray water from household appliances. "History of Rainwater Harvesting" below describes how early civilizations dealt with water scarcity and offers twenty-first-century water-harvesting ideas.

Rain Barrels and Cisterns

Rain barrels and cisterns are easy and inexpensive ways to maintain a household reservoir of water. Rainwater is free and safe, and by collecting it to irrigate the garden, you conserve potable water for drinking, bathing, and washing clothes and dishes. This simple system consists of four components: capture, conveyance, storage, and distribution. Roof gutters capture the rain and convey it to downspouts, which flow into rain barrels or into above- or below-ground containers. By installing filters or gutter guards, you prevent leaves and debris from blocking the flow. A spigot

History of Rainwater Harvesting

Roman villas and even whole cities were designed to capture rainwater for drinking and domestic uses beginning around 2000 B.C. In northern Egypt, water tanks holding up to 530,000 gallons have been used for the past two thousand years. Many of these are still operational today. The technology also has a two-thousand-year history in Asia, where rainwater collection was practiced in Thailand. The world's largest rainwater tank is probably the Yerebatan Sarayi in Istanbul, Turkey, constructed during the rule of Caesar Justinian (A.D. 527–565). It has a capacity of 21 million gallons (Kafin and Van Ooyen, "Rainwater Harvesting 101").

Figure 7.9. A rain barrel (*top left*), a series of barrels (*above*), or a cistern (*left*) can be used to capture rainwater from roofs to use during drought times.

Did you know? One inch of rain on a 2,000-square-foot roof generates more than 1,000 gallons of water.

at the receptacle's base allows gardeners to use a watering can or hose to distribute the water to the plants. If the barrel has no top, cover it with a wire or dense mesh to prevent contamination from leaves and to keep out insects, such as mosquitoes. Rain barrels are sold at many garden centers or can be made at home inexpensively.

Air-Conditioning Condensate

Air-conditioning condensate is clean wastewater that can easily be caught and stored in a container. Locate the point where the unit drains water and put a garbage can or other covered container under it. You may have to dig a hole in the ground under the drain pipe to be able to slide the container under the pipe. If the air conditioner produces 10 gallons of water each day, then 280 gallons can be collected in one month.

Gray Water

Gray water presents possibilities for using the nontoilet wastewater produced in a home. This includes discarded water from cooking, bathing, showering, washing dishes, washing machines (rinse cycle), dishwashers, and dehumidifiers. Gray water may contain grease, hair, detergent, cosmetics, dead skin, food particles, and small amounts of fecal matter, so check with the local health department or environmental regulatory agency about local regulations before using gray water for landscape irrigation.

Order of gray water desirability (from most to least desirable)

- Cooking
- Shower and bathtub
- Bathroom and utility sinks
- Washing machine
- Kitchen sink and dishwasher (This is the least desirable because it contains grease, food particles, and other materials.)

Recycling water from a washing machine that was used to wash cloth diapers may contain fecal matter. Recycling from this source should be avoided. Here are other questions regarding the use of gray water:

Are Soaps and Detergents Harmful to Soil and Plants?

Soaps and detergents are biodegradable, but they can present problems when gray water is used over an extended period. Cleaning agents contain sodium salts that, if present in excessive amounts, can damage soil microbes and create an alkaline condition that may damage plants. Phosphates in detergents can be good for plant growth, but unfortunately, detergents highest in phosphates usually contain the greatest amount of sodium. (*Note*: High phosphate levels also contribute to algae blooms in ponds and lakes.) If reusing washing machine water, eliminate bleach from your laundry routine, and do not use detergents or additives that contain boron. They are especially toxic to plants. Rotate gray water with freshwater to flush out sodium and excess salts.

Is There Any Danger of Spreading Disease
by Using Gray Water in the Garden?

Recycled water from the bath, shower, or washing machine may contain disease-causing organisms. However, when it is poured onto soil rich in organic matter, harmful bacteria and viruses die quickly. But if any survive, they can be absorbed by plant roots and transferred to the edible portion of food plants. For safety's sake, use gray water to irrigate lawns and ornamental plants only.

How Should I Apply Gray Water?

Gray water can be transported to the garden in several ways, beginning with a basic bucket. To the amusement of my neighbors, I carried pots and buckets of water from cooking and bathing to soothe my thirsty plants during the severe drought of 2008. My plants survived, and I got the added benefit of step aerobics biweekly. More sophisticated systems involve siphoning or pumping water from the bathtub to the yard through a garden hose. In addition, the plumbing system can be adapted to pipe gray water to the garden. Check with the local board of health to ensure that no sanitary codes are violated.

Managing Storm Water to Enhance Nature

How gardeners manage their landscapes directly affects the health of nearby streams, rivers, and lakes. That's because we all live in a watershed or land drainage area, and water resources are connected above and below ground. Water flows from the mountain ridges, hilltops, and higher ground to the lowest points, which are rivers, streams, and lakes. Rain infiltrates the soil and is absorbed by plant roots. The excess water drains into underground reservoirs that intersect with streams and rivers. Eco-minded gardeners can have a positive impact on stream water quality by understanding the dynamics of gardening in populated areas and then trying to prevent pollutants from leaving their property.

Urban areas present special challenges. They are densely populated and contain large areas of impervious surface that collect pollutants from many people and their lifestyles, which may include behaviors that run the gamut from littering or driving cars that leak gas and oil to walking dogs and not picking up their waste. Add to this scenario gardeners who improperly apply fertilizers and pesticides on their landscapes. The result is great quantities of pollutants flushing off hardscapes and landscapes into storm drains and surface water during each rain. In addition, rain cannot penetrate pavement and enter the ground. Instead, it rushes off these surfaces, causing stream surges or floods.

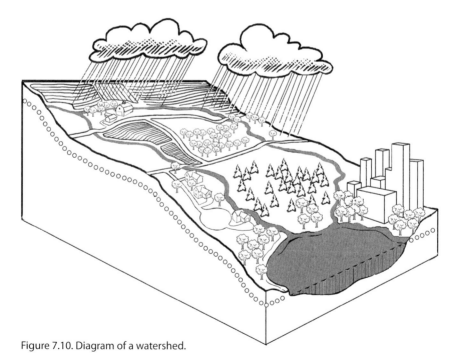

Figure 7.10. Diagram of a watershed.

Many older cities such as Atlanta, New Orleans, and New York share a dirty secret. During heavy storms, rainwater surges into the same pipes that carry untreated wastewater into nearby rivers. To avoid the exorbitant cost of separating storm and sewer pipes, city engineers are finding ways to use vegetated land to absorb storm water and pollutants before they enter the pipes.

Storm water is a valuable resource if gardeners can keep it on their property. Slowing its flow over the land and capturing it provides needed moisture for plants. Creating landscape features such as rain gardens and swales allows water to be collected and filtered so that potential contaminants—such as the nitrogen, potassium, and metals found in fertilizers, pesticides, and pet waste—are degraded and don't end up in streams. Increasing vegetated areas and decreasing impervious surfaces and bare soil allow more water to penetrate the soil to recharge underlying aquifers. Managing storm water in landscaping and gardening requires attention to the four major areas outlined below.

Reduce Pollution Sources

Landscape pollutants can include loose soil, excess fertilizer, pesticides, pet waste, and yard waste such as grass clippings. Developing some good habits to keep these pollutants contained on the property will make you deeply appreciated by your downstream neighbors.

Cover Bare Soil with Plants

Sediment is the number-one stream pollutant in many areas of the country, especially where construction is prevalent. Loose soil erodes off the land and is carried into nearby storm drains or surface waters. Vegetated land holds the soil in place and slows the flow of water, giving plant roots an opportunity to absorb rain. It also increases soil organic matter, thereby increasing infiltration of water into the soil.

More Fertilizer Is Not Better

When applying fertilizer, read the label carefully and follow the instructions. Never apply more than the recommended amounts. And never ap-

Figure 7.11. Stream polluted with sediment.

ply fertilizer before a rainstorm. The roots won't have time to absorb it, and it will be carried off the land. Don't spread fertilizer when plants or grass are dormant. The plant roots can't use it so it becomes a pollutant. Gardeners who live near a creek, river, stream, or lake should maintain a 25-foot buffer of natural vegetation near the water body to filter chemicals migrating off the landscape.

Minimize Pesticide Use

Pesticides are toxic, so use them sparingly. Use pesticides only after all other nontoxic options are exhausted (see chapter 8). Choose the least toxic pesticide to accomplish the job. Read the label and apply at the recommended rate. Calibrate all application equipment. Store and dispose of pesticides properly.

Scoop the Poop

Fecal matter from pets is a major source of bacteria in urban streams. Scoop it up and dispose in the toilet or trash can, or even better, throw it in the compost pile, where the heat generated reaches (~131°F)—it can kill pathogens. Monitor pets when they frolic in or near streams and lakes.

Dispose of Yard Waste Properly

Keep yard waste out of streams. If clippings fall on driveways or walkways, sweep them back onto the lawn so they don't get washed off the pavement into the storm sewer. Keep the compost pile at least 50 feet from the water's edge.

Increase the Flow of Water into the Soil

Particularly in urban areas, most rainwater hits the roofs and pavement and drains into sewers or water bodies. It is standard building practice to direct downspouts onto driveways. This system prevents storm water from filling groundwater aquifers. To restore water flowing into the earth, a gardener can do a number of things.

- Replace pavement with plants.
- Create paths, driveways, and patios with wood chips, small stones, and pavers.
- Redirect downspouts from driveways or patios onto grass, swales, or flower beds, where rain can percolate into the soil.
- Enhance treatment/filtration

Rain Gardens

Rain gardens are landscape features that help manage flooding and pollutants associated with storm-water runoff. They are shallow depressions that contain deeply rooted plants that absorb storm water from landscapes and hardscapes. As the water enters the soil, the plants, mulch, and soil use a combination of natural physical, biological, and chemical processes to degrade pollutants into compounds plants can use. Rain gardens also provide wildlife habitat.

Figure 7.12. Hardscapes (*top*) prevent water from entering the ground while the vegetated landscape allows rain to penetrate the soil.

Figure 7.13. Pathways made of small stones (*top*) and wood chips and stepping stones (*left*) allow rain to seep into the soil and underlying aquifers.

Figure 7.14. Downspout empties onto a permeable layer of rocks (*above*) and into a rain garden (*below*) to increase water filtration into soil.

Did you know? Rain gardens remove 99 percent of storm-water pollutants. (Dietz and Clausen, "Saturation to Improve Pollutant Retention")

When deciding where to put the rain garden, take the following precautions in determining its location. Locate it:

- At least 10 feet from the house so infiltrating water doesn't seep into the foundation
- More than 25 feet from a septic system drain field
- More than 25 feet from a well head
- In full or partial sun—not directly under a big tree
- Where the water table is 2 feet or more below the soil surface
- Away from an area where water ponds

Bioswales

Bioswales are simpler than rain gardens and are usually lined with grass, gravel, or riprap. They tend to be long, narrow, shallow depressions located parallel to streets, parking lots, and other hardscapes to catch storm-water runoff. Positioned under roof gutters as pictured in figure 7.14, swales can direct water onto landscapes.

Choosing Plants for Rain Gardens and Bioswales

Use noninvasive species that can withstand brief periods of pooling as well as dry periods between rainfall events. A variety of plants with large root structures make the rain garden more effective and less susceptible to disease. It is also better to use mature plants with developed root systems instead of starting plants from seed. Seeds will have a hard time getting

Caution: Water should be absorbed in the rain garden a few hours after rainfall. This is important to assure that plants survive and that mosquitoes do not breed in the water.

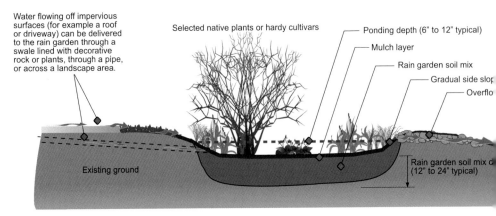

Water flowing off impervious surfaces (for example a roof or driveway) can be delivered to the rain garden through a swale lined with decorative rock or plants, through a pipe, or across a landscape area.

Selected native plants or hardy cultivars

Ponding depth (6" to 12" typical)

Mulch layer

Rain garden soil mix

Gradual side slop

Overflo

Existing ground

Rain garden soil mix d (12" to 24" typical)

Figure 7.15. Diagram of a rain garden.

established in rain-garden conditions and will expose the soil, leaving it prone to erosion.

Create a Rain Garden

There are many good online resources for designing and maintaining rain gardens. Figure 7.15 is a good overview of a simple rain garden and its elements.

Install a Bioswale

The Center for Watershed Protection is an excellent resource for homeowner storm-water management practices. Their website contains a wealth of information including designs, construction, and maintenance information for rain gardens and bioswales.

Gardening in the twenty-first century requires an adept understanding of how to make every water drop count. Gardeners no longer have the luxury of turning on sprinklers at random times throughout the day and irrigating the landscape—and maybe even the driveway, roadway, and walkway—for hours. Today's gardeners are replacing irrigated lawns with water-wise landscapes. Rain gauges, soil-moisture sensors, watering cans, and drip irrigation tubing are gardeners' water-management tools. And when the rains don't come, gardeners have a ready supply of water in rain barrels and cisterns.

Did you know? A study of two Burnsville, Minnesota, neighborhoods showed that the neighborhood where rain gardens were installed reduced storm-water runoff by 89–92 percent compared with the neighborhood with no rain gardens. (Barr Engineering Co., "Burnsville Rainwater Gardens")

Storm-water management programs throughout the Southeast are connecting citizens with their watersheds. Gardeners can take the important first step toward enhancing the water quality of streams and rivers by minimizing landscape chemicals. And when gardeners take measures that increase the flow of rainwater into the landscape, both landscapes and underground aquifers benefit alike. Using pervious pavement, directing rain gutters onto the landscape, and creating rain gardens and swales to catch rainwater before it leaves the property give nature a helping hand in managing storm water and degrading pollutants.

8

Manage Pests Naturally

If all mankind were to disappear, the world would regenerate back
to the rich state of equilibrium that existed ten thousand years ago.
If insects were to vanish, the environment would collapse into chaos.

E. O. Wilson, Pulitzer Prize–winning author and ecologist

Gardening in the Southeast is challenging. The hot, humid weather provides the perfect growing environment for pests such as bugs, weeds, and diseases. They lurk everywhere. Crabgrass invades lawns, hornworms devour tomatoes, and black spot blights roses. Left unchecked, pests can transform a beautiful garden into an unsightly mess. The good news is that 80 percent of pest problems result from poor site conditions or weather, much of which a gardener can manage or mitigate. Only 20 percent are due to living organisms, including humans.

Garden pests that damage cultivated plants are classified as weeds, diseases, and insects. In the natural world, however, it is truly difficult to label an organism as a pest. That's because diverse microbes, insects, birds, amphibians, and other animals interact and prey upon one another in a complex food web. But plant-eating insects hold a special and very important niche in the food web. When they are eaten, they transfer energy directly from plants to animals. The world-renowned ecologist, entomologist, and naturalist E. O. Wilson calls insects "the little things that run the world."

Did you know? Of the 9 million insect species, only 1 percent interacts with humans in a negative way. The other 99 percent pollinate plants, return nutrients to the soil, keep insect pests in check, and aerate and enrich the soil.

Insects and other pest problems have plagued gardens and farms since biblical times. The Old Testament, for instance, contains many references to familiar diseases and insect pests found in today's gardens, including this passage from Amos 4:6–9. "I struck you with blight and mildew; your many gardens and your vineyards, your fig trees and your olive trees the locust devoured; yet you did not return to me."

A quick look back at the development of today's petrochemical pesticides helps us understand the path that gardeners and farmers have traveled to arrive at today's pest-management strategies aimed at preserving nature.

Before scientists understood the dangers of synthetic pesticides, homeowners and professional landscapers often sprayed the entire landscape to destroy a few weeds, insects, and diseases. Although this treatment killed pests, it also destroyed many beneficial insects such as lady beetles, which prey on aphids, and honeybees, which pollinate flowers.

Many synthetic pesticides, which include herbicides, insecticides, and fungicides, are toxic to people and animals. Like synthetic fertilizers, they are derived from petroleum products and require a great deal of energy to manufacture, package, and transport. As stated in greater detail in other chapters, improperly applied pesticides may wash off landscapes and pollute nearby streams, rivers, ponds, and lakes. They may even seep through the soil and pollute groundwater.

In the 1970s, scientists and environmentalists understood the dangers of synthetic pesticides to people and wildlife and wanted effective, environmentally friendly alternatives. The search for safer options led to the development of a program of environmentally friendly pest control called Integrated Pest Management (IPM). IPM emphasizes creating conditions for plants to thrive and then using nontoxic means to control infestations. Using this strategy, gardeners strive to maintain nature's equilibrium and, therefore, its natural ability to minimize the impact of pest outbreaks.

Did you know? One billion pounds of synthetic pesticides are used each year in the United States to control weeds, insects, and other pests. (Grube et al., "Pesticide Industry Sales and Usage 2006–2007")

History of Pest Control

In 2500 B.C., Sumerians controlled insects by using sulfur on crops. By the fifteenth century, toxic elements such as arsenic, mercury, and lead were the pesticides of choice. In the seventeenth century, pests met their demise with nicotine sulfate extracted from tobacco leaves. Pyrethrum, derived from chrysanthemums, was introduced in the nineteenth century. The manufacture of synthetic pesticides from petroleum products was launched from 1940 to 1950. DDT, among the early synthetic pesticides, was used to control vectors of typhus and malaria during World War II. After the war, it became a broad-spectrum agricultural pesticide used in industrial agriculture. In her best-selling book *Silent Spring*, Rachel Carson exposed the dangers of many synthetic pesticides. Ten years later, in 1972, the U.S. Environmental Protection Agency banned DDT because it was a threat to wildlife, especially the bald eagle. As a result, the U.S. Department of Agriculture promoted Integrated Pest Management as the best method to control pests without degrading the natural environment. ("Pest Control," Wikipedia)

Ancient farmers used various products found in nature to safeguard their harvest from pest damage. When humans decided to tinker with nature to find alternatives to natural pest control, problems began. The history of pest control shows we are circling back to reexamine some of these earlier remedies.

Maintain Nature's Balance

A garden that is rich in plant and wildlife diversity benefits from a resulting system of checks and balances that prevents any one organism from dominating the ecosystem. Plants that are unable to adapt will eventually weaken and die. Fertile soil, renewed through the cycle of plant and animal growth and decay, enables adapted plants to flourish.

Healthy plants, like healthy people, can more easily ward off infection than those that are ailing. In fact, disease is nature's way of getting rid of sick and dying organisms. Plants are no exception. When they are stressed from a variety of factors such as placement in the wrong environment, poor soils, improper planting, and so on, the plants will eventually get weak or sick. So the best thing gardeners can do is to provide a growing environment where plants can flourish. The following general recommendations can lead you down the path to natural pest control.

Cultivate Healthy Soil

Soil rich in organic matter supports plant health. In addition to the benefits derived from using compost and mulch to restore organic matter, organic-rich soil reduces compaction and retains moisture better. Test the soil every two to three years to see if the pH is appropriate for the plants and if sufficient nutrients are available. Also, avoid using uncomposted animal manure; it may harbor diseases and weed seeds. For more details, follow the recommendations described in chapter 2.

Select Plants Adapted to the Site

Consider temperature range, sun/shade needs, moisture requirements, soil nutrients, and optimum pH, as well as a plant's mature height and width when choosing varieties for your landscape. When possible, use plants that are naturally pest-resistant. Replace plants that continually attract pests with others that are resistant.

Plant Diversity: Avoid Monocultures

Swaths of a single species may be lovely and dramatic, but they also invite pests with an appetite for this kind of plant. Monocultures provide pests with an abundant food supply and support their prolific growth and reproduction. Limit the size of annual and perennial beds composed of a single species. Also avoid planting the same species for both hedges and shade trees to prevent such catastrophes as Dutch elm disease, which was inadvertently brought to our shores in 1930 and quickly decimated thousands of American elms along main streets across the nation. Use a mixture of grass seed species for the lawn. Consider replacing portions of the lawn with hardy ground covers. More tips for creating a landscape filled with diverse native plants are provided in chapter 4.

Attract Beneficial Insects

Include nectar- and pollen-producing plants that attract beneficial insects in the landscape. Supply flower-rich foraging patches for spring, summer, and fall to provide insects with ample food throughout the growing seasons. The Xerces Society provides a comprehensive guide to attracting pollinators for different areas of the country. In addition, incorporate native plants into the landscape for natural pest control, as described in chapter 4.

Provide Habitat for Natural Predators

A range of birds, insects, spiders and mites, and other animals ensures healthy biological pest control. Chapter 10 describes how to create different kinds of wildlife habitats in the garden.

Adopt Integrated Pest Management (IPM)

Pest problems occur only after plants are stressed or injured and are then susceptible to infection from nearby insect pest or disease pathogens. Three factors contribute to infection: (*a*) the presence of a pathogen or pest; (*b*) a susceptible plant; and (*c*) an environment where the disease or pest can thrive. The red area or triangle in figure 8.1 represents situations where all

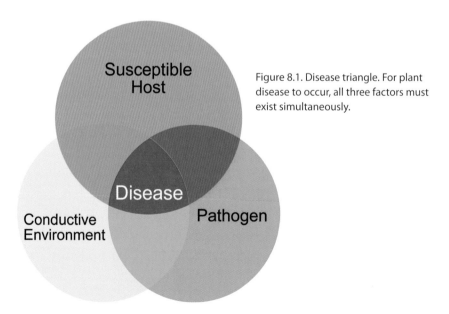

Figure 8.1. Disease triangle. For plant disease to occur, all three factors must exist simultaneously.

three factors are present. By eliminating one factor, an infestation can be thwarted. The aim of the following five-step Integrated Pest Management (IPM) program is to eliminate the factors that cause infestations. And when pest problems appear, the IPM program emphasizes using natural controls over pesticides. The following tactics are listed in order of most sustainable to least sustainable.

Step 1: Patrol for Pests

Walk through the garden weekly or more often to note any changes. By monitoring the landscape regularly, gardeners learn what insects occur seasonally and what plants they feed on. For example, southern landscapes that include azaleas are often visited by azalea lace bugs in spring. Be careful not to confuse seasonal changes in plants for disease. A beginner gardener, for instance, may mistake spores on ferns for insect eggs or disease.

If a plant appears unhealthy, take a closer took. A hand lens or magni-

Figure 8.2. Fern spores can resemble insect eggs.

fying glass is useful in finding and identifying small insects. Inspect the leaves, especially the undersides. Look at the stems, flowers, and, if possible, the roots. Examine the healthy parts of the plant as well since they serve as a basis of comparison to problem areas.

Collect specimens of diseased leaves and branches, insects, and weeds for later identification. Put specimens in small containers or plastic bags. Make a note that includes information about the plant name, date, and weather conditions as well as the location of plant damage, such as underside of leaves, the center of flower buds, or tender, green stems.

Look for weeds and damage to the lawn. Are there patches of yellowing, dead, or dying grass? Are they circular or irregularly shaped? Most weeds can grow in adverse conditions. Where a lawn is bare, thin, diseased, or insect-ridden, weeds often stake a claim. Weeds typically grow along fencerows, banks, driveways, and walkways, and around ornamental beds.

By walking through the landscape often, gardeners notice pest issues when they arise. Watch closely to see if the problem persists, worsens, or improves. Early detection gives gardeners the opportunity to use nonchemical controls that work best when pest populations are low. Early intervention saves plants and the environment.

Step 2: Identify the Problem

The best way to identify the problem is to first identify the host plant. By knowing the kind of plant that harbors the pest, you can research the specific diseases and insects that are associated with it. This limits the field of possibilities. Searching through picture books and websites to match up diseases and insects is time-consuming and may lead to the wrong conclusion. Sending a digital image of the plant to the Extension office is the easiest way to identify it. Master Gardeners can also help with identification.

Look for changes in the plant's appearance that would be unexpected at this time of year, such as yellowing or curling leaves or sudden leaf drop. In effect, you have to become a sleuth looking at clues or signs and symptoms that will lead to identifying the culprit or pest. The process is similar to a doctor trying to figure out what is wrong with a patient. The doctor asks the patient many questions to narrow down the possibilities and make an accurate diagnosis. Since plants can't talk, the gardener must carefully examine the affected plant, looking for symptoms and signs listed below, and then rule out the unlikely scenarios. Through a process of elimination, the remainder of pests and diseases become possibilities. Use this checklist to help diagnose the problem.

Symptoms

Plants

- Tattered leaves or flowers can be caused by grasshoppers, caterpillars, or adult or immature beetles.
- Stippled, bleached, or bronzed foliage may be caused by insects with piercing mouth parts such as lace bugs or plant bugs. Mites or thrips may also cause this type of damage.

Figure 8.3. Eggplant leaf chewed by a grasshopper.

Figure 8.4. Bleached leaves from thrips' damage.

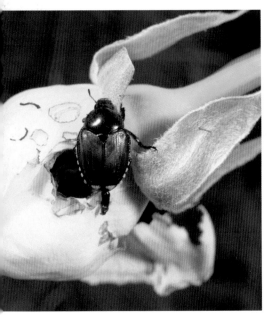

Figure 8.5. Dieback on roses from Japanese beetles.

Figure 8.6. Eastern tent caterpillars.

- Dieback of plant parts is often caused by scale insects or by beetles or moth larvae that bore inside the stems.
- Evidence of insects may include webs, tents, cases, flocculence (cottony material), frass or fecal material, and sawdust.
- Chewed or shredded leaves can be caused by armyworms, sod webworms, billbugs, cutworms, or chinch bugs.
- Patches of yellowing or dying grass in circular patterns usually indicates a disease.
- Mushrooms in a ring, or fairy ring, are the fruiting bodies of a large underground fungal network that indicate a healthy conversion of decaying matter into soil. They are not harmful to the grass.

Figure 8.7. *Top:* Lawn damaged by chinch bugs; *bottom, left:* full winged chinch bug adult on St. Augustinegrass blade; *bottom, right:* fall armyworm in Bermudagrass.

Figure 8.8. Large dead patch or brown patch on lawn is caused by a disease.

Figure 8.9. Fairy ring with mushrooms does not attack the grass but breaks down organic matter in the soil.

Signs

- Evidence of disease such as leaf spot or insects leaving spittle-like substance on the leaves (figure 8.11).
- Mechanical damage from string trimmers, mowers, lightning.
- Chemical residue such as from pesticides.
- Secretions from the plant.
- Damage pattern—random or regular.
- Damage from weather such as early or late freeze or hail.
- Compacted or soggy soil.

Identify the Affected Part of the Plant

- Flowers
- Fruits
- Limbs
- Leaves
- Roots
- Stems or twigs
- Crown

Evaluate the Situation

Eighty percent of landscape problems are related to weather or the planting site. Moisture—either too much or too little—makes up 70 percent of

Figure 8.10. Black spot on rose leaf.

Figure 8.11. Spittle-like substance indicates presence of spittle bugs.

Figure 8.12. Lightning damage.

those weather-related problems. Temperature, light, wind, hail, lightning, sunburn, or sunscald can all damage or kill plants, and so can air pollution. Site problems including soil compaction, topography, nutritional deficiencies, pH, improper application of fertilizers and pesticides, and mechanical injury may also be responsible for plant health issues.

The remaining 20 percent of plant problems are caused by a range of living organisms that includes pathogens, insects, mites, pets, birds, and even people. Ultimately, gardeners who incorrectly plant, water, site, and prune their plants stress those plants and make them vulnerable to pests.

Step 3: Determine the Source of the Problem—Living or Nonliving

Garden problems resulting from nonliving sources generally do not progress and do not spread to neighboring plants. Typically, they occur randomly and are not species-specific. If damage occurs across large areas where plants of multiple species are impacted, then the cause is usually nonliving. Freeze damage, poor soils, overfertilizing, and herbicide drift are all contenders.

When insects and diseases find a suitable host plant, they tend to spread throughout plantings of the same species in a random fashion. Closely monitor the landscape for a progression of pests.

Narrow the Field

Since most problems are linked to nonliving causes, let's begin here. Think about recent weather events. Did the tree die during an extended drought? Did the dogwood blossoms and hydrangea buds turn brown after a late frost? Did the tree suddenly perish after an electrical storm?

What about the family pets? Do they run loose in the yard leaving yellow spots on lawns and shrubs? Did the lawn turn brown after it was mowed closely during a drought? Did you notice the tree base scraped after lawn mowing? Are tree roots popping up through the lawn and thinning it? Is the site right for the plant?

The local Cooperative Extension office, the Internet, or Master Gardeners can help you determine whether the plant's environmental needs are being met. Does the plant have the right sun exposure? Many plants and trees

Case Study

During the summer of 2004, I noticed my big, beautiful Yoshino cherry tree, planted by the previous homeowners, was losing its leaves. This tree was located on a slope planted with junipers as a ground cover to hold the soil. A quick call to the Extension pathologist gave me a diagnosis I didn't want to hear: My tree was most likely dying from the extended drought and the competition for soil moisture from the junipers. Sure enough, my tree lost all its leaves that summer and died. I replaced it with a native dogwood on a terraced area and dug out the water-sucking junipers. Spring flowers fill that little corner of my yard again.

such as hostas, azaleas, rhododendrons, camellias, dogwoods, and redbuds thrive best under large shade trees or in other shaded areas. If you put them out in the full sun, you stress them.

Look closely at how the plant was installed. Was it placed higher or lower than the surrounding soil? Take a look at the soil. Is there good drainage or does the soil need some compost to break apart the clay? Is it situated in a low-lying boggy area that holds water when it prefers drier conditions? Does it have the right nutrients and pH? A soil test gives this information.

Step 4: Pest Identification

If there is evidence of damage or presence of disease, insects, and weeds, then the problem comes from a living organism. Research the common pest problems for this plant and its larger plant family using Extension publications, Master Gardeners, *Southern Living Answer Book*, and *Ortho Problem Solver*. Refer to your notes on the time of year and the type and location of the plant damage. This information will offer clues to the pest.

Look at the life cycle of the suspected pest or disease. Match up the pest specimens you collected with a photo of the pest at one stage of its life. Learn about the environment in which the disease or pest thrives, such as wet foliage or soggy soils, poor air circulation, or high humidity. All this information will help identify the weak link or vulnerable areas that you can control. Since wet foliage can lead to disease, watering the plant at the base and not on the leaves can help reduce the risk of disease.

Knowing a pest's life cycle reveals at what stages the pest is most susceptible to control methods. It also gives information about the number of pests the plant can tolerate before severe damage occurs. You will also learn what elimination tactics are the most effective. If you are stumped, you can photograph the insect, pest, diseased plant part, or troublesome weed with a digital camera or hand-held device and submit the photos electronically to the local Cooperative Extension office for correct identification.

Once the affected plant and its pest are identified, assess the extent of the damage. Answering the following questions will help you determine if control methods are needed and, if so, the best approach to take.

- Is the damage cosmetic, or is the plant's health deteriorating?
- How much of the plant is affected? Is it the entire plant or just part of it?
- Do the symptoms or visible changes in the plant's appearance occur on new growth, old growth, a single branch or leaf, or at random locations?
- Is just one plant affected or does the damage extend to an entire row or clump or even to other plant species?

Detecting plant damage does not necessarily mean you need to take action to control the problem. Remember, a plant can be productive with up to 20 percent damage. Is the damage escalating, or has it affected more than 20 percent of the plant?

Ensure that the pest population level or the plant damage level is sufficiently high to merit control intervention. Plant seedlings are more vulnerable to such things as a few chewed leaves than older plants are. If the pest is confined to just part of a plant, perhaps the affected portion can easily be removed or pruned.

Compare the benefits versus the risks of taking action to control a pest problem. Consider the value of the plant or plant part, the cost of the control action (money, time, and labor), environmental impact, and human safety. If one species of plant continually draws pests year after year, then perhaps the best pest control is to remove it.

Step 5: Implement IPM Tools

Integrated Pest Management offers many pest control options to gardeners. There is no single right way. In fact, many different practices can be used on the same plant to keep damage below an acceptable threshold. Acceptable level varies among plants and people. Complete eradication is not the goal. Instead, the goal should be to intervene only when the plant's health is at risk.

Cultural Controls

The following general garden practices are preventative with the goal of creating a healthy landscape.

- Use resistant plant varieties and turfgrasses suited for the local conditions of rainfall, temperature, sunlight, etc.
- Follow all the proper planting procedures outlined in chapter 5.
- Manage soil to maintain organic matter, nutrients, and pH, and to alleviate compaction.
- Shift planting dates to avoid any damaging levels of pests that may occur early or late in the season.
- Observe all watering recommendations in chapter 7.
- Rotate annual plants and vegetables to avoid recurring pest problems such as root rots and root-knot nematodes.
- Use plants that are free of insect pests and disease.
- Remove diseased or insect-infested plant debris and destroy it by burying it.
- Maintain mulched beds to manage weeds in vegetable and flower gardens.
- Refrain from using toxic pesticides to avoid killing beneficial insects.

Special Instruction for Vegetables

- Use good-quality, clean seed. Seeds often carry diseases.
- Avoid wet soils unless the plants thrive under those conditions.
- Plant all but shade-loving plants in sunny, well-ventilated areas.
- Shift planting dates.
  - Plant squash early to avoid vine borers, which become active in June.
  - Plant corn early to avoid earworm.
  - Plant winter squash before June 1 to give the rind time to harden before pickleworm pulls in.
- Refrain from overhead irrigation; hand-water or use drip irrigation instead and avoid splashing the leaves.
- Avoid planting crops in the same group in the same location for multiple years. Rotate the crops as recommended in table 8.1.

Special Instruction for Lawns

- Use high-quality certified seed and weed-free sod.
- Many varieties of perennial ryegrass and fescue seeds are enhanced

Table 8.1. General crop rotation

Rotate crops in one group with any of those in another group.

Group A	Group B	Group C	Group D	Group E	Group F
Cantaloupe	Brussels sprouts	Eggplant	Beet	Sweet corn	Bean
Cucumber	Cabbage	Irish potato	Carrot		Cowpea
Honeydew melon	Cauliflower	Okra	Garlic		Pea
Pumpkin	Collards	Pepper	Onion		
Squash	Lettuce	Tomato	Shallot		
Watermelon	Mustard		Sweet potato		
	Radish				
	Rutabaga				
	Spinach				
	Swiss chard				
	Turnip				

Source: Little, "Sustainable Management of Common Garden Diseases."

with endophytes (fungi) that are toxic to webworms, chinch bugs, and billbugs. When reseeding or renovating the lawn, use these varieties.

- Don't overapply nitrogen. Too much causes brown patch.
- Water at recommended times and only when grass is stressed (see chapter 6).
- Mulch ornamental plants to control weeds and prevent them from spreading into grass.
- Mow at the recommended height. Don't mow when grass is wet. Keep blades sharp so grass is not torn, making it easier for disease to gain traction.
- Remove excess thatch, which harbors disease and insects.
- Avoid soil compaction; core aerate as needed.
- Reduce fertilizer use by 20–50 percent in the shade. Do not fertilize during a drought.

Mechanical Controls

These methods use hand removal and equipment to mechanically reduce pest populations.

- Remove insects, egg clusters, beetles, and caterpillars on plants by hand. Before Japanese beetles overwhelm roses, get out early in the day when they move more slowly and pick them off, dropping them into a bucket of soapy water.
- Using a hose, spray plants infested with aphids, lace bugs, and other pests to reduce their numbers.
- Prune or cut out diseased or insect-infected plants or plant parts.
- Eastern tent caterpillars can be removed from trees by using a stick to pull off the silk tent and then removing the caterpillars.
- Traps of all sorts such as baits, pheromones, sticky boards, traps that attract pests, and spraying water can be used for specific pests.
- Dig out weeds from flower beds early in the season, when the weeds are small.
- Place landscape fabrics and even newspaper or cardboard under mulch to serve as a barrier against weeds in flower beds.
- Use netting over vegetables to keep flying adult insects from laying eggs.
- Put sticky barriers around tree trunks to prevent caterpillars from crawling up to eat the tree's leaves.

Special Instructions for Vegetable Gardens

- Pick off insects such as tomato hornworms before they ruin the possibility for fresh salsa.
- Pick and destroy spinach infested with leaf miners and tomato leaves infected with leaf spots.
- Cultivate or till soils to mechanically destroy pests and crop residue that may harbor pests.
- Use cardboard and foil collars around vegetable stems to protect young plants from cutworms. Cardboard tubes from toilet paper and paper towels work well. Cut off the collars when the plants are 12 inches tall.

Special Instructions for Lawns

- Dig out weeds such as goose grass and knotweed that grow in compacted soil along fencerows and walkways early in the season, when it's easiest.

Figure 8.13. Cardboard collar on tomato plant.

The Dandelion Stomp

A soccer dad once noticed that dandelions bloomed in his son's field only outside the play area. He figured that they had perished from the pounding inflicted by the players. So he devised his own nontoxic dandelion-control method. He ground his heel into the dandelion crown and twisted it. It opened up the plant to disease and infection, which killed it!

- Remove perennial weeds such as crabgrass and dandelions that show up in thinning lawn areas.
- Mow cool-season grasses at a height of 2.5–3 inches to prevent annual weeds from seeding. Annual weeds—including chickweed, henbit, and crabgrass—grow, flower, and seed in a single season.
- Fire ants don't damage the lawn. However, they can sting children and adults playing in the yard and ruin a garden party. Direct a strong spray of water at the mound and use nontoxic baits available at garden centers.

Biological Controls

Natural biological control occurs when predators, parasitoids, disease, and larger fauna such as birds attack and consume insect pests. This form of natural control in the landscape works to prevent infestations. Cultivate biological controls in your garden by creating a habitat in which they can thrive. Learn to recognize these beneficial insects at their various life stages. It is important to note, for example, that larvae of the lady beetle look very

Did you know? Clover is a "nitrogen fixer," which means it converts nitrogen from the atmosphere to a useable form for plants. Clover mixed in with grass benefits the soil.

Figure 8.14. *From left*: larva, egg, and adult lady beetle.

different from the adults, but these immature insects have a voracious appetite for aphids.

Many beneficial insects feed on nectar during the adult stage but are parasitic or predatory as larvae. A good example is the soldier beetle, which is frequently found on flowers as an adult, but whose larvae eat aphids, caterpillars, grasshopper eggs, and other beetles.

Here is quick overview of how predators, parasites, and diseases work to decimate pests.

Predators include insects such as lacewings, bigeyed bugs, rove and ground beetles, pirate bugs, and aphid midges. Mantids, festive tiger beetles, assassin bugs, and dragonflies and damselflies are also insect predators. In addition, centipedes, spiders, and predatory mites, as well as larger fauna such as frogs, toads, lizards, and birds eat insects.

Did you know? Most spiders are beneficial to the garden. They have eight legs, which makes them arachnids, not insects.

Figure 8.15. Bigeyed bug.

Figure 8.16. Ground beetle getting ready to eat a caterpillar.

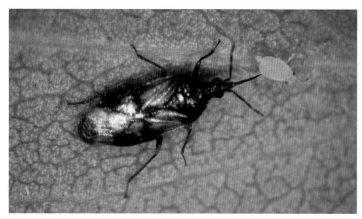

Figure 8.17. Minute pirate bug eating an aphid.

Figure 8.18. European mantid.

Figure 8.19. Festive tiger beetle.

Figure 8.20. Assassin bug.

Figure 8.21. Dragonfly.

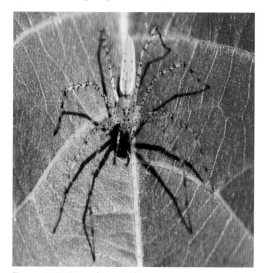

Figure 8.22. Green lynx spider.

Figure 8.23. Yellow garden spider.

Figure 8.24. Tobacco hornworm caterpillar is parasitized by a Braconid wasp that laid her eggs inside the caterpillar. Wasp larvae hatch, eat the caterpillar's insides, and then emerge through its skin to form egg-like cocoons.

Parasitoids

Parasitoids comprise a diverse range of insects that lay their eggs on or in the body of another insect host, which is then used as food by developing larvae. Parasitic wasps and flies take much longer than other predators, such as spiders, to consume their victims. If the larvae ate much too quickly, they would run out of food before they became adults. Most parasitoids have a very narrow host range.

Debilitating or Deadly Plant Diseases

Debilitating or deadly plant diseases can be caused by a range of organisms, including bacteria, fungi, viruses, protozoa, and nematodes. These disease-causing agents are relatively specific in terms of host plants, and they also have been the focus of natural pest control innovations. Several have been produced commercially for gardeners to use in their landscapes to control insect pests.

Biological control involves conserving naturally occurring predators, parasitoids, and diseases in the landscape.

- Learn to identify naturally occurring beneficial insects in the landscape. Become familiar with their various stages of development.

- Plant ground covers to reduce dust, which interferes with the activity of some desirable predators and parasites and favors the development of mite pest populations.
- Provide for a biodiverse landscape to lure desirable insects and wildlife to your garden where they can feed on pests.
- Entice beneficial insects by using various small-flowered, nectar- and pollen-rich plants that bloom for long periods. Flowers in the carrot (*Apiaceae*), daisy (*Asteraceae*), and mint (*Lamiaceae*) families work well. Carrot family plants include caraway, dill, fennel, lovage, and parsley. Daisy plants include coneflowers, daisies, and yarrow. Mint family members include catnip, lemon balm, rosemary, and thyme.
- Create habitats that attract birds and other wildlife that prey on insects. Include trees and plants that produce nuts, berries, and seeds to attract wildlife. Both the National Wildlife Federation and the National Audubon Society provide guidelines for backyard habitats. Chapter 10 explores this subject in detail.
- Several bacteria, fungi, nematodes, and viruses that infect insects are produced commercially as microbial insecticides. *Bacillus thuringiensis,* or Bt, for example, occurs naturally and is most effective when pests are young. It is used to destroy caterpillars of destructive or undesirable moths, butterflies (such as cabbage butterflies), beetles, and flies. Bacteria used for biological control infect insects via their digestive tracts, so insects with sucking mouth parts like aphids and scale insects are difficult to control with bacterial biological control.

Special Instructions for Vegetable Gardens

Put plants that attract beneficial insects—such as yarrow, goldenrod, rosemary, purple coneflower, dill, fennel, alyssum, and buckwheat—in close proximity to the vegetable garden.

Special Instructions for Lawns

By adding compost to the lawn, you increase soil fertility and microbial diversity to combat insect pests and disease.

Chemical Controls

Chemical pesticides should be the pest control method of last resort. These chemical compounds range in toxicity from insecticidal soaps and horticultural oils, which degrade quickly, to toxic synthetic pesticides that last longer in the environment and can be harmful to people, pets, and beneficial insects. When trying to control pest outbreaks, begin with the least toxic chemicals. Spray affected areas only. Even insecticidal soaps can temporarily reduce the beneficial insect population. Give careful thought before using synthetic pesticides, which can hurt nature's defense mechanisms. This issue is discussed more extensively in the section devoted to synthetic pesticides later in this chapter.

Chemical controls are grouped according to the following categories: botanical, inorganic, and synthetic. Many are available at garden centers.

Botanical Controls

Some botanicals are made from ground plant materials such as flowers, roots, stems, or seeds. Others are extracted from plants and refined and purified. Botanical pesticides have broad-spectrum activity, which means they kill a wide variety of insects, including beneficial insects. Use botanicals for spot spraying only. They work better for some pests than for others. Since they are produced from natural materials, they break down quickly in the environment.

Insecticidal Soaps

Insecticidal soaps are made with natural soaps and cause cell membranes of soft-bodied insects to collapse and leak. This method also can burn plant leaves if they are thin and the sun is shining.

- *Targeted pests*—Aphids, mealybugs, scale insects, whiteflies, and thrips. Fungicidal versions are also available to control powdery mildew, black spot, brown canker, leaf spot, and rust on ornamentals or food plants.
- *Application method*—Spray

Horticultural Oils

Horticultural oils control a wide variety of insect pests by smothering them. Horticultural oils are less toxic to beneficial insects than insecticidal soaps.

Avoid using oils on plants that are diseased and when daytime temperatures are likely to exceed 85°F or night temperatures fall below freezing.

- *Targeted pests*—Aphids, scale insects, mealy bugs, and spider mites on a diversity of fruit, nut, ornamental and shade trees.
- *Application method*—Spray

Neem

Neem is an insecticide extracted from seeds of the neem tree that is common to Africa and India. It works by making the plant unappetizing to insects. Neem has some systemic effect. It kills a wide range of pests and can be used on vegetables and fruits as well as on ornamentals.

- *Targeted pests*—Aphids, gypsy moths, leaf miners, loopers, mealy bugs, thrips, whiteflies, and more difficult pests like Colorado potato beetles, corn earworms, cucumber beetles, flea beetles, and Mexican beetles. Research shows that neem may also have some effect against diseases such as powdery mildew and rust.
- *Application method*—Spray

Pyrethrum

Pyrethrum, derived from chrysanthemums, acts as an insect nerve poison that kills insect pests on contact. It is approved for controlling pests on vegetables, fruits, and flowers.

- *Targeted pests*—Aphids, cabbage loopers, celery leaftiers, codling moths, Colorado potato beetle, leafhoppers, Mexican bean beetles, spider mites, stick bugs, thrips, tomato pinworms, and whiteflies.
- *Application method*—Spray or dust

Spinosad

Spinosad was developed from a soil bacterium discovered in 1982 on land surrounding an abandoned rum distillery. It can be used on outdoor ornamentals, lawns, vegetables, and fruit trees. To be effective, the insect must ingest Spinosad; therefore, it has little effect on sucking insects and nontarget predatory insects. Spinosad is relatively fast-acting and kills an insect within one to two days after it ingests the active ingredient.

- *Targeted pests*—Caterpillars, thrips, leafminers, borers, and fruit flies
- *Application method*—Spray

Special Instructions for Lawns

Corn Gluten

Corn gluten is a very effective preemergent herbicide, according to research, that gets rid of crabgrass, dandelion, pigweed, and many other
annual and perennial weeds. By consistently applying it year after year,
a gardener can reduce weeds the first year by 50–60 percent, the second
year by 80–85 percent, and the third year by 90 percent. Corn gluten
suppresses the germination of weed seeds. It also suppresses grass seed
germination. Avoid using this product when the lawn is reseeded. Apply
it shortly after spring frost and again in the fall at the rate of 20 pounds
per 1,000 square feet.

Herbicidal Soaps

Herbicidal soaps are nontoxic, nonselective contact herbicides. They are effective against annual weeds such as chickweed, spurge, and crabgrass and
less effective against perennial weeds with tap roots, such as dandelions.
Since they are nonselective, they will affect the grass also. Spray directly
only on the weeds.

Inorganic Controls

Inorganic pesticides are made from natural, nonliving materials. They are
applied mostly for disease control. Some precautions must be taken when
using some of the fungicides since they are toxic. The two most common
inorganic controls, copper and sulfur, are deadly poisons and should be
used with care. As fungicides, they inhibit the germination and growth of
fungal spores; however, they won't stop the growth of fungal spores once
infection has occurred. Use only when the threat of disease is great.

Copper

Copper has been used as a pesticide since the 1700s. It has both herbicidal
and fungicidal properties and works by inactivating enzyme systems in
fungi, algae, and other plants.

- *Targeted pests*—Anthracnose, bacterial leaf spot, black rot, blights,
  downy mildew, peach leaf curl, and Septoria leaf spot.
- *Application method*—Dust, wettable powder, sprayable solution

Sulfur

Sulfur, a natural mineral, has been used for centuries to control plant pathogens, pests, and mites. It works well as an insecticide against insects and mites on fruit trees. Since it is moderately toxic to humans and pets, wear protective clothing when applying it and keep children and pets away from areas where it is applied.

- *Targeted pests*—Apple scab, brown rot of stone fruits, powdery mildew, rose black spot, rusts, and other plant diseases on vegetables and fruits.
- *Application method*—Dust, wettable powder

Bordeaux Mix

Bordeaux mix combines copper sulfate and hydrated lime. It acts as a fungicide with insect-repellent properties. It can burn plant foliage, so read the label carefully.

- *Targeted pests*—Anthracnose, bacterial leaf spots and wilt, black spot, fire blight, peach leaf curl, powdery mildew, and rust.
- *Application method*—Wettable powder can be dusted onto plants or mixed with water and applied as a spray.

Diatomaceous Earth

Diatomaceous earth is produced from the fossilized remains of tiny marine organisms called diatoms. Sharp microscopic shells cut the insects' bodies, causing them to lose their fluids and die. It is nonselective and will kill beneficial insects as well as pests.

- *Targeted pests*—slugs and snails when dusted on the soil, and soft-bodied pests like aphids, caterpillars, leaf hoppers, thrips, and mites when applied to plant foliage.
- *Application method*—Dust

Kaolin

Kaolin is naturally occurring clay found in huge deposits around the world. It is generally inert and does not react with other materials. It is insoluble in water. When kaolin is sprayed as a powdered suspension on crops, it forms a film that repels and prevents targeted pests from penetrating leaves or other parts of the plant. It is approved for use on a wide range of fruit and vegetable crops, including beans, potatoes, eggplant, citrus fruits, apples, apricots, and berries.

- *Targeted pests*—Insects, mites, fungi and bacteria.
- *Application Methods*—Kaolin is sprayed as a suspension as needed.

Synthetic Controls

Synthetic chemicals are made in a laboratory and are toxic, ranging from somewhat toxic to potentially fatal in small amounts. Follow label directions carefully as some can harm or kill people and animals if they come into contact with skin or are inhaled or ingested, and some are potential carcinogens. Some of the newer synthetic chemicals target particular pests better and are less toxic to other living organisms and the environment. They kill beneficial insects as well as pests. Careful assessment of the pest situation is warranted before using toxic chemical pesticides. Be sure you have identified the pest correctly.

Is Chemical Treatment Worth It?

If your landscape is diverse and contains native plants, if you cull out pest-attracting plants, and if you monitor the landscape regularly and use cultural, mechanical, and biological controls, there should be little need for synthetic chemical pesticides. They should be used only in the following limited circumstances:

- a serious pest infestation
- a life-threatening problem
- a threatened heirloom shrub, substantial-sized tree, or other valuable plant where other measures have not worked
- all nontoxic measures have failed

Before Buying Synthetic Pesticides, Read the Label

Information on the label helps you determine if the product is right for your circumstances and specifies where the pesticide can be used. It also lists pests that the pesticide is intended to control. Strive to use the least toxic pesticide to do the job. How dangerous the pesticide is will be indicated by the words "Caution," "Warning," and "Danger." "Caution" identifies the least toxic group of pesticides when used according to label directions. "Warning" indicates that the pesticide has moderate toxicity to humans and animals. "Danger" means the pesticide is toxic by one route of exposure—through skin contact, inhalation, or ingestion—and can kill in very small amounts. If the word "Poison" is also listed on the front label in red letters with the word "Danger," then the pesticide is highly toxic by all routes of contact. This last group of pesticides should be handled by licensed professionals only. Children should never come in contact with them.

The formulation of the pesticide is listed on the label. There are dusts, granules, baits, wettable powders, and emulsifiable concentrates. Many pesticides are premixed and packaged as aerosols or pump sprays for the homeowner market. They are usually more expensive but safer and more convenient because the gardener does not have to measure or mix concentrates.

Selecting the Right Pesticide

Base your selection on the pest you wish to control, the plants you wish to protect, the application equipment you have, and the hazards of the pesticide. While broad-spectrum insecticides kill many pests, they also are usually more dangerous. Choose newer formulations, which have much lower rates of active ingredients and thus have generally lower toxicity levels, too.

- *Pyrethroids* are newer products indicated on the label by words such as Permethrin, Bifenthrin, Cypermethin, Cyfluthrin, Deltamethrin, Esfenvalerate, Fluvalinate, and Lambda-cyhalothrin. Pyrethroids work by inhibiting the functioning of insects' nervous systems.
- *Insect growth regulators* work by preventing molting. They can be found in fire ant baits. They are slow-acting and contain the ingredients Methoprene, Hydroprene, and Fenoxycarb.
- *Systemic insecticides*—This group will have words such as Imidacloprid and Fipronil, and these insecticides are absorbed by the plant's leaves and roots and move throughout a plant's entire system, including flowers and nectar.
- *Fungicides*—Look for ingredients such as Myclobutinal, Chlorothalonil, Mancozeb, Maneb, Tecuconazole, Thiophanate-methyl, and

Propiconazole. Many fungicides are applied to prevent an outbreak of a fungal disease and are less effective in controlling the spread of fungal diseases.

Guidelines for Applying Pesticides

- Wear protective clothing to prevent the pesticide from coming into contact with the skin, eyes, and respiratory system.
- Follow label directions for the time of day to apply.
- Never spray on a windy day to reduce the risk of the pesticide drifting onto unintended plants.
- Avoid spraying when plant foliage is wet and when flowers are blooming.
- Apply pesticides to the pest or infested area only. This will avoid killing beneficial insects or even plants. For example, if herbicides are sprayed accidently on vegetable plants, they may get damaged.
- Keep children, other individuals, and pets out of the treated area until the pesticide has dried.

Handling and Storing Pesticides

- Wash hands after spraying.
- Clean up any pesticide that spills onto pavement. For a dry formulation, scoop it up with an outdoor broom and dustpan and put it back into the original container. If it is liquid, cover it with an absorbent material like cat litter or sand. For disposal, follow the pesticide label directions or call the Cooperative Extension office for advice.
- Store pesticides safely and out of reach of children. Never store any pesticide in a food or drink container.
- Dispose of pesticides properly. Pesticide containers can be disposed of in the household trash if they are rinsed three times and the rinse water is disposed of in an approved site listed on the label.
- Call Poison Control immediately if you have any reactions to the pesticide.

For me, trying to maintain a presentable yard without incessantly running to the garden center and searching through shelves of sprays and potions to manage beetles and black spot was once a challenge. First, I worried that toxic sprays might harm the environment, my children, and the two family cats, and second, I had little time between carpooling and working to run to the store and read the fine print on the labels. However, as I became aware of the link between increasing biodiversity and natural pest control, I slowly retrofitted my landscape with native plants. As the biodiversity increased, the pest problems decreased. Now I find that I can handle most pest problems by hosing down a few plants, cutting out diseased leaves and limbs, and removing caterpillars and worms by hand. I no longer have to read the fine print, store smelly chemicals, or temporarily cordon off sections of a pesticide-treated landscape. And I feel good knowing that my Integrated Pest Management strategies are working in harmony with Mother Nature and helping safeguard the plants in my garden.

9

Grow Food Organically

Ripe vegetables were magic to me. I would quicken at the sight of a ripe tomato, sounding its redness from deep amidst the undifferentiated green. To lift a bean plant's hood of heart-shaped leaves and discover a clutch of long slender pods hanging underneath could make me catch my breath.

Michael Pollan, *The Omnivore's Dilemma*

Who can resist the flavor of a homegrown tomato? Use it for homemade salsa, and you're the hit of the garden party. Or put a thick tomato slice between two pieces of bread, and you've got the perfect summer sandwich. Homegrown tomatoes are the ultimate fast food, just a few steps from your doorway. And your environmental conscience can rest easy, too—no greenhouse gases are emitted transporting it. Growing some of your own food, even if it is just a pot of patio tomatoes or a window box of herbs, is a healthy choice for the body, the spirit, and the earth. In a home garden, fruits and vegetables can be grown organically, which means using no synthetic pesticides or fertilizers.

All human food, except some mushrooms, comes directly or indirectly from plants. In the United States, just 103 plant species supply more than 90 percent of the calories we consume, even though tens of thousands of other plant species have been used by human beings for food at some time or in some place. The diversity of our food choices has been dramatically reduced (Neff, *Introduction to the U.S. Food System*).

Industrialized agriculture, an efficient means to feed the earth's massive human population, has an environmental downside. From fertilizer manufacture to food storage, packaging, and transportation, it is responsible for approximately 10 percent of U.S. greenhouse-gas emissions, according to the U.S. Environmental Protection Division. These processes have transformed a system that in 1940 produced 2.3 calories of food

Did you know? Most food travels 1,500 miles from farm to table. It is common for lettuce grown on a California farm to be shipped 3,000 miles to a New York City table. (Pirog et al., "Food, Fuel, and Freeways")

from every calorie of fossil fuel burned to one that today produces one calorie of food for every 10 calories of fossil fuel used (Pollan, "Farmer in Chief").

In 2005, out of concern for climate change and food safety issues, four California women birthed the locavore movement, which encourages eating locally produced food. This movement led to increased interest among gardeners to grow some of their own fruits, vegetables, and herbs. The concept of the World War II Victory Garden, where 40 percent of the nation's fruits and vegetables were grown in home gardens or in empty lots, is experiencing a revival today. Eco-minded gardeners are cultivating vegetable gardens for "victory over global climate change."

Since home gardeners eat what they grow, it makes sense to cultivate food that uses organic practices that rely on natural systems. This chapter explains how to grow vegetables and fruits to maintain soil nutrients, enhance biodiversity, conserve water, and protect the surrounding environment.

Growing Vegetables

Most gardeners would agree with *Rodale's Encyclopedia of Organic Gardening* (P. Pears, ed.): "Growing vegetables organically is a positive, empowering, rewarding and (for some) spiritual experience." And it saves money, too. A small 4 × 8-foot raised vegetable garden can reduce your grocery bill by six hundred dollars a year (Ball, "Down-to-Earth Plan").

Vegetables can be grown in pots, raised beds, backyards, or anywhere there is sufficient sunlight. They can even be mixed in with flowers and shrubs. Before digging in, determine how much space you want to devote to a vegetable garden, how much time you have to maintain it, and whether you have a suitable site or will need to make room by altering a section of the landscape.

What Do Farmers and Grocers Mean by Organic?

In the United States, organic agriculture is a certification program administered through the U.S. Department of Agriculture that gives farmers the right to use the label "organic" if they satisfy certain requirements. These include developing a farm-management plan and keeping careful records documenting soil-improvement strategies such as reduced tillage, use of cover crops, crop rotation, and the use of organic fertilizers. This holistic management system stresses soil management to furnish nonsynthetic nutrients and natural control of weeds, diseases, and insects. Organic agriculture enhances biodiversity, biological cycles, and soil microbiology. This chapter describes organic practices for home gardeners.

Location, Location, Location

Vegetable gardens need a sunny spot, well-drained soil, and a water source. They require at least 6 hours of sunlight a day—and 8–10 hours is best. If you suspect drainage is going to be a problem, try the quick test described in chapter 2. If it turns out that drainage is an issue, consider making raised beds where soil can be improved and managed according to the plants' needs. Select a location near the house if possible, because it is easier to maintain a garden located just a short distance from your doorstep.

Plan the Produce

Begin by deciding whether you want to cultivate vegetables year-round or just during the summer. In many southeastern states (Georgia, Florida, Alabama, Mississippi, Louisiana), food can be grown year-round. If you are a newcomer to home vegetable gardening, begin small. A 4 × 8-foot raised bed (figure 9.1) is a good start if you have the space and sun. A 4-foot-wide bed allows you to reach across the bed without having to walk on the soil and compact it.

If you decide on summer veggies, consider planting the garden with a winter cover crop that holds and builds the soil.

Figure 9.1. Raised beds are a great way to start.

Cover Crops

Cover crops (figure 9.2) have many benefits. They reduce erosion, improve soil structure, increase the water-holding capacity of the soil, reduce winter weed growth, penetrate hardpan in the winter, and, if the cover crop is a legume, they also provide nitrogen. Cover crops come in two types—legumes and nonlegumes. Legume cover crops, like vetch and clover, add nitrogen to the soil. Nonlegume crops, such as wheat and rye, can grow in poor soils and erosive soils. Plant legumes earlier than grasses so they can become established. Check with the Cooperative Extension in your area for

Figure 9.2. Cover crop of crimson clover and rye grown together.

the best time to plant. When spring arrives, till the cover crop to help feed the summer garden.

Draw Up a Plan

Before purchasing seeds or plants, draw a plan for the season or the year. This will serve as a guide to how many plants and varieties your garden space can accommodate; it provides a historical record and can be used in determining future crop rotations. Select vegetables you love to eat. Choose some of the easiest southern favorites to grow such as tomatoes, cucumbers, green peppers, squash, and zucchini. Place tall plants on the north or west side of the garden so they won't shade lower-growing plants. For larger vegetable gardens, include enough space between rows to walk between them.

Since, on average, one in three bites of food comes from pollination, vegetable gardens need a ready, nearby supply of pollinators to accomplish the task. Some crops are self-pollinating, such as tomatoes, peas, and beans, but they still need to be shaken by the wind or visited by bees to transfer pollen from the male anther to the female stigma for fertilization. Vegetables such as cucumber, squash, and melon produce separate male and female flowers and depend on pollinators for fertilization.

To help with pollination and pest control, reserve space in the planning phase for flowers and herbs that attract pollinators and other beneficial insects and repel nematodes. These include plants such as purple coneflower and common herbs such as yarrow, lavender, rosemary, dill, and fennel. Plants with small flowers like alyssum, buckwheat, and goldenrod work well, too. Marigolds, especially French marigolds, suppress nematodes when planted en masse.

Once you decide what to plant, an important next step is to list the vegetable plants according to their botanical family. That way you can avoid planting vegetables in the same botanical family next to one another since they may share the same soil-borne pests and diseases. For example, tomatoes, eggplant, and potatoes are botanical cousins and should not be neighbors in the garden; the same holds true for cucumbers, zucchini, and summer squash. Pests and diseases for specific plant families can become established in areas where crops are not rotated from one season to the next (see table 8.1). Vegetables differ in their nutrient needs, so it's wise to plant those with the same nutritional needs together, for example those from the same family: cabbage, broccoli, cauliflower, arugula, and kale. The major vegetable plant families are briefly described below.

Cabbage Family (Brassicaceae)

Cabbage family plants are grown for their leaves, buds, roots, stems, or flowers. Turnips, kale, and other cabbage cousins thrive in cool, moist climates and are very nutritious. They are heavy feeders, meaning they use high quantities of nitrogen. Cabbage family vegetables can be grown either where the nitrogen-fixing pea and bean family were grown last season (discussed later in this chapter) or any place where compost is added.

The cabbage family includes arugula, broccoli, cabbage, kale, radish, rutabaga, Brussels sprouts, cauliflower, and turnips.

Onion Family (Amaryllidaceae, formerly Alliaceae)

Onion family members include hardy cool-climate crops grown for their bulbs and stems. After harvesting, many can be stored for extended periods of time. They prefer well-drained, relatively fertile soil. The onion family includes garlic, leek, onion, and shallot.

Cucumber Family (Cucurbitaceae)

Plants are usually annual vines, with *five-lobed or divided leaves* and *spring-like tendrils*. A single plant is monoecious, which means it has both male and female flowers and needs cross-pollination from bees. After the male flower falls off, the female flower grows to produce the fruit. Make sure you allow space for the trailing vines to grow. The cucumber family includes zucchini, cucumber, melon, pumpkin, watermelon, and winter squash.

Pea and Bean Family (Fabaceae)

This vegetable family is also known as legumes. They are grown for their fleshy seeds and pods. Their roots fix nitrogen in the soil, which means they use nitrogen from the air and convert it into a form that can be used by

Figure 9.3. Red cabbage.

Figure 9.4. Red onions.

Figure 9.5. Mexican zucchini squash.

Figure 9.6. Green bean.

plants. They accomplish this through nodules on the roots. Nitrogen-fixing plants infuse the soil with nitrogen that heavy feeders such as members of the cabbage family can use. This family is important for good crop rotations. The pea and bean families include string bean, snow peas, fava bean, runner bean, green beans, winter peas, peanuts, soybeans, and clover.

Beet Family (Amaranthaceae, formerly Chenopodiaceae)

Beet family members include leaf and root crops suitable for warm and cool climates. Spinach is best sown during cool temperatures of fall and early spring. The beet family includes beet, chard, spinach, and red orach.

Lettuce Family (Asteraceae)

Lettuce family plants range from annual lettuce to the perennial 6-foot-tall globe artichoke. Depending upon the species grown, the leaves, shoots, flower buds, roots, and stem tubers can all be eaten. In temperate climates,

Figure 9.7. Freshly pulled beets.   Figure 9.8. Lettuce.

lettuce can provide salad year-round. The lettuce family includes chicory, endive, lettuce, globe artichoke, Jerusalem artichoke.

Tomato/Potato Family (Solanaceae)

Tomato/potato family members are planted in spring in fertile soil rich in organic matter. They follow a winter rye cover crop well. Heirloom varieties are becoming popular. When planting potatoes, be sure the tubers are certified to ensure that they are healthy, disease-free, and without varietal mixture. Tomatoes come in all varieties—from cherry-sized to large tomatoes that can make an entire meal. There is a whole range of peppers, too, from sweet to hot, for every gardener's taste. Members of this family include tomato, potato, sweet pepper, chili pepper, hot pepper, and eggplant.

Carrot Family (Apiaceae)

Carrot family members include a diverse group of crops characterized by umbrella-shaped flower heads, which attract beneficial insects. It includes root crops such as carrots and fennel, the herb parsley, and the versatile

Figure 9.9. Cherry tomatoes.   Figure 9.10. Freshly pulled carrots.

celery, grown for its stalk and leaves. Soil conditions for this group vary, so check the requirements first and amend the soil accordingly. This family includes carrot, celery, parsley, parsnip, and fennel.

Prepare Soil for High Yields

Good soil is the single-most important factor in successful vegetable gardening. Submit a soil-test sample to the local county Extension office several months prior to planting the garden to determine lime and fertilizer needs. Apply dolomitic lime, if recommended, to raise the soil pH to 6.0–6.5. For best results, incorporate lime into the soil two to three months before planting seeds or seedlings to give it time to be assimilated. Apply fertilizer as recommended by the soil test.

Till the soil to a depth of 6 inches to bury crop residue and vegetation. This also aids in disease and insect control. Do not till wet soils as this may compact the soil and destroy soil structure. The soil is too wet to till if you can squeeze a handful of it and water is visible in your hand or it ribbons out between your fingers.

Plow organic materials into the garden soil. These materials include ma-

Try Heirloom Vegetables

Heirloom or heritage vegetables have been selected by farmers and gardeners over the centuries because they are tasty and produce well in local conditions. Using heirloom vegetables helps to increase plant varieties and preserve genetic diversity. Among the advantages of using heirloom vegetables are their exceptional taste, interesting colors, and unusual shapes. Most fresh vegetables found in the supermarkets are hybrids that are bred for yield, disease resistance, and shelf life, but not necessarily for flavor or texture. Heirloom varieties are open-pollinated, which means the seeds can be saved and sown year after year (assuming you don't plant other cultivars that could cross-pollinate nearby) to produce a similar vegetable next generation. The best-saved heirlooms are ones that are self-pollinated such as tomatoes and peppers. Heirloom vegetables usually can be harvested over an extended period of time, too. Heirloom seeds are available through seed exchanges, and some cultivars are available through seed companies and nurseries.

Figure 9.11. Heirloom tomatoes come in many varieties.

nure, compost, leaves, and green plant material. If manure is not composted, it must be spread in the fall before spring planting. Well-composted manure can be added at any time. Decayed organic matter increases the nutrient- and water-holding capacity of the soil. Vegetables are classified as heavy, medium, or light feeders based on their fertilizer requirements as shown in table 9.1.

After amending the soil and improving its structure, avoid tilling it again. The "no dig" method, described in chapter 2, conserves soil health. It works well in beds where the soil is protected from foot traffic and other activities that cause soil compaction. If green manure or cover crops are used, they can be mowed in the spring and left on the soil to decompose until planting.

Table 9.1. Fertilizer requirements for vegetables

Heavy	Medium	Light
4–5 lb. of 10–10–10 per 100 sq. ft.	2–3 lb. of 10–10–10 per 110 sq. ft.	1–1½ lb. of 10–10–10 per sq. ft.
Cabbage	Artichoke	Southern peas
	Pumpkin	
	Cucumbers	
	Radish	
Celery	Asparagus	
	Okra	
	Eggplants	
	Pepper	
Lettuce	Beans	
	Peas	
	Greens	
	Rhubarb	
Onions	Beets	
	Herbs	
	Squash	
Potatoes, Irish	Cantaloupes	
	Swiss chard	
Potatoes, Sweet	Carrots	
	Watermelon	
	Tomatoes	
	Sweet corn	

Plant a Sustainable Vegetable Garden

The following recommendations can help you plant a garden that will be a health-promoting, attractive asset for the environment and the menu.

1. Select high-quality vegetable seeds from a reputable company.
2. Opt for pest-resistant varieties.
3. Choose seedlings that are free of diseases, insects, and nematodes.
4. Follow the recommended planting dates and spacing for the vegetable plants you choose. If this information is not provided on the plant tag or seed packet, then check with the local Cooperative Extension office, which can supply guidelines.
5. Include plants that attract pollinators and beneficial insects.
6. Seeds should be planted in a well-prepared, weed-free bed. Plant tall crops that need support in the middle of the bed with smaller crops on either side. Work from the paths to avoid stepping on the soil and compacting it.
7. Rotate crops among plant families yearly to avoid depleting the soil and to discourage diseases and pests associated with some vegetables from becoming entrenched in one area.

Manage Vegetable Plants to Safeguard the Harvest

Mulch beds with organic material such as straw, leaves, compost, pine straw, or bark to conserve soil moisture, control weeds, and reduce cultivation. Maintain a 2- to 4-inch mulch layer after the first application of mulch settles. Newspaper placed under the mulch provides an extra barrier to weeds. Pull back mulch 3–4 inches from the plant stem to prevent the spread of disease. Mulched beds also guard against disease-causing molds and bacteria that can splatter onto the plant leaves when water strikes the soil and splashes onto the leaves.

Water

Water is critically important during two periods in the life of vegetable plants. The first occurs during the two initial weeks of growth. The second period takes place during bloom and fruit set. Inadequate moisture during either of these two periods reduces yields. Use caution when watering. Wet foliage increases the likelihood of disease, especially if leaves are wet for an extended period of time.

Seedlings and transplants should never be allowed to dry out.

1. Water early in the morning so the foliage can dry quickly.
2. Use a gentle stream of water directed at the base of the plant to avoid splashing.
3. Water when the soil's surface feels dry. Excess watering can lead to surface-water runoff.
4. Use a soaker hose to avoid wetting the leaves.

Feed

Feed vegetables according to soil-test recommendations and the condition of your soil. Soils with high organic matter require less fertilizer; however, all soils will require some additional fertilizer for optimum yield. One-third to one-half of the fertilizer should be applied prior to planting with the remainder applied when the crop is one-third to one-half grown.

Control Weeds, Insects, and Diseases

Control weeds, insects, and diseases to ensure good-quality produce. Keep weeds from choking out the plants and prevent worms, beetles, bugs, and borers from devouring the harvest. Since healthy vegetable plants are more resistant to pests than poorly planted and maintained ones, follow these general recommendations to minimize pests. If pest problems arise, refer to chapter 8.

1. Weeds can be removed by hand or by lightly cultivating or hoeing between the plants to avoid using herbicides. Cultivating too often dries out the soil. Mulched beds effectively control most weeds.
2. Insects can be removed by hand. Wrap aluminum foil around tomato and pepper plant stems so 2 inches of the foil is below the soil surface and 2 inches is above it to prevent cutworms from feeding on the plant. Insecticidal soaps, oils, and Bt qualify as organic pest

Edible Landscape

Today's gardeners are finding practical and attractive ways to plant vegetables and herbs in their annual and perennial beds and even in sections of the lawn. Edging beds with lettuce and kale and planting tomatoes and cabbage in a flower bed can be appealing to the eye and satisfying to the palate. Herbs such as parsley, tarragon, lamb's ear, chives, and thyme placed throughout the landscape provide texture and color, attract beneficial insects, and offer fresh flavors for cooking.

Be bold—how about planting corn in the front yard? (But be sure to check with your homeowners association if you have one.) Gardeners living in apartments can grow vegetables in pots on their porches or balconies.

Figure 9.12. *Top*: Corn provides a visual accent and food for the homeowner. *Bottom*: Vegetables planted in the lawn.

control. Early plantings of vegetables generally help deter pest pressure later in the season.

3. Diseases—Water plants at the base to keep the leaves from becoming wet for an extended period. Remove diseased plants or plant parts to prevent further infection. Separate vegetable groups when planting, putting a good distance between crops of the same family, such as melons and cucumbers.

Harvest

Harvest vegetables as soon as they are ripe. Leaving vegetables on the plant for too long leads to disease and insect problems. It also causes crops such as beans, okra, squash, and cucumbers to become overripe, and the plants will stop producing.

Planting Fruits

Fruits have been on the human menu since hunters and gatherers began picking berries from bushes and vines more than 2 million years ago. Producing them in the landscape gives the gardener a flower show in the spring and a luscious harvest in the summer or fall. And like any other food grown in a home garden, fresh-picked fruits taste better and save miles in transportation. Fruit gardening also connects gardeners with the seasons. Fruit can be grown in small or large gardens. Even a pocket garden may have a sunny corner for a few blueberry bushes, raspberry vines, or a strawberry jar with strawberry plants. And if you have enough sun on your front or back porch, you can grow dwarf varieties of blueberries and raspberries in pots.

Deciding what to grow depends on the following aspects:

Sunshine

Sunshine is the most important factor in growing fruit. Insufficient sun limits the possibilities. Table 9.2 outlines the sun/shade needs of fruit trees, shrubs and vines.

Table 9.2. Sun requirements for fruits

Fruits for full sun	Fruits that tolerate partial shade
Apples	Blackberries
Apricots	Currants
Blueberries	Gooseberries
Figs	Raspberries
Grapes	Sour cherries
Peaches	
Pears	
Plums	
Nectarines	
Strawberries	
Sweet cherries	

Climate

Climate plays an important role in successfully growing fruit. The low number of chilling hours and mild winters found in the South are particularly conducive for peach and plum production. A protected location such as the south side of a house coupled with the mild winters makes fig production possible. Muscadine grapes, blackberries, and rabbiteye blueberries are native to the Southeast and make a great addition to a garden. Many fruits grown in northern climates, including many cultivars and varieties of raspberries and apples, can be grown in the Southeast. Avoid planting fruit trees in frost pockets where an early frost will freeze the flowers and damage the harvest. Also, stay away from windy locations, which make it difficult for pollinators to settle on flowers and consequently limits yield.

Space

Space rarely stops a gardener from growing fruit. Dwarf varieties such as BrazelBerries®, for example, are available and work well in small gardens and containers. Strawberries can grow in pots and raspberries and black-berries can be draped over a fence or propped against the side of a house or apartment building. Small fruit trees can be espaliered on a fence or rock wall. Some trees and shrubs (blueberries, for example) require compatible cultivars for cross-pollination, so make room for two plants if you select these types of fruits.

Soils

Soils that are deep, rich, and drain well allow plant roots to reach deeply for water and nutrients. Prepare the soil as you would for a vegetable garden and adjust the pH if needed for fruits such as blueberries that prefer acid soils with a pH of 5.5.

Choosing Cultivars

Choosing cultivars, like selecting any outdoor plant, requires an under-standing of local conditions and space availability. Look for pest-resistant varieties. Find out about pollination requirements. Many fruits such as plum and cherry are self-sterile. Some apples also need two different cul-tivars for pollination. Blueberries have the same requirement. Be sure the two varieties are compatible, with similar bloom periods, so they can cross-pollinate. In addition, compatible cultivars have to be within bee-flying dis-tance of one another for pollination to take place. Your local Cooperative Extension office will have a list of fruit trees and vines adapted to your con-ditions and how to care for them. In addition, you can access other states land-grant universities' information through the new national extension website (http://about.extension.org/). Figure 9.13 shows some easy-to-grow fruits for most southern landscapes.

General Instructions for Planting, Watering, and Pruning

Using knowledge acquired from planting and watering trees, bushes, and vines comes in handy when you decide to grow fruits. The one big differ-ence is pruning the plants. Pruning fruit trees is important to maximize the harvest. The purpose is to remove dead and diseased material, open up

Figure 9.13. *Top*: Titan blueberries, blackberries. *Center:* raspberries, strawberries. *Bottom*: figs, Pink Lady® apples.

the branches to allow air to circulate and sun to reach the fruit, and shape the tree for vigor. There are many good publications that provide pruning information, including those published by state Cooperative Extension offices such as those in Arkansas, North Carolina, and Georgia (fruit trees and vines).

Humans are not the only ones who enjoy fruits. Birds may become a nuisance, eating the blueberries and blackberries off the bush and vines. It may be necessary to cover the plants with netting or a fruit cage after they set fruit to safeguard the harvest.

Herbal Delight

An herb garden is a sensory experience of fragrance, color, taste, and texture. Herbs have been grown throughout the centuries to flavor food and drinks, to help people sleep, to ward off demons, and to heal illness. Fresh or dried, they flavor stew, fish, tea, vinegar, and many other dishes. Scented herbs such as lavender also can be gathered to make potpourri to add fragrance to your home. Even today, in many countries such as Costa Rica and the Bahamas, an ailing person may go out into the garden to snip a few leaves to make a tea, salve, or potion to cure a variety of ills. Many ingredients used in medicines today, such as aspirin and digitalis, come from plants.

Some kinds of herbs have been around for thousands of years and, if planted in the right place, are very resilient. Herbs often offer the additional qualities of drought-tolerance, pest-resistance, and low-maintenance. Although dry conditions are usually best for most herbs, the range of varietal choices means gardeners can find herbs that will grow well in almost any region and in an array of conditions. Lavender and rosemary, for instance, prefer sun; foxglove and creeping Jenny tolerate shade. For gardeners short of space, herbs can be grown in pots on the patio or deck or even in window boxes.

Practice natural pest control by mixing flowering perennial herbs throughout your garden beds to attract beneficial insects. Growing herbs also increases biodiversity in the landscape, especially because bees, butterflies, moths, and birds are attracted to the nectar, pollen, and seeds.

The Basics

Herbs may be annuals, biennials, or perennials. They may be bulbs, shrubs, climbers, or trees. Annuals and biennials can be grown from seed. Vegetative propagation is a good option for many herbs. Before planting an herb garden, answer these few questions to assess your herbal and flavoring needs.

1. How will these herbs be used—for cooking, potpourri, tea, or medicinal purposes—or for visual appeal and interest?
2. Which herbs will fill these needs?
3. Will I go into full-scale drying, which requires additional resources, or do I need a few herbs for personal use only?
4. Is there enough space with the right growing environment?

Once you know what you want to grow, assess the environment the herbs will need. Then group them according to growing requirements:

1. Sun-loving—Find a spot with six to eight hours of sun. Full sun all day is better. Check the soil requirements of the herbs. Some may prefer fertile soil (basil, chives, parsley); others are drought-tolerant and require low-nutrient (rosemary, thyme, lavender), well-drained soils. Group plants according to soil and water needs.
2. Shade-tolerant—Typically these herbs like more fertile soil than the sun-loving and drought-tolerant herbs. And they prefer dappled shade over full sun.
3. Drought-tolerant—Often blue-green in color, these herbs grow in low-nutrient and well-drained soil. Use a light-colored gravel mulch at the base of the plants to control weeds.

Planting Ideas

Dedicated Garden: Formal or Informal

A formal herb garden can be a feast for the eyes and the palate, but it also is high-maintenance. Its well-groomed beds and paths must be trimmed and weeded frequently to maintain a formal appearance. In an informal garden, herbs can be planted randomly, so they tumble and creep throughout a designated area, making the garden easier to manage and appear more casual.

Table 9.3. Growing conditions for herbs

Herbs for sun	Herbs for shade	Drought-tolerant
Chives	Creeping Jenny	Lavender
Tarragon	Foxglove	Lavender cotton
Dill	Periwinkle	Lamb's ear
Fennel	Bugle	Yarrow
Mint	Parsley	Thyme
Basil		Rosemary
		Sage

Mingling herbs throughout perennial and vegetable beds has many advantages. Many herbs attract pollinators and beneficial insects that are necessary for pollination of other landscape plants, and as previously mentioned, some herbs also can provide a measure of biological pest control. As long as the herbs are planted in conditions suited to their needs, they make a good addition to flower and vegetable gardens. Since many herbs are blue-green, they also add color and texture to the beds as well as diversity.

Containers

Many drought-tolerant herbs grow well in containers. Invasive herbs such as mint can be kept under control by confining them to pots. For container-grown herbs, use either a light soil mixture or one with one part gravel

Figure 9.14. Easy-to-grow herbs. *Left:* thyme. *Facing page, top row*: lavender, chives blooming. *Second row:* sage, Tuscan blue rosemary. *Third row*: Italian parsley, lamb's ear. *Bottom row*: mint, sweet basil.

Figure 9.15. Different herbs within a container produce pleasing sights. *Above, foreground*: oregano, parsley, chives, thyme, sage; *background*: basil, dill, cilantro; *lower corner (almost out of sight)*: peppermint and spearmint. *Below, left:* Wooden crate filled with herbs is a focal point. *Below, right*: Pot of herbs containing thyme, sage, chives, marjoram, parsley, and lemon balm.

Figure 9.16. With results ranging from the aesthetically pleasing (*above*) to the imaginative and funky (*left*), growing herbs sparks all the senses.

and five parts soil. Be sure the bottom of the container has drainage holes. Herbs will grow in a great variety of containers (figures 9.15 and 9.16). Have fun, be creative, and consider most any receptacle as a potential pot.

Walkways

Seeds of Corsican mints and creeping thymes can be sown as a ground cover between stepping-stones to elicit an interesting appearance and a savory smell. They also tolerate some light foot traffic.

Caution: Most herbs are safe, but some contain toxic chemicals. Before you use herbs for medicinal purposes, consult a doctor or other medical expert.

Caring for Herbs

Many herbs don't require specific growing conditions in order to thrive. Most can be grown in low-nutrient, well-drained soils. The same recipe for container-grown herbs also works in a garden setting—mix one part gravel or sand with five parts soil to create a well-drained soil. For continuous production, prune herbs such as lavender and rosemary in the spring after flowering and pinch back flower heads on basil and parsley to encourage bushy growth. Invasive herbs, such as some of the mints, need pruning and containing to keep them manageable.

Besides reducing greenhouse emissions associated with transporting food from a distant farm to your table, cultivating vegetables, fruits, and herbs in a home garden produces a plethora of benefits. Homegrown food bestows a new appreciation for farmers who not only work hard but also have an extensive knowledge of soils, nutrients, water conservation, and pest management. It also allows us to expand our horizons beyond the limited supply of vegetables and fruits available in supermarkets and to try heirloom varieties. It is a great way to exercise and a wonderful intergenerational activity for parents and grandparents to share with their children and grandchildren. It provides an easy avenue to explore the natural world and to understand our reliance on it for our sustenance.

10

Bring Wildlife Home

Wildlife is disappearing at an alarming rate in the Southeast. As natural areas are bulldozed for development, especially near metro areas, wildlife corridors are becoming increasingly fragmented, and the resulting wildlife islands are often not large enough to support the nutritional and nesting needs of animals that once inhabited the larger expanses. Inadvertently adding to these habitat pressures are landscapers and homeowners who spray pesticides on plants with abandon, turning gardens into virtual wildlife deserts. As non-native species come to dominate more and more landscapes and as invasive species gain ground in woodlands, wetlands, and grasslands, native wildlife habitat continues to shrink.

Gardeners can help stage a comeback for wildlife by making some simple changes in how they garden, creating habitats that are oases for a variety of insects, birds, reptiles, amphibians, and mammals.

By restoring native plants to your landscape and linking to other natural areas nearby, you will increase the native habitat size. This is a vital step since some animals need a considerable range in which to live and reproduce. For example, the U.S. Forest Service estimates the average size of a red fox range is about 18 miles and that of an eastern screech owl is about 10 miles.

Good wildlife habitat contains sufficient food and water to support wildlife adults and their young; adequate nesting spots; and places to escape predators. By creating specific habitats for pollinating insects, as well as birds, reptiles, and amphibians, gardeners can restore ecosystem stability.

Creating a Wildlife Habitat

By using the practices outlined below, gardeners can implement a number of specific measures to attract wildlife to their gardens and surrounding landscapes.

Eliminate Pesticide Use

Eliminate pesticide use to protect the pollinators and other beneficial insects as well as birds and other animals that prey upon pests. Some pesticides can be harmful to pets and people too, especially children. You can achieve natural pest control by creating a diverse habitat of native plants. For more on pest control, see chapter 8.

Reduce Lawn Size

Reduce lawn size and replace grass with ground covers, flowers, trees, shrubs, and even vegetables. Grass is neither a food source nor a sheltering cover for wildlife.

Conserve Natural Areas

Conserve natural areas that already exist on the property. If a greenway borders your property, connect with it. This enlarged habitat provides a greater range that many species rely on for hunting. An added benefit is that being surrounded by greenways increases property values.

Remove Invasive Non-Natives

Remove invasive non-native plants and restore native plants to bring wildlife to your landscape. For more on this subject, see chapter 4.

Did you know? Proximity to parks in urban areas has been shown to account for up to 15–20 percent of a property's value. (Crompton, "The Impact of Parks on Property Values")

Collect Rain

Collect rain in cisterns and rain barrels to have a ready supply of pure, nonchemically treated water for wildlife and to water your landscape during drought periods.

Mulch with Organic Material

Mulch beds with organic material preferably created from your backyard compost pile. Let some leaves lie after they have fallen to the ground. They provide foraging places for ground-dwelling birds and other wildlife.

Furnish Food Sources

Include native trees, shrubs, flowers, and vines in the landscape to provide the foliage, nectar, pollen, berries, seeds, and nuts that many species of wildlife require to survive and thrive. The National Wildlife Federation recommends woody plants that include such natives as sweetgum, sumac, blueberry, bayberry, several types of holly, viburnum, cotoneaster, and crab apple. Chapter 4 contains a list of trees and perennials that attract diverse wildlife (see table 4.1).

Include a Water Source

Wildlife, like humans, need a continual source of clean water. A birdbath, a water feature such as a pond (figure 10.1), or just simply a terra-cotta dish with water will attract birds, small mammals, amphibians, and butterflies. Keep the water clean and 1 to 1½ inches deep. But remember, a pool of stagnant water can breed mosquitoes. Change the water when it becomes cloudy and filled with debris and feathers. Sometimes it may need changing every day. Avoid using chemicals such as chlorine to clean the container; they may contaminate the water. Create cover around the edges of the water source by adding rocks, logs, and plant material for birds. This will give wildlife a refuge from predators.

Provide Protective Cover

A place to take shelter protects wildlife from bad weather and predators. Protective cover forms the foundation for nesting, sleeping, and feeding

Figure 10.1. Koi pond provides water for thirsty wildlife.

areas. It also provides safe corridors during migration. Wildlife will benefit from the following additions.

1. Brush piles made with fallen branches, Christmas trees, and plant clippings provide cover for rabbits, thrushes, towhees, and others. Dense shrubs also provide good shelter.

2. Standing dead trees not too close to the house make ideal homes for many species of insects, reptiles, and amphibians that hide in their bark. Some gardeners actually "plant" a dead snag to attract birds and mammals that nest in dead limbs and tree trunks. According to the U.S. Forest Service, there are 85 cavity-nesting bird species in North America.

3. Leaf litter provides cover for a variety of amphibians—frogs, salamanders, and toads—and offers foraging opportunities for southern birds such as towhees, sparrows, juncos, and doves that spend much of their time searching for food on the ground. Mammals such as squirrels, chipmunks, rabbits, and shrews rummage through the litter for nuts, leaves, roots, and bark.

4. Rock and stone piles supply places for chipmunks, skinks, toads, and salamanders to hide. Place a flat rock in a sunny place on which lizards and butterflies can bask.

Include Places to Raise Young

Every animal needs a safe place to raise its young. For birds it is often a tree or shrub, but it could also be a ground cover. For rabbits and mice, it's a brush pile. Snakes and salamanders lay their eggs under rocks or logs or in rotting wood, while frogs, newts, and dragonflies deposit their eggs in water. Cavity-nesting birds—such as the turkey vulture, barred owl, red-headed woodpecker, Carolina chickadee, and the eastern bluebird—raise their young in tree cavities. If there are no dead trees, nesting boxes will do.

Design Habitat for Specific Wildlife

One way to enrich your garden is to create plantings for waning wildlife that needs an ecological boost. Honeybees and amphibians, in particular, are on the decline. You can do your part to increase their numbers by providing sanctuaries for them.

Pollinator Garden

Through pollination, an essential process for the planet's ecological survival, flowers are fertilized when pollen grains from the male *anther* land on the female *stigma*, and the process produces seeds surrounded by fruit tissue. Although many trees, grasses, and flowers are wind-pollinated, most fruit and vegetable plants grown in American gardens rely primarily on insect pollinators. For example, honeybees alone pollinate a third of the nation's food supply. Without pollinators, the human race and all of earth's ecosystems would be in peril. Pollinators can be insects, birds, bats, and other animals; however, among animal pollinators, bees do the majority of the labor. There are four thousand species of native bees in North America, but their numbers are fast declining.

Honeybees Threatened

According to the U.S. Department of Agriculture's *Report on the National Stakeholders Conference on Honey Bee Health*, U.S. beekeepers reported losing 33 percent of their honeybee colonies each year due to a syndrome known as colony collapse disorder. Across the country, bees are abandoning their nests and the colony is literally collapsing.

A nationwide team of scientists is studying the problem and its causes, which include loss of habitat, pesticide use, bee pests such as the varroa mite, malnutrition, and pathogens. Gardeners can help restore honeybee populations by adopting and promoting the pollinator-friendly landscape practices outlined by University of Georgia bee expert Keith Delaplane in *Bee Conservation in the Southeast.*

Figure 10.2. Honeybee pollinating watermelon flower. Note the full pollen baskets on her legs.

Minimize Pesticide Use

Female honeybees, which are the worker bees, may fly 1–2 miles from their hives to collect pollen and nectar for their colonies. If flowers are sprayed with pesticides, bees and other pollinators may be adversely affected by the chemicals within this range. If you must use pesticides, switch to those that are targeted to specific pests and spray only when pollinators are not in your garden, such as at night or when flowers are not blooming.

Color Matters

Different-colored flowers attract different kinds of pollinators. Plan your garden to sport a wide variety of colorful nectar-producing blooms throughout the spring and summer. Bees and other pollinators see a wider spectrum of light rays than humans; many flowers have ultraviolet patterns that guide pollinators to the nectaries so that pollinators can visit more flowers and collect more nectar without wasting time getting oriented.

Go Native

Focus on plants native to your region and those that will attract many of your local pollinators.

Create a Big Target

Arrange a variety of pollinator-attracting plants in masses rather than as individual plants. This helps pollinators find flowers more easily.

Plant Nectar- and Pollen-Producing Plants for Prolonged Blooming

Grow an assembly of diverse and native plants that bloom continuously to build local bee populations. Delaplane's *Bee Conservation in the Southeast* lists trees, shrubs, and plants that provide successive blooming times to sustain bees in the garden. Examples include early bloomers like flowering dogwood, redbud, blueberry, and pine, followed by midseason blooming plants such as oak, holly, honeysuckle, coneflower, buckeye, and crimson clover. Among late bloomers are aster, goldenrod, and milkweed.

Use Flower Power to Attract Butterflies

Butterflies and moths, members of the order Lepidoptera, are second-string pollinators (figure 10.3). While some plants are pollinated exclusively by specific Lepidopterans, most flowers are pollinated by bees (or wind). A long list of "other" pollinators includes flies and beetles, hummingbirds, and even bats. In addition to pollinating flowers, monarchs, swallowtails, and various other butterflies and moths bring an ethereal, transient beauty to your landscape. Attracting them is easy. Begin with native plants that supply nectar for adult butterflies or moths and serve as host plants for their larvae. You need both kinds of food for the butterfly or moth to complete its life cycle (figure 10.4). Beware of non-natives such as butterfly bush (*Bud-*

Figure 10.3. Fritillary butterfly pollinating a marigold.

Life Cycle of a Monarch Butterfly

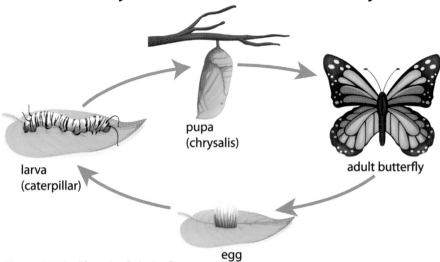

pupa
(chrysalis)

larva
(caterpillar)

adult butterfly

egg

Figure 10.4. The life cycle of a butterfly.

dleia species) that provide nectar to some butterflies but cannot serve as a larval host plant. Many native plants multitask as nectar sources for adult butterflies and as larval host plants. Among them are milkweeds (*Asclepias*), which include butterfly weed, common milkweed, and swamp milkweed. No serious butterfly gardener should be without them. They provide a continuous display of pink and orange flowers from June until September and attract many species of butterflies, including the monarch. Black-eyed Susans (*Rudbeckia hirta)* and coneflowers (*Echinacea* genus) perform both functions also. Dozens of butterfly species are attracted to their colorful flowers.

If spicebush is native to your region and you have space in your garden, plant it to attract the spicebush swallowtail that lays her eggs on the leaves. The caterpillar (figure 10.5) has "eyes" that are actually markings on the caterpillar's rear end. The markings mimic a tree snake to ward off potential bird predators.

Since moths are night pollinators, they are attracted to plants with pale or white flowers and strong fragrance, so the blossoms can be seen and smelled in moonlight. Native species such as evening primrose (*Oenothera biennis*), night-blooming jessamine (*Cestrum nocturnum*), and Ad-

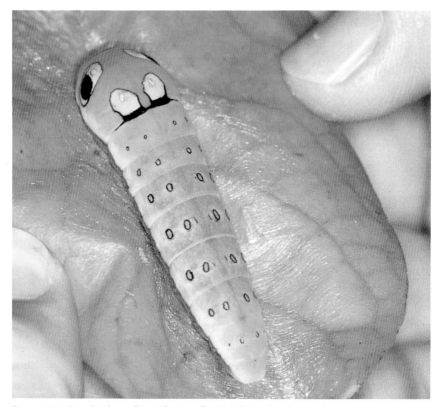

Figure 10.5. Spicebush swallowtail caterpillar (*Papilio troilus* Linnaeus).

am's needle (*Yucca filamentosa* L.) attract moths. Some moths, including the luna moth and the cecropia silk moth, do not feed as adults, but luna caterpillars feed on native trees such as sweet gum (*Liquidambar styraciflua*), persimmon (*Diospyros virginiana*), hickories (*Carya* spp.), and sumacs (*Rhus* spp.), and cecropia caterpillars eat leaves of wild cherries and plums (*Prunus* spp.), apples (*Malus* spp.), dogwood (*Cornus florida*), and willows (*Salix* spp.).

For information on the best regional native plants to attract butterflies and moths, visit the National Wildlife Federation website at www.nwf.org. Montana State University hosts a Butterflies and Moths of North America website that allows the public to put in their state and county and find out what butterflies and moths are native to their area and the plants that support them. Table 10.1 is a general list of southeastern plants that attract pollinators.

Table 10.1. Southeastern plants that attract pollinators

Plant	Attracted pollinators	Requirements & cautions
Goldenrods (*Solidago* spp.)	Butterfly Bee	Full sun; this is not an allergy-causing flower; its pollen is transferred by insects and is not carried on the wind
Sedum (*Sedum* spp.)	Butterfly Bee	Full sun/partial shade; choose a variety native to your region: eastern/central U.S.: Woodland stonecrop (*Sedum ternatum*)
Milkweeds (*Asclepias*)	Butterfly	Full sun
Sunflowers (*Helianthus* spp.)	Butterfly Bee	Full sun; beware that the following varieties can be invasive: Common sunflower (*Helianthus annuus*); Texas blueweed (*Helianthus ciliaris*)
Berry bushes: blueberry, huckleberry (*Vaccinium* spp.)	Butterfly Bee	Full sun/partial shade
Salvias (*Salvia* spp.)	Butterfly Bee Hummingbird	Full sun; beware that the following varieties are invasive: Mediterranean sage (*Salvia aethiopis*); introduced sage (*Salvia pratensis*); European sage (*Salvia sclarea*)
Anise hyssop/giant hyssop (*Agastache* spp.)	Butterfly Bee Hummingbird	Full sun; choose a variety native to your region: eastern/north central: purple and yellow giant hyssop
Red columbine (*Aquilegia canadensis*)	Bee Hummingbird	Full sun/partial shade
Beebalm/Oswego tea (*Monarda didyma*)	Butterfly Bee Hummingbird	Full sun
Blazing-star/gayfeather (*Liatris* spp.)	Butterfly Bee Hummingbird	Full sun/partial shade; good alternative to the invasive species purple loosestrife
Trumpet (coral) honeysuckle (*Lonicera sempervirens*)	Hummingbird	Full sun/partial shade
Purple coneflower (*Echinacea purpurea*)	Butterfly Bee	Full sun
Red buckeye (*Aesculus pavia*)	Butterfly Bee Hummingbird	Sun/shade
Zinnia (*Zinnia* spp.)	Butterfly Bee	Full sun
Cosmos (*Cosmos*)	Butterfly Bee	Full sun
Scarlet penstemon (*Keckiella* spp.)	Bee Hummingbird	Full sun

Source: The Pollinator Partnership™/North American Pollinator Protection Campaign, "Selecting Plants for Pollinators."

Figure 10.6. Plants that attract pollinators.
Left: butterfly weed; *above*: purple coneflower;
and *below*: autumn sedum.

Make Your Garden Bird-Friendly

What would a neighborhood be without birds and their songs? Pretty sorry and sad to both the eyes and ears! But more important, birds indicate the state of the environment because they are sensitive to habitat change. If bird numbers and species decline, something is amiss. Either the habitat is fragmented, destroyed, or polluted, or consists of mostly non-native species.

The U.S. Fish and Wildlife Service estimates that between 1,080 and 1,350 bird species can be found in the fifty states, Puerto Rico, and other U.S. territories. Many of these birds are migratory. Songbirds such as thrushes and warblers, shorebirds that include sandpipers and plovers, and waterfowl such as green-winged teal fit this description. Migratory stopover areas are essential links to their survival. From songbirds to shorebirds to waterfowl, migratory birds must have places to rest and fuel up during their travels. Interior wetlands, coastal wetlands, and riparian zones (the lush forest and shrub vegetation that grows along stream and riverbanks) are particularly important migratory bird staging habitats.

By following the preceding general recommendations for attracting wildlife, you will entice a greater variety of birds to your property. To increase avian activity in the yard, consider the following suggestions.

1. Vary the heights of vegetation to mimic natural landscape structure and to provide birds areas for nesting, perching, and shelter. Plant large and small trees, shrubs, herbaceous undergrowth, ground covers, and vines. Implement the tiered landscape approach even for meadows and wetlands, designing with plants of different heights. Avoid overclearing woodland or forest habitat. Leave plenty of undergrowth for nesting and for shelter from predators.

Did you know? Birds eat up to 98 percent of budworms and up to 40 percent of all nonoutbreak insect species in eastern forests. (Sterling, "How Birds Keep our World Safe")

2. Look for native plants that offer food sources year-round, including nectar and edible fruits, nuts, or seeds. Consult the local nature center or Audubon chapter to learn what native plants provide this extended buffet. Examples include cherry, crab apple, dogwood, hawthorn, holly, mountain ash, mulberry, peach, plum, serviceberry, and viburnum. Needle-leaved and broadleaved evergreen trees and shrubs provide winter protection as well as food. Expect these to attract blue jays, chickadees, nuthatches, and finches, to name a few.

3. Increase the number of clean, shallow-water sources including birdbaths, small pools, and ponds. Place the birdbath or water feature in a shaded area where there is plenty of cover nearby. Birds are drawn to running water so consider a recirculating fountain that also will help clean the water. Birds not only drink from these sources but also bathe in them to keep their feathers free of dirt, debris, and parasites.

4. Connect various planted and landscaped areas—from your front yard to backyard, and from your yard to your neighbors' yards—to create a bird corridor.

5. Plant in masses of several species rather than an individual plant here and there: it's more aesthetically pleasing and provides more value to wildlife.

6. Retain dead trees and snags where safety permits to provide foraging, nesting, and perching opportunities for birds and other wildlife.

7. Spread leaf litter under and in front of shrubs to provide a mulch cover for plants and a foraging area for ground-feeding birds. Similarly, stack brush into piles that provide areas of shelter and protection for wildlife.

8. Use natural borders rather than fencing. Native shrubs create a hedgerow beneficial to wildlife and are aesthetically pleasing and low-maintenance.

Use Bird Feeders to Supplement Natural Food Sources

Feeders can help migratory birds on their way south make the trip and help tide them over during periods of inclement weather. Birds will eat

Figure 10.7. Wildlife-friendly habitat.

a variety of foods, but certain species show a preference for particular foods. To avoid wasting seed, fill each feeder with a single type of seed. Sunflower seed is popular with the majority of seed-eating birds, including tufted titmice, evening grosbeaks, purple finches, and cardinals. Peanut butter, peanuts, and nutmeats attract blue jays, thrashers, chickadees, and small mammals. Suet feeds woodpeckers and other insectivorous birds. Hummingbird feeders filled with sugar water attract a horde of hummingbirds.

Cats Cause Catastrophes

Cats kill thousands of birds each day in North America. Outdoor family cats, feral cats, and abandoned cats can all take a toll on the bird population. Bells, declawing, and keeping the cats well fed don't work to protect birds

Did you know? America's cats, including housecats that venture outdoors and feral cats, kill between 1.3 billion and 4.0 billion birds per year. (Loss, Will, and Marra, "The Impact of Free-Ranging Domestic Cats")

and other wildlife. Keeping the cat inside is the best solution. The cat will also be safe from mishaps with predators and vehicles.

Attracting Frogs and Toads

According to the 2004 Global Amphibian Assessment, one-third of frogs, toads, and salamanders are threatened with extinction. Habitat loss and destruction are among the reasons for this decline. Amphibians are widely regarded as "canaries in the coal mine" since their highly permeable skin is more immediately sensitive to changes in the environment, including changes to freshwater and air quality. Not only are their numbers declining but a higher rate of deformity has also been documented, which is attributed to environmental factors. Amphibians need our help and protection, and gardeners can respond by creating a pond or toad abode and by protecting existing amphibian habitat.

Become a Citizen Scientist

From retirees to home-schooled kids, people of all ages and abilities can contribute to the advancement of science, and it's a rewarding and fun adventure. By helping supply the tens of thousands of data points required to understand sweeping ecological changes, citizen scientists can partner with the limited number of scientists collecting such data and help expand their research efforts. Anyone with the time and inclination can submit data that helps scientists determine many important parameters such as bird migratory patterns and population trends, the influence of non-native species on native species, and the effect of climate change on plants and animals. A number of citizen scientist partnerships are listed in the following sections. Many more are available for you to participate in, depending on your interests and inclinations and the time you want to devote to collecting data.

Passion for Birds

Each day, bird-watchers throughout the world report their observations to the Cornell Laboratory of Ornithology and contribute to the world's most dynamic and powerful source of information on birds. Here are several ways you can get involved.

The Great Backyard Bird Count

Launched in 1998 by the Cornell Lab of Ornithology and National Audubon Society, the Great Backyard Bird Count was the first online citizen-science project to collect data on wild birds and to display results in near real-time. Since then, more than one hundred thousand people of all ages and walks of life have joined the four-day count each February to create an annual snapshot of the distribution and abundance of birds. You can count from any location, anywhere in the world! (See http://gbbc.birdcount.org/about/.)

Project FeederWatch

Each year, approximately fifteen thousand people across the nation count birds at their feeders, contributing valuable data to scientists who monitor changes in the distribution and abundance of birds. This program has enabled scientists to study the influence of non-native species on native bird communities, examine the association between birds and habitats, and track unpredictable movements in winter bird populations. This project is also important to see how a warming climate may change bird species ranges (see www.birds.cornell.edu/pfw/).

Celebrate Urban Birds

The project assesses the value of green spaces for birds, ranging in size from a potted plant to half a basketball court (see www.birds.cornell.edu/celebration).

Christmas Bird Count

Begun in 1900, the longest-running citizen science survey in the world provides critical data on population trends. Before this time, people engaged in a holiday tradition known as the Christmas "Side Hunt": a hunting competition won by bringing in the biggest pile of dead feathered (and furred) quarry. Conservation was new at the turn of the twentieth century, and observers and scientists were becoming concerned about declining bird populations. On Christmas Day 1900, ornithologist Frank Chapman, an officer in the budding Audubon Society, proposed a new holiday tradition—a "Christmas Bird Census"—that would count birds during the holidays rather than hunt them (see http://birds.audubon.org/christmas-bird-count).

BumbleBeeWatch

The Xerces Society and other partners inaugurated this citizen science project to track and conserve North America's bumblebees. Anyone can upload digital photos of bumblebees that are then verified by experts to help researchers determine the status and conservation needs of bumblebees. It is a super opportunity for citizens to learn about bumblebees and for scientists to continue ongoing research needed to expand their numbers (see www.BumbleBeeWatch.org).

FrogWatch USA

Volunteers learn to identify native frog and toad species by their calls during the breeding season and how to report their findings accurately. By mastering these skills, volunteers gain increased experience and control over asking and answering scientific questions, which, in turn, augments science literacy, facilitates conservation action and stewardship, and increases knowledge of amphibians. FrogWatch USA Chapters are hosted and managed by zoos, aquariums, and like-minded organizations (see www.aza.org/frogwatch/).

Project BudBurst

This national field campaign is designed to engage the public in the collection of important ecological data based on the timing of leafing, flowering,

Figure 10.8. Frogs and toads are disappearing at an alarming rate. Help scientists identify native species in your area.

and fruiting of plants. This is especially important in monitoring how climate change is affecting plants and their range and distribution (see www.budburst.org/).

Create a Certified Wildlife Habitat

The National Wildlife Federation recognizes people who garden to create wildlife sanctuaries with a certification program. It's simple. When you demonstrate you have food, water, cover, and places for wildlife to raise their young, your landscape qualifies as a Certified Wildlife Habitat. You then have the privilege of displaying their official sign in your yard (figure 10.9) (see www.nwf.org/habitats).

Figure 10.9. Certify your landscape as a wildlife habitat with the National Wildlife Federation.

Make Places for People, Too

Don't forget to add pathways, benches, decks, and patios for humans to observe wildlife in their home landscapes. Sit, stroll, and pause to observe the unveiling of nature everywhere. Why not stage a bird-watching party on your deck or patio? Create an inventory of birds, animals, trees, and wildflowers in your yard. Offer the list to your homeowners association if you have one.

Making a garden wildlife-friendly not only gives gardeners the satisfaction of doing their part to protect the earth but also gives them a ringside seat on the natural world. Watching birds forage for seeds and bugs, observing bees and butterflies flit from flower to flower as they pollinate and sip nectar, listening to birds call one another across the woods, watching squirrels scamper in every direction or try a new tactic to eat from the bird feeder, and hearing insects' buzzing—all these offer a relaxing way to unplug our information-overloaded psyches and restore our equilibrium.

Acknowledgments

This book would not have happened without my dear husband's support over the many years it took to write the manuscript and find a publisher. Ivan's skill as a photographer produced many quality photos in this book, and his attention to detail in preparing the photos, illustrations, tables, and manuscript for publication saved me months of time. Thank you is woefully inadequate for the man who has given me so much and with whom I have shared the last forty years.

Judy Purdy, my good friend, the former editor of the University of Georgia research magazine and an ecologist, spent countless hours, days, and nights editing and rewriting sections of the book to make it uplifting and scientifically accurate. I am deeply indebted to her.

Scott Angle, the dean of the University of Georgia College of Agriculture and Environmental Sciences, allowed me to pursue this project, which took nearly eight years from conception to completion. His leadership of our college has allowed it to become one of the premiere colleges of agriculture in the nation and the world. I am deeply honored to be among the faculty.

My colleagues at the University of Georgia patiently reviewed chapters pertaining to their expertise and provided some excellent photos, giving me confidence that the book would be scientifically sound and well-illustrated. Allan Armitage, a world-class horticulturist, took a chance on this project from the onset and wrote the foreword. Gary Wade, Extension horticulturist, reviewed the first five chapters; Dr. Clint Waltz, turfgrass specialist, reviewed and improved chapter 6; and Dr. Frank Henning, horticulturist and water conservation and storm-water management expert, supplied information for chapter 7. Dr. Kris Braman, an entomologist and the associate dean for the University of Georgia Griffin Campus, and Elizabeth Little, a pathologist, reviewed chapter 8. Dr. David Knauft, professor of horticulture and faculty leader for the Organic Agriculture Certificate program, evaluated chapter 9; and Jamie Hawk, executive director of the Atlanta Audubon, reviewed chapter 10. And Dr. Dayton Wilde, a geneticist who works with native plants, reviewed the entire manuscript.

The College's talented communications staff provided editing, illustrations, and additional photos for the book. Amanda Swennes, former editor at the College, slogged through the whole manuscript and offered very helpful suggestions. Jay Bauer created most of the illustrations, helping readers understand concepts such as watersheds and land-use plans. Carol Williamson's lovely drawings will encourage readers to pause and learn the information. And my son Neil, industrial designer extraordinaire, pitched in to refine images and draw several illustrations. I thank the University Press of Florida for seeing the importance of providing southeastern gardeners with sustainable practices. Meredith Morris-Babb and Marthe Walters have provided expert guidance in helping me shape the manuscript. Susan Murray did a superb editing job. And my appreciation goes to Robyn Taylor, who made this book so visually appealing.

Finally, I am forever grateful to this nation's land-grant universities and their many experts, too numerous to name, who have furnished the wealth of information and photos I used for this book. From the University of California and the University of Minnesota to North Carolina State and the University of Florida, so many experts willingly offered their help. My heartfelt thank you to all of you!

References

Alliance for Community Trees. "Benefits of Trees and Urban Forests: A Research List." August 2011. www.ACTrees.org.

Alliance for Water Efficiency. "Promoting the Efficient Use of Water." 2010. www.allianceforwaterefficiency.org/Drip_and_Micro-Spray_Irrigation_Introduction.aspx.

Alvarado, Katie Hoover. Coastal Georgia NEMO PowerPoint presentation. 2007 Association of Natural Resource Extension Progessionals (ANREP) Conference, August 21, 2007, Dahlonega, Ga.

American Chestnut Foundation. Ashville, N.C. www.acf.org/.

American Forestry Association. *Tree Facts: Growing Greener Cities*. Booklet. 1992.

Arbor Day Foundation. "Benefits of Trees: The Value of Trees to a Community." www.arborday.org/trees/benefits.cfm.

Armitage, Allan M. *Armitage's Native Plants for North American Gardens*. Portland, Ore.: Timber, 2006.

Ball, George. "Down-to-Earth Plan Will Put Green in Your Wallet." *Atlanta Journal-Constitution*, December 19, 2008.

Barr Engineering Company. "Burnsville Rainwater Gardens—A Nationally Significant Demonstration Project." http://northlandnemo.org/images/BurnsvilleRaingardens.pdf.

Barringer, Felicity. "Lawn Mowers on the Pollution Hit List." *New York Times*, April 24, 2006.

Bremer, Dale. "Carbon Sequestration in Turfgrass: An Eco-Friendly Benefit of Your Lawn." *Turfnews*, October 2007.

Center for Invasive Species and Ecosystem Health. University of Georgia. www.bugwood.org.

Cerling, Thure E., Jonathan G. Wynn, Samuel A. Andanje, Michael I. Bird,

David Kimutai Korir, Naomi E. Levin, William Macel, Anthony N. Macharial, Jay Quade, and Christopher H. Remien. "Woody Cover and Hominin Environments in the Past 6 Million Years." *Nature*, August 4, 2011, 51–56.

Chivian, Eric, and Aaron Bernstein, eds. *Sustaining Life: How Human Health Depends on Biodiversity*. New York: Oxford University Press, 2008.

Climate Change Resource Center. U.S. Department of Agriculture. Forest Service. www.fs.usda.gov/ccrc/.

Coder, Kim D. *Identified Benefits of Community Trees and Forests*. University of Georgia School of Forest Resources Extension Publication FOR 96–039. October 1996.

———. "Using Gray Water in the Landscape." University of Georgia College of Agricultural and Environmental Sciences. March 25, 2013. www.caes. uga.edu/topics/disasters/drought/home/graywater.html.

Crompton, John L. "The Impact of Parks on Property Values: A Review of Empirical Evidence." *Journal of Leisure Research* 33, no. 1 (2001): 1–31.

"Dandelion Removal." Grinning Planet. www.grinningplanet.com/2006/03-16/dandelion-removal-article.htm.

Delaplane, Keith S. *Bee Conservation in the Southeast*. University of Georgia College of Agricultural and Environmental Sciences Publication 1164. April 30, 2013.

Dietz, Michael E., and John C. Clausen. "Saturation to Improve Pollutant Retention in a Rain Garden." *Environmental Science and Technology* 40, no. 4 (February 15, 2006): 1335–40.

Dig It! The Secrets of Soil. Exhibit. July 18, 2008–January 10, 2010. Smithsonian National Museum of Natural History. http://forces.si.edu/soils/.

Dirr, Michael A. *Manual of Woody Landscape Plants*. Champaign, Ill.: Stipes, 1998.

"Don't Bag It™—Compost It!" Earth-Kind Landscaping, chap. 1, "The Decomposition Process." AgriLife Extension, Texas A&M University. February 2009. http://aggie-horticulture.tamu.edu/earthkind/landscape/dont-bag-it/.

Durham, Sharon. "Designing the Best Possible Conservation Buffers." *Agricultural Research Magazine* (U.S. Department of Agriculture), December 2003. www.ars.usda.gov/is/pr/2003/031201.htm.

Ellis, Barbara W., and Fern Marshall Bradley, eds. *The Organic Gardener's*

Handbook of Natural Insect and Disease Control. Emmaus, Pa.: Rodale, 1996.

"Environmental Benefits of a Healthy, Sustainable Lawn." Sustainable Urban Landscape Information Series. University of Minnesota. 2006. www.sustland.umn.edu/maint/benefits.htm.

Falcon-Lang, Howard J., John W. Nelson, Scott Elrick, Cindy V. Looy, Philip R. Ames, and William A. DiMichele. "Incised Channel Fills Containing Conifers Indicate That Seasonally Dry Vegetation Dominated Pennsylvanian Tropical Lowlands." *Geology* 37 (2009): 923–26.

Flanders, Aron A., William P. Kuvlesky Jr., Donald C. Ruthven III, Robert E. Zaiglin, Ralph L. Bingham, Timothy E. Fulbright, Fidel Hernández, and Leonard A. Brennan. "Effects of Invasive Exotic Grasses on South Texas Rangeland Breeding Birds." *American Ornithologists Union* 123, no. 1 (January 2006): 171. http://connection.ebscohost.com/c/articles/19713699/effects-invasive-exotic-grasses-south-texas-rangeland-breeding-birds.

"Florida-Friendly Landscape." Florida-Friendly Plant Database. www.florida-yards.org/fyplants/index.php.

Fourth Assessment Intergovernmental Panel on Climate Change, Climate Change 2007, Mitigation of Climate Change section, IPCC Secretariat, c/o WMO, 7bis, Avenue de la Paix, C.P.N. 2300, 1211 Geneva 2, Switzerland: 512. www.ipcc.ch/publications_and_data/ar4/syr/en/contents.html.

Georgia Urban Forest Council. *Shade: Healthy Trees, Healthy Cities, Healthy People.* Booklet. Decatur: Georgia Urban Forest Council, 2005.

Gilman, Edward F. *Dispelling Misperceptions about Trees.* University of Florida Extension Publication No. SSORH3. 2013.

Global Amphibian Assessment. "Amphibians in Dramatic Decline—Nearly One in Three Species Faces Extinction 2004 to 2014." NatureServe. www.natureserve.org/conservation-tools/projects/global-amphibian-assessment.

Glover, Tony, "CSI Southeast Plant Diagnostics." Alabama Cooperative Extension. PowerPoint presentation at IPM workshop for Master Gardeners, Lawrenceville, Ga., September 1, 2010.

"Going Native: Urban Landscaping for Wildlife with Native Plants." North Carolina Cooperative Extension. www.ncsu.edu/goingnative/howto/mapping/invexse/.

"Green Spaces 'Improve Health.'" BBC News. October 15, 2009. http://news.bbc.co.uk/2/hi/health/8307024.stm.

Grube, Arthur, David Donaldson, Timothy Kiely, and La Wu. "Pesticide Industry Sales and Usage 2006–2007 Market Estimates." U.S. Environmental Protection Agency, Office of Prevention, Pesticides and Toxic Substances, EPA-733-R-11-001. February 2011. www.epa.gov/pesticides/pestsales/07pestsales/market_estimates2007.pdf.

Hauck, Morris J. "Windbreaks—Their Use." PowerPoint. U.S. Department of Agriculture. Natural Resources Conservation Service. www.nrcs.usda.gov/Internet/FSE_PLANTMATERIALS/publications/txpmcot5584.pdf.

Hawkinson, Candice. "The Pollinators: Moths." Beneficials in the Garden. Extension Horticulture. Texas A & M University. http://aggie-horticulture.tamu.edu/galveston/beneficials/beneficial-65_pollinators-moths.htm.

Hippe, D. J., and J. W. Garrett. "The Spatial Distribution of Dissolved Pesticides in Surface Water of the Apalachicola–Chattahoochee–Flint River Basin in Relation to Land Use and Pesticide Runoff—Potential Ratings, May 1994." In *Proceedings of the 1997 Georgia Water Resources Conference*, edited by K. J. Hatcher. Athens: University of Georgia, 1997.

International Society of Arboriculture. "Benefits of Trees." 2011. www.treesaregood.com/treecare/resources/benefits_trees.pdf.

Ingham, Elaine R., Andrew R. Moldenke, and Clive A. Edwards. "Soil Biology." U.S. Department of Agriculture. Natural Resources Conservation Service. http://soils.usda.gov/sqi/concepts/soil_biology/biology.html.

Jenkins, Virginia Scott. *The Lawn: A History of an American Obsession*. Washington, D.C.: Smithsonian Institution Press, 1994.

Kafin, Ribert J., and Marcel Van Ooyen. "Rainwater Harvesting 101." GrowNYC. August 2008. www.grownyc.org/files/osg/RWH.how.to.pdf.

Kaplan, R., and S. Kaplan. *The Experience of Nature: A Psychological Perspective*. Cambridge, Mass.: Harvard University Press, 1989.

Kirkman, Katherine L., Claud L. Brown, and Donald J. Leopold. *Native Trees of the Southeast: An Identification Guide*. Portland, Ore.: Timber, 2013.

Klein, Alexandra-Maria, Bernard E. Vaissière, James H. Cane, Ingolf Steffan-Dewenter, Saul A. Cunningham, Claire Kremen, and Teja Tscharntke. "Importance of Pollinators in Changing Landscapes for World Crops." *Proceedings of the Royal Society* 274, no. 1608 (February 2007): 303–13.

Klingeman W. E., S. K. Braman, and G. D. Buntin. "Azalea Growth in Response to Azalea Lace Bug (Heteroptera: Tingidae) Feeding." *Journal of Economic Entomology* 94, no. 1 (February 2001): 129–37.

Klingeman W. E., G. D. Buntin, and S. K. Braman. "Using Aesthetic Assessments of Azalea Lace Bug (Heteroptera: Tingidae) Feeding Injury to Provide Thresholds for Pest Management Decisions." *Journal of Economic Entomology* 94, no. 5 (2001): 1187–92.

Kowalchik, Claire, and William Hylton. *Rodale's Encyclopedia of Herbs*. Emmaus, Pa.: Rodale, 1987.

Kuo, Frances E., and William C. Sullivan. "Environment and Crime in the Inner City." *Environment and Behavior* 33, no. 3 (May 2001): 343–67.

Leslie, Anne R. *Handbook of Integrated Pest Management for Turf and Ornamentals*. Boca Raton, Fla.: CRC, 1994.

Little, Elizabeth. Homeowner and IPM educator, University of Georgia. Personal communication with the author. September 29, 2010.

———. "Sustainable Management of Common Garden Diseases." Homeowner Integrated Pest Management Workshop, Advanced Master Gardener Training, September 2010, Lawrenceville, Ga.

Loss, Scott R., Tom Will, and Peter P. Marra. "The Impact of Free-Ranging Domestic Cats on Wildlife of the United States." *Nature Communications* 1396. www.nature.com/ncomms/journal/v4/n1/abs/ncomms2380.html.

Maas, Jolanda, Robert A. Verheij, Sjerp de Vries, Peter Spreeuwenberg, Francois G. Schellevis, and Peter P. Groenewegen. "Morbidity Is Related to a Green Living Environment." *Journal of Epidemiology and Community Health* 63, no. 12 (October 15, 2009). http://jech.bmj.com/content/early/2009/10/15/jech.2008.079038.

Maclean, Ilya M. D., and Robert J. Wilson. "Recent Ecological Responses to Climate Change Support Predictions of High Extinction Risk." *Proceedings of the National Academy of Sciences* (2011). DOI: 10.1073/pnas.1017352108.

Mader, Eric, Matthew Shepherd, Vaughn Mace, Scott Hoffman Black, and Gretchen LeBuhn. *Attracting Native Pollinators: The Xerces Society Guide*. North Adams, Mass.: Storey, 2011.

Mann, Charles C. "Where Food Begins, Our Good Earth." *National Geographic Magazine*, September 2008, 80.

Martin, Jane C., Alyn Eickholt, and Joanne Dole. "Natural Organic Lawn Care for Ohio." Ohio State University Extension Fact Sheet 2001. http://ohioline.osu.edu/hyg-fact/4000/4031.html.

McPherson, E. G. "Atmospheric Carbon Dioxide Reduction by Sacramento's Urban Forest." *Journal of Arboriculture* 24, no. 4 (1998): 215–23.

McPherson, E. G., and Rowan A. Rowntree. "Energy Conservation of Potential of Urban Tree Planting." *Journal of Arboriculture* 19, no. 6 (November 1993): 321–31.

McPherson, E. G., and J. R. Simpson. "Shade Trees as a Demand-Side Resource." *Home Energy Magazine* 12, no. 2 (March/April 1995). www.homeenergy.org/show/article/id/1115.

Meerow, A. W., and R. J. Black. *Enviroscaping to Conserve Energy: Determining Shade Patterns for South Florida*. University of Florida Extension Publication No. EES48. 2008.

Milesi, C., S. W. Running, C. D. Elvidge, J. B. Dietz, B. T. Tuttle, and R. R. Nemani. "Mapping and Modeling the Biogeochemical Cycling of Turf Grasses in the United States." *Environmental Management* 36, no. 3 (2005): 426–38.

Miller, Tyler G., and David Brewer. *Living in the Environment*. Belmont, Calif.: Wadsworth/Thomson Learning, 2002.

National Audubon Society. "Welcome Birds and Butterflies . . . and Toads and Dragonflies . . . and . . ." Audubon at Home. 2003. http://web4.audubon.org/bird/at_home/wildlife.html.

———. "What Is a Healthy Yard?" Audubon at Home. http://web4.audubon.org/bird/at_home/Healthy_Yard.html.

National Oceanic and Atmospheric Administration. "Leatherback Turtle (Dermochelys coriacea)." www.nmfs.noaa.gov/pr/species/turtles/leatherback.htm.

———. "Toward a Climate-Smart Nation." Fact Sheet. 2013. www.noaa.gov/factsheets/new%20version/TowardAClimateSmartNation_Final-Links_2013.pdf.

National Pesticide Information Center. "Fungicides." Topic fact sheet. Oregon State University and U.S. Environmental Protection Agency. http://npic.orst.edu/ingred/ptype/fungicide.html.

———. "Pesticides and the Environment." http://npic.orst.edu/envir/index.html.

———. "Plant-Pesticide Interaction." Oregon State University and U.S. Environmental Protection Agency. http://npic.orst.edu/envir/plantint.html.

———. "Pyrethrins and Pyrethroids." Fact sheets. Oregon State University and U.S. Environmental Protection Agency. http://npic.orst.edu/factsheets/pyrethrins.pdf.

———. "Signal Words." Topic fact sheet. Oregon State University and U.S. Environmental Protection Agency. www.npic.orst.edu/factsheets/signal words.html.

National Research Council of the National Academies. *The Status of Pollinators in North America*. Washington D.C.: National Academies Press, 2007.

National Turfgrass Association. www.ntep.org/pdf/turfinitiative.pdf.

Native Plant Database. Lady Bird Johnson Wildlife Conservation Center. www.wildflower.org/explore/.

National Wildlife Federation. "Simple Tips for Attracting Birds, Butterflies and Other Wildlife—5 Ways to Enjoy Nature in Your Own Backyard." www.nwf.org/News-and-Magazines/National-Wildlife/Gardening/Archives/2010/Five-Ways-to-Enjoy-Nature-in-Your-Own-Backyard.aspx.

Neff, Roni. *Introduction to the U.S. Food System: Public Health, Environment and Equity*. New York: Wiley and Sons, 2015.

Niemiera, Alex X. *Conserving Energy with Landscaping*. Virginia Cooperative Extension. Virginia Polytechnic Institute and State University. Publication No. 426–712. 2009.

Nowak, David J., Daniel E. Crane, and Jack C. Stevens. "Air Pollution Removal by Urban Trees and Shrubs in the United States. *Urban Forestry and Urban Greening* 4 (2006): 115–23.

Nowak, David J., Jack C. Stevens, Susan M. Sisinni, and Christopher J. Luley. "Effects of Urban Tree Management and Species Selection on Atmospheric Carbon Dioxide." *Journal of Arboriculture* 28, no. 3 (May 2002): 113–22.

Pears, Pauline, ed. *Rodale's Illustrated Encyclopedia of Organic Gardening*. London: DK, 2005.

———. *Rodale's Illustrated Encyclopedia, Organic Gardening: The Complete Guide to Natural and Chemical-Free Gardening*. New York: DK, 2002.

"Pest Control." Wikipedia. http://en.wikipedia.org/wiki/Pest_control.

Pickering, John. Founder of Discover Life, University of Georgia. E-mail with author. June 8, 2011.

Pirog, R., T. Van Pelt, K. Enshayan, and E. Cook. *Food, Fuel, and Freeways: An Iowa Perspective on How Far Food Travels, Fuel Usage and Greenhouse Gas Emissions*. Ames, Iowa: Leopold Center for Sustainable Agriculture, 2001. http://ngfn.org/resources/ngfn-database/knowledge/food_mil.pdf.

Planet Natural for Earth Friendly Products for Home, Lawn and Garden. www.planetnatural.com/site/monterey-garden-insect.html.

Pollan, Michael. "Farmer in Chief." *New York Times Magazine*, October 12, 2008, 62–71, 92.

———. *The Omnivore's Dilemma*. New York: Penguin, 2006.

The Pollinator Partnership™/North American Pollinator Protection Campaign. "Selecting Plants for Pollinators: A Regional Guide for Farmers, Land Managers, and Gardeners in the Southeastern Mixed Forest Province." http://pollinator.org/PDFs/Guides/SoutheastMixedForestrx5FINAL.pdf.

Powell, Alvin. "'Settle Down,' Warns E. O. Wilson." *Harvard Gazette*, September 24, 2010.

Pugliese, Paul. "Turfgrass IPM Strategies." PowerPoint presentation at University of Georgia workshop. Gwinnett County, September 8, 2010.

Qian, Y., and R. F. Follett. "Assessing Soil Carbon Sequestration in Turfgrass Systems Using Long-Term Soil Testing Data." *Agronomy Journal* 94 (2002): 930–35.

Qian, Yaling, Ronald F. Follett, and John M. Kimble. "Soil Carbon Sequestration & Greenhouse Gas Mitigation: Soil Organic Carbon Input from Urban Turfgrasses." *Soil Science Society American Journal* 74 (2010): 366–71.

Raven, Peter H. "Plants in Peril: What Should We Do?" Keynote address presented at XVI International Botanical Congress, St. Louis, Mo., August 1, 1999.

Relf, Diane. *Conserving Energy with Landscaping*. Virginia Cooperative Extension, Virginia Polytechnic Institute and State University. May 1, 2009.

Richter, Amanda. "Fertilizer: Knowing What's in the Bag." *Irrigation and Green Industry*, March 2008, 30–34.

———. "Harvesting Rainwater." *Irrigation and Green Industry*, March 2008, 12–18.

Robins, Sandy. "Gimme Shelter." *Backyard Birding*, vol. 1, pp. 94–103.

Samuelson, Lisa. "Trees of Alabama and the Southeast." Auburn University, School of Forestry and Wildlife Sciences. 2012. www.auburn.edu/academic/forestry_wildlife/dendrology/dendrology/.

Sauer, J. R., J. E. Hines, and J. Fallon. "The North American Breeding Bird Survey: Results and Analysis, 1966–2004." Version 2005.2. Laurel, Md.: USGA Patuxent Wildlife Research Center, 2005.

Scherr, Sara J., and Sajal Sthapit. "Farming and Land Use to Cool the Planet." Chapter 3 of *State of the World: Into a Warming World*. Washington, D.C.: World Watch Institute, 2009.

Schmidt, R. C., E. F. Hoener, E. M. Milner, and C. A. Morehouse, eds. *Natural and Artificial Playing Fields: Characteristics and Safety Features*. Ann Arbor, Mich.: American Society for Testing and Materials—Significant Tests of Petroleum Products (ASTM STP), June 1990.

Schueler, Tom. Center for Watershed Protection. 1992. www.cwp.org/.

Schwarz, Mary, and Jean Bonhotal. *Composting at Home—The Green and the Brown Alternative*. Ithaca, N.Y.: Cornell Waste Management Institute, Cornell University, 2011. http://cwmi.css.cornell.edu/compostingathome.pdf.

Seymour, Rose Mary. "Reclaim Your Rain: Rain Gardens for Home Landscapes." Clean Water Atlanta. 2010. www.cleanwateratlanta.org/environmentaleducation/reclaim.htm.

Shapiro, Howard-Yana, and John Harrison. *Gardening for the Future of the Earth*. New York: Bantam, 2000.

Shrewsbury, P. M., and S. R. Leather. *Using Biodiversity for Pest Suppression in Urban Landscapes*. 2012. Wiley Online Library.

Singh, Mamta H. "Soil Organic Carbon Pools in Turfgrass Systems in Ohio." Ph.D. diss., Ohio State University, 2007.

Slusher, John. P., and Doug Wallace. *Planning Tree Windbreaks in Missouri*. University of Missouri Extension Bulletin No. G5900. Revised 1997.

Snedeker, Suzanne M. "Breast Cancer Environmental Risk Factors in New York State, Pesticides and Breast Cancer Risk, An Evaluation of DDT and DDE." Fact Sheet #2. Cornell University Program on Breast Cancer and Environmental Risk Factors in New York State. Revised April 2001.

Snyder, S. A. "*Canis lupus*, Gray Wolf." Index of Species Information. U.S. Department of Agriculture. Forest Service. 1991. www.fs.fed.us/database/feis/animals/mammal/calu/all.html.

Soil Science Society of America. *Soils Matter: Get the Scoop!* August 29, 2013. https://soilsmatter.wordpress.com/2013/08/29/soil-formation/.

Southeast Exotic Pest Plant Council. www.se-eppc.org/.

Stangel, Peter. "Avoid Cat-astrophes." *Backyard Birding*, vol. 1, p. 49.

Sterling, John. "How Birds Keep Our World Safe from the Plagues of Insects." Smithsonian Migratory Bird Center. January 1, 1995. http://nationalzoo.si.edu/scbi/migratorybirds/fact_sheets/?id=2.

Sullivan, Janet. "*Megascops asio*, eastern screech-owl." Index of Species Information, U.S. Department of Agriculture. Forest Service. 1995. www.fs.fed.us/database/feis/animals/bird/meas/all.html.

Tallamy, Douglas W. *Bringing Nature Home: How Native Plants Sustain Wildlife in Our Gardens*. Portland, Ore.: Timber, 2007.

Taylor, Andrea Faber, Frances E. Kuo, and William C. Sullivan. "Coping with ADD: The Surprising Connection to Green Play Settings." *Environment and Behavior* 33 (January 2001): 54–77.

Taylor, Cory, Tim Davis, and Frank Henning. "Advanced Concepts in WaterSmart Landscape Design." Webinar. 2008 Advanced Master Gardener Training. August 19, September 16, October 14, 2010.

Tesky, Julie L. "*Vulpes vulpes*, red fox." Index of Species Information. U.S. Department of Agriculture. Forest Service. 1995. www.fs.fed.us/database/feis/animals/mammal/vuvu/all.html.

Thomas, Paul, and Gary Wade. "Mulching Helps Plants Retain Valuable Moisture." University of Georgia College of Agricultural and Environmental Sciences Cooperative Extension. www.caes.uga.edu/topics/disasters/drought/home/mulching.html.

"Tri-State Water Wars." Southern Environmental Law Center. www.southern environment.org/cases/tri_state_water_wars_al_ga_fl/.

Union of Concerned Scientists. "The Climate-Friendly Gardener: A Guide to Combating Global Warming from the Ground Up." April 2010. www.ucsusa.org/sites/default/files/legacy/assets/documents/food_and_agriculture/climate-friendly-gardener.pdf.

United Nations. *Millennium Ecosystem Assessment*. 2005. www.millennium assessment.org/en/About.html.

———. Department of Economic and Social Affairs. Population Division. "Population Distribution across the Continents 1950–2100." 2013. www.geohive.com/earth/his_proj_continent.aspx.

University of Georgia Extension. "On-Site Beneficial Use of Scrap Wallboard," Special Bulletin B1223. www.extension.uga.edu/publications/detail.cfm?number=B1223.

U.S. Census Bureau. "Population Change in Metropolitan and Micropolitan Statistical Areas: 1990–2003." September 2005. www.census.gov/prod/2005pubs/p25-1134.pdf.

U.S. Department of Agriculture. Forest Service. "Cavity-Nesting Birds of North American Forests." November 1997. www.na.fs.fed.us/Spfo/pubs/wildlife/nesting_birds/index.htm.

———. Forest Service. Climate Change Resource Center. www.fs.usda.gov/ccrc/.

———. Forest Service. "Native Gardening." www.fs.fed.us/wildflowers/Native_ Plant_Materials/Native_Gardening/index.shtml.

———. Forest Service. "Plant Pollination Strategies." www.fs.fed.us/wildflowers/ pollinators/.

———. Forest Service. "Restoring a Disappearing Ecosystem: The Longleaf Pine Savanna." May 2013. www.fs.fed.us/pnw/sciencef/scifi152.pdf.

———. Forest Service. "Tree List." www.fs.fed.us/database/feis/plants/tree/ index.html.

———. National Invasive Species Information Center. "Dutch Elm Disease." www.invasivespeciesinfo.gov/microbes/dutchelm.shtml.

———. Natural Resources Conservation Service. "History of NRCS." www. nrcs.usda.gov/wps/portal/nrcs/main/national/about/history/.

———. Natural Resources Conservation Service. Plants Database. www. plants.usda.gov.

———. Natural Resources Conservation Service. Plants Database. "*Andropogon gerardii.*" http://plants.usda.gov/core/profile?symbol=ANGE.

———. National Resources Conservation Service. Plants Database. "*Cestrum nocturnum* L., night jessamine." http://plants.usda.gov/core/ profile?symbol=CENO.

———. Natural Resources Conservation Service. Plants Database. "*Oenothera biennis* L., common evening primrose." http://plants.usda.gov/core/ profile?symbol=OEBI.

———. Natural Resources Conservation Service. Plants Database. "*Yucca flaccida* Haw., weak-leaf yucca." http://plants.usda.gov/core/ profile?symbol=YUFL2.

———. Natural Resources Conservation Service. "Tree Planting" (Backyard Conservation Tip Sheet.) April 1998. www.nrcs.usda.gov/Internet/FSE_ DOCUMENTS/stelprdb1186060.pdf.

———. "Organic Agriculture." www.usda.gov/wps/portal/usda/usdahome?co ntentidonly=true&contentid=organic-agriculture.html.

———. *Report on the National Stakeholders Conference on Honey Bee Health.* Alexandria, Virginia, October 15–17, 2012.

———. Southern Region Forest Service. *Benefits of Urban Trees. Urban and Community Forestry: Improving Our Quality of Life.* Forestry Report No. R8–FR 71. September 2003.

U.S. Department of Interior. Fish and Wildlife Service. Southeast Region.

Carolina National Wildlife Refuge Comprehensive Conservation Plan. August 2010.

U.S. Environmental Protection Agency. "Beneficial Landscaping: Environmentally-Friendly Landscaping." Green Communities. www.epa.gov/greenkit/landscap.htm.

———. "Bird Conservation Overview." Water: Wetlands. http://water.epa.gov/type/wetlands/birds-index.cfm.

———. "Conserving Water." www.epa.gov/greenhomes/ConserveWater.htm.

———. "Global Anthropogenic Non-CO_2 Greenhouse Gas Emissions: 1990–2020." http://nepis.epa.gov/Adobe/PDF/2000ZL5G.PDF.

———. "Greenscaping: The Easy Way to a Greener, Healthier Yard." June 2006. www.epa.gov/osw/conserve/tools/greenscapes/owners.htm.

———. "Healthy Lawn, Healthy Environment—Caring for Your Lawn in an Environmentally Friendly Way." U.S. Environmental Protection Agency Publication No. 735-K-04-001. September 2004. www.epa.gov/oppfead1/Publications/lawncare.pdf.

———. "Heat Island Impacts." www.epa.gov/heatislands/impacts/index.htm.

———. "Improving Air Quality in Your Community, Outdoor Air—Transportation: Lawn Equipment—Additional Information." www.lincolntown.org/DocumentCenter/View/6607.

———. "Lawn and Garden (Small Gasoline) Equipment." Nonroad Engines, Equipment and Vehicles. www.epa.gov/otaq/smallsi.htm.

———. "Managing Nonpoint Source Pollution from Households." http://water.epa.gov/polwaste/nps/outreach/point10.cfm.

———. "Municipal Solid Waste Generation, Recycling, and Disposal in the United States: Facts and Figures for 2012." www.epa.gov/osw/nonhaz/municipal/msw99.htm.

———. "Preliminary Risk Assessment for Creosote." Pesticides: Topical & Chemical Fact Sheets. August 2007. www.epa.gov/pesticides/factsheets/chemicals/creosote_prelim_risk_assess.htm.

———. "Water Sense." www.epa.gov/WaterSense/pubs/indoor.html.

U.S. Fish and Wildlife Service. "Endangered Species." www.fws.gov/endangered/.

———. "Frequently Asked Questions about Invasive Species." www.fws.gov/invasives/faq.html#q7.

———. "Pollinators." www.fws.gov/pollinators/.

U.S. National Park Service. *Economic Impacts of Protecting Rivers, Trails, and*

Greenway Corridors. 4th ed. Rivers and Trails Conservation Assistance Program. Washington, D.C.: U.S. Department of Interior, 1995.

Varlamoff, Susan M., Wayne Gardener, and Robert R. Westerfield. *Homeowner Best Management Practices for Georgia Urban Landscapes—A Training Manual.* Athens: University of Georgia, 2000.

"Victory garden." Wikipedia. http://en.wikipedia.org/wiki/Victory_garden.

Wade, Gary L., James T. Midcap, Kim D. Coder, Gil Landry, Anthony W. Tyson, and Neal Weatherly. *Xeriscape: A Guide to Developing a Water-Wise Landscape.* Cooperative Extension. University of Georgia College of Agricultural and Environmental Sciences Bulletin No. 1073. Revised May 2007. www.caes.uga.edu/extension/whitfield/anr/documents/Xeriscape waterwise.pdf.

Wade, Gary, Elaine Nash, Ed McDowell, Brenda Beckham, and Sharlys Cusafulli. "Native Plants for Georgia. Part I: Trees, Shrubs and Woody Vines" (B 987). August 17, 2011. http://extension.uga.edu/publications/ detail.cfm?number=B987.

Walker, Cameron. "What's Causing Bird and Amphibian Decline?" *National Geographic News*, November 8, 2004. http://news.nationalgeographic. com/news/2004/11/1108_041108_birds_frogs.html.

Waltz, Clint. "Turfgrass." Chapter 14 of *Georgia Master Gardener Handbook,* edited by Marco T. Fonseca and Kristin L. Slagle. 7th ed. Athens: University of Georgia Cooperative Extension, 2011.

———. "Water Lawns Wisely." Bulletin 151. UGA Center for Urban Agriculture, University of Georgia College of Agriculture and Environmental Sciences. http://ugaurbanag.com/content/water-lawns-wisely.

Welsh, Douglas F., ed. "Humus—It's the Dirt!" Horticulture update. Extension Horticulture, Texas Agricultural Extension Service. Texas A&M University System. July/August 2001.

Westmiller, Robin. "Fertilizers: Organic vs. Chemical." *Irrigation and Green Industry*, February 18, 2010. www.igin.com/article-1300-fertilizers_ organic_vs_chemical.html.

Wilson, E. O. "The Little Things That Run the World (The Importance and Conservation of Invertebrates)." *Conservation Biology* 1, no. 4 (December 1987): 344–46.

"Woody Plants of the Southeastern U.S." http://bioimages.vanderbilt.edu/ metadata.htm?//se-trees/list/se-trees.

Illustration Credits

Unless otherwise noted, all photos are courtesy of the author.

Figure 1.3. Courtesy of the National Oceanic and Atmospheric Administration.

Figure 1.6. Courtesy of Barr Engineering Co. and the City of Burnsville, Minnesota.

Figure 1.8. Courtesy of United States Department of Agriculture (usda.gov).

Figure 1.9. Illustration by Jay Bauer, University of Georgia.

Figure 1.10. Illustration by Jay Bauer, University of Georgia.

Figure 2.4. Adapted from the Natural Resource Conservation Service.

Figure 2.7. Courtesy of USDA Natural Resources Conservation Service (http://soils.usda.gov/sqi/soil_quality/soil_biology/soil_food_web.html).

Figure 2.8. Photo by Paula Flynn, Iowa State University Extension.

Figure 2.9. Photo by Petr Kratochvil.

Figure 2.11. Photo by Robbie Honerkamp, licensed under the CC-BY-SA-3.0 (https://creativecommons.org/licenses/by-sa/3.0/us/).

Figure 2.13. Illustration by Jay Bauer, University of Georgia.

Figure 2.14. Photo by Sharon Dowdy, University of Georgia.

Figure 2.15. Photo by Ivan Varlamoff.

Figure 2.16. Photo by Clarity Jones, licensed under the CC BY 2.0 (http://creativecommons.org/licenses/by/2.0/).

Figure 3.2. Courtesy of U.S. Environmental Protection Agency.

Figure 3.3. Photo by Jessica McCorvey, Joseph W. Jones Ecological Research Center.

Figure 3.4. Courtesy of the Arbor Day Foundation.

Figure 3.6. Courtesy of University of Minnesota Sustainable Urban Landscape Information Series (http://www.extension.umn.edu/garden/landscaping/).

Figure 3.7. Courtesy of University of Minnesota Sustainable Urban Landscape Information Series (http://www.extension.umn.edu/garden/landscaping/).

Figure 3.8. Courtesy of University of Minnesota Sustainable Urban Landscape Information Series (http://www.extension.umn.edu/garden/landscaping/).

Figure 4.1. Photo by Jennifer Anderson, hosted by the USDA-NRCS PLANTS Database.

Figure 4.3. Photo by Dave Powell, USDA Forest Service, Bugwood.org, licensed under the CC BY 3.0 US (http://creativecommons.org/licenses/by/3.0/us/).

Figure 4.4. Photo by John Ruter, University of Georgia, Bugwood.org, licensed under the CC BY-NC 3.0 US (http://creativecommons.org/licenses/by-nc/3.0/us/). Used with permission.

Figure 4.5. Photo by Paul Bolstad, University of Minnesota, Bugwood.org, licensed under the CC BY 3.0 US (http://creativecommons.org/licenses/by/3.0/us/).

Figure 4.6. Courtesy of the American Chestnut Foundation.

Figure 4.7. Photo by Sharon Dowdy, University of Georgia.

Figure 4.8. Photo by James H. Miller, USDA Forest Service, Bugwood.org, licensed under the CC BY 3.0 US (http://creativecommons.org/licenses/by/3.0/us/).

Figure 5.1. Photo of pansies by spiderwort, licensed under the CC BY-ND 2.0 (https://creativecommons.org/licenses/by-nd/2.0/).

Figure 5.2. Photo of money plant by TeunSpaans, licensed under the CC BY-SA 3.0 (http://creativecommons.org/licenses/by-sa/3.0/deed.en) via Wikimedia Commons (http://commons.wikimedia.org/wiki/File:Lunaria_annua_flowers.jpg#mediaviewer/File:Lunaria_annua_flowers.jpg). Photo of dianthus by Jim, the Photographer, licensed under the CC BY 2.0 (https://creativecommons.org/licenses/by/2.0/).

Figure 5.4. Photo of flame azalea by Walter Reeves. Used with permission.

Figure 5.6. Illustration by Jay Bauer, University of Georgia.

Figure 6.1. Photo by Clint Waltz, University of Georgia.

Figure 6.5. Courtesy of North Carolina State University, Crop Science Department.

Figure 6.6. Photo by Jack Kelly Clark. Courtesy of University of California Statewide IPM Program.

Figure 6.7. Photo by Charles T. Bryson, USDA Agricultural Research Service,

Bugwood.org, licensed under the CC BY 3.0 US (http://creativecommons. org/licenses/ by/3.0/us/).

Figure 6.9. Photo by John D. Byrd, Mississippi State University, Bugwood.org, licensed under the CC BY 3.0 US (http://creativecommons.org/licenses/ by/3.0/us/).

Figure 6.17. Photo by Clint Waltz, University of Georgia.

Figure 6.18. Illustration by Jay Bauer, University of Georgia.

Figure 6.19. Photo on top by Walter Reeves. Used with permission.

Figure 7.1. Diagram by Tom Schueler, 1992.

Figure 7.2. Photo by Joy Stewart, from WaterSense's Water-Smart Landscape Photo Gallery.

Figure 7.9. Photos by Mark Risse and Jon Calabria, University of Georgia.

Figure 7.10. Illustration by Jay Bauer, University of Georgia.

Figure 7.12. Photo on top by Interlocking Concrete Pavement Institute, licensed under the CC BY 2.0 (https://creativecommons.org/licenses/by/2.0/).

Figure 7.14. Photo on top by Center for Neighborhood Technology, licensed under the CC BY 2.0 (https://creativecommons.org/licenses/by/2.0/. Photo on bottom by BrianAsh Source on English Wikipedia, licensed under the CC-BY-SA-3.0-2.5-2.0-1.0 (http://creativecommons.org/licenses/ by-sa/3.0), via Wikimedia Commons (http://commons.wikimedia.org/ wiki/File:2006NeighborsNewRG2.JPG#filehistory).

Figure 7.15. Courtesy of Washington State University Extension.

Figure 8.3. Photo by Derek Ramsey (Ram-Man), licensed under the GFDL 1.2 (http://www.gnu.org/licenses/old-licenses/fdl-1.2.html), via Wikimedia Commons (http://commons.wikimedia.org/wiki/File:Grasshopper_Eating _Eggplant_Leaf_3008px.jpg).

Figure 8.4. Photo by Clemson University USDA Cooperative Extension Slide Series, Bugwood.org, licensed under the CC BY 3.0 US (http://creative commons.org/licenses/by/3.0/us/).

Figure 8.5. Photo by Clemson University USDA Cooperative Extension Slide Series, Bugwood.org, licensed under the CC BY 3.0 US (http://creative commons.org/licenses/by/3.0/us/).

Figure 8.6. Photo by Jerry A. Payne, USDA Agricultural Research Service, Bugwood.org, licensed under the CC BY 3.0 US (http://creativecommons. org/licenses/by/3.0/us/).

Figure 8.7. *From left*: Courtesy of NC State University; photo by David Shetlar, The Ohio State University, Bugwood.org, licensed under the CC BY-NC 3.0 US (http://creativecommons.org/licenses/by-nc/3.0/us/), used with permission; photo by Charles T. Bryson, USDA Agricultural Research Service, Bugwood.org, licensed under the CC BY 3.0 US (http://creative commons.org/licenses/by/3.0/us/).

Figure 8.8. Photo by Clint Waltz, University of Georgia.

Figure 8.9. Photo by Clint Waltz, University of Georgia.

Figure 8.10. Photo by Clemson University USDA Cooperative Extension Slide Series, Bugwood.org, licensed under the CC BY 3.0 US (http://creative-commons.org/licenses/by/3.0/us/).

Figure 8.11. Photo by Graham Wise, licensed under the CC BY 2.0 (https://creativecommons.org/licenses/by/2.0/).

Figure 8.12. Photo by G. Keith Douce, University of Georgia, Bugwood.org, licensed under the CC BY 3.0 US (http://creativecommons.org/licenses/by/3.0/us/).

Figure 8.14. Photo by Clemson University USDA Cooperative Extension Slide Series, Bugwood.org, licensed under the CC BY 3.0 US (http://creative-commons.org/licenses/by/3.0/us/).

Figure 8.15. Photo by Bradley Higbee, Paramount Farming, Bugwood.org, licensed under the CC BY 3.0 US (http://creativecommons.org/licenses/by/3.0/us/).

Figure 8.16. Photo by A. Steven Munson, USDA Forest Service, Bugwood.org, licensed under the CC BY 3.0 US (http://creativecommons.org/licenses/by/3.0/us/).

Figure 8.17. Photo by Bradley Higbee, Paramount Farming, Bugwood.org, licensed under the CC BY 3.0 US (http://creativecommons.org/licenses/by/3.0/us/).

Figure 8.18. Photo by Whitney Cranshaw, Colorado State University, Bug-wood.org, licensed under the CC BY 3.0 US (http://creativecommons.org/licenses/by/3.0/us/).

Figure 8.19. Photo by Sturgis McKeever, Georgia Southern University, Bug-wood.org, licensed under the CC BY-NC 3.0 US (http://creativecommons.org/licenses/by-nc/3.0/us/). Used with permission.

Figure 8.20. Photo by Whitney Cranshaw, Colorado State University, Bug-wood.org, licensed under the CC BY 3.0 US (http://creativecommons.org/licenses/by/3.0/us/).

Figure 8.21. Photo by Russ Ottens, University of Georgia, Bugwood.org, licensed under the CC BY 3.0 US (http://creativecommons.org/licenses/by/3.0/us/).

Figure 8.22. Photo by Russ Ottens, University of Georgia, Bugwood.org, licensed under the CC BY 3.0 US (http://creativecommons.org/licenses/by/3.0/us/).

Figure 8.23. Photo by Ronald F. Billings, Texas Forest Service, Bugwood.org, licensed under the CC BY-NC 3.0 US (http://creativecommons.org/licenses/by-nc/3.0/us/). Used with permission.

Figure 8.24. Photo by Robert L. Anderson, USDA Forest Service, Bugwood.org, licensed under the CC BY 3.0 US (http://creativecommons.org/licenses/by/3.0/us/).

Figure 9.13. Photo of blackberries by Thomas's Pics, licensed under the CC BY 2.0 (https://creativecommons.org/licenses/by/2.0/). Photo of figs by Clive Darra, licensed under the CC BY-SA 2.0 (https://creativecommons.org/licenses/by-sa/2.0/).

Figure 9.14. Photo of chives by Crystal, licensed under the CC BY 2.0 (https://creativecommons.org/licenses/by/2.0/).

Figure 9.15. Photo on top by Thomas Kriese. Photo on right by Tristan Ferne. Both are licensed under the CC BY 2.0 (https://creativecommons.org/licenses/by/2.0/).

Figure 10.1. The Varlamoff family pond; photo by Ivan Varlamoff.

Figure 10.2. Photo by Stephen Ausmus, USDA ARS.

Figure 10.5. Photo by Jerry A. Payne, USDA Agricultural Research Service, Bugwood.org, licensed under the CC BY 3.0 US (http://creativecommons.org/licenses/by/3.0/us/).

Figure 10.7. Adapted from the National Audubon Society.

Index

Page numbers in *italics* refer to illustrations.

232; fertilizer requirements, *230*; harvesting, 231, 234; heirloom, 229, *229*; herbicides and, 217; IPM for, 200, 202, 210; managing, 231; in organic food gardening, 220–34; watering, 231–32

Vegetated landscape, *178*

Victory Gardens, 220

Vincas, 25, 100

Virginia pine (*Pinus virginiana*), 69

Virginia spiraea, 77

W

Walkways, 16, 20, 69, 146, 151, 243

Washington hawthorn (*Crataegus phaenopyrum*), 62

Water: for bird-friendly gardens, 258; collection, 5, 15; conservation, 3, 4, 15; contamination, 157; hydrologic cycle, 9–11; measuring, 168; purification, 11, 12; scarcity, 3; sources in wildlife habitat, 247, *248*; standing water, *32*; sufficient in sustainable lawn care, 128; trees for collecting and filtering storm, 56–57; use, 157, *158*. *See also* Alternative water sources; Rain; Rain gardens

Water cycle, *11*

Watering: annuals, 167; after backfilling trees with soil, 72–73; drip irrigation, 165, *166*; in establishing new lawn, 148–49; in extreme drought and restrictions, 169; fruits, 236, 238; hand, 164–66; lawns, 168; overhead sprinklers, 165, *167*; perennials, 167; resilient landscapes, 117–19; system selection in water-wise gardening, 164–66; time of day, 168–69; tips, 118–19; trees and shrubs, 168; trees during establishment, 75; vegetables, 231–32

Water oak (*Quercus nigra*), *61*

Watershed: Center for Watershed Protection, 182; degradation, *158*; diagram, *174*

Water-wise gardening, *160*; alternative water sources, 170–73; bioswales, 181–82; cover bare soil with plants, 175; fecal matter, 177; fertilizers and, 175–76; increase water flow, 177; overview, 157–58; pesticides and, 176; rain gardens in, 177, *180*, 181–83; reduce pollution sources, 175; step 1—group plants according to water needs, 159; step 2—build soil fertility, 160; step 3—right plant for right place, 160–61; step 4—downsize irrigated lawn, 161, *161*; step 5—water efficiently, 161–62; step 6—mulching, 162; step 7—keep landscape healthy, 162–64; stormwater management in, 159, 173–83; watering guidelines, 167–69; watering system selection, 164–66; yard waste disposal, 177

Water-wise landscape, *24*; defining, 24–25; high water-use zones, 25; low water-use zones, 25–26; moderate water-use zones, 25; xeriscape, 24–25

White ash (*Fraxinus americana*), *60*

White oak (*Quercus alba*), *61*

White pine (*Pinus strobus*), 69

Wildlife corridors, 22, 245, 248, 258

Wildlife habitat, 5, *81*, *259*; attracting wildlife, 15; bird-friendly gardens, 257–60; BumbleBeeWatch, 262; citizen scientists and, 260–61; creating certified, 263, *264*; food sources, 247; frogs and toads, 260, 262, *263*; lawn size and, 246; mulching, 247; overview, 245; passion for birds, 261–62; people in, 264–65; pesticide elimination, 246; place to raise young, 249; pollinator gardens for, 249–56; Project BudBurst,

SUSAN VARLAMOFF is director of the Office of Environmental Sciences at the University of Georgia, a certified Georgia Master Gardener, and the 2012 recipient of the University of Georgia Sustainability Award. She is a lifelong gardener whose interest in the environment took off in 1982, when she spearheaded an effort to shut down a toxic landfill in her Eden Prairie, Minnesota, neighborhood, an effort that she later chronicled in her award-winning book, *The Polluters: A Community Fights Back*.